What **JESUS** Said About
SUCCESSFUL
LIVING

PRINCIPLES *from the*
SERMON ON THE MOUNT
for TODAY

HADDON W. ROBINSON

DISCOVERY HOUSE

P U B L I S H E R S®

Feeding the Soul with the Word of God

Previously published as *The Christian Salt & Light Company*
Copyright © 1988 by Haddon W. Robinson and *The Solid
Rock Construction Company* Copyright © 1989 by Haddon
W. Robinson

Discovery House Publishers is affiliated with RBC Ministries,
Grand Rapids, Michigan.

Discovery House books are distributed to the trade exclusively
by Barbour Publishing, Inc., Uhrichsville, Ohio.

Library of Congress Cataloging-in-Publication Data
Robinson, Haddon W.
      [Christian salt and light company]
      What Jesus said about successful living : principles from
the Sermon on the mount for today / by Haddon W. Robinson
      p.   cm.
A combined edition of The Christian salt and light company,
© 1988, and The solid rock construction company, © 1989.

ISBN 0-929239-43-1

1. Christian life—Biblical teaching. 2. Sermon on the
mount. I. Robinson, Haddon W. Solid rock construction
company. 1991. II. Title
BS2417.C5R6333   1991   241.5'3—dc20   91-18351
                                                 CIP

Printed in the United States of America
10 11 12 13 14 / / 13 12 11 10 9

To my precious friend, Bonnie,
who has demonstrated to me
what it means to live life with skill.

and

To Carey William, my grandson.
Perhaps at some future time
you will read these words and
understand why your parents
and grandparents prayed that you
would live life to the hilt
as God intended.

CONTENTS

∎

Part 2 • *The Solid Rock Construction Company*

PART I

■

THE CHRISTIAN SALT AND LIGHT COMPANY

LEARNING ABOUT THE COMPANY

■

I have given my life to the study and teaching of homiletics, the preparation and the delivery of sermons. For some that sounds as exciting as watching iron rust.

I have found the study of preaching deeply challenging and satisfying. The great preachers—whether known or unheralded—have always spoken to the needs and issues of their times. What is more, they cared about people caught in the minefields of life. They cared enough to warn them and to guide them. And, when they found men and women wounded by the shrapnel, they preached to comfort them. Above all, they were heard. At times some were despised, a few almost worshiped, others applauded or castigated by the press. But even when they were not heeded, they were heard. Those who served God and their congregations best spoke from the Scriptures to the condition of their people in words that ordinary folks in their audience could understand.

Because of my interest in preachers and preaching, I have studied the sermons of the noted preachers of history—John Chrysostom, Alexander Maclaren, George Whitefield, F. S. Boreham, and Charles Spurgeon, among many others. I have also given special attention to the sermons that Luke recorded in his Acts of the Apostles on the assumption that any theory of preaching that cannot explain why Peter's sermon at Pentecost proved as powerful as the mighty wind and fire is not worth talking about.

For some reason I did not give the same diligence to Jesus' Sermon on the Mount until a few years ago. When I did begin to work with it, a disturbing thing happened. Instead of my studying the sermon, the sermon studied me. The preaching of Jesus jumped out of the pages of Matthew, and, rather than hearing Jesus address His disciples and the Pharisees of the first century, I heard Him speak to the pharisee in me.

For almost a year I taught the Sermon to a group of businessmen who struggled out of bed early in the morning to hear the Sermon again. They bought tapes and listened to each lesson several times and assured me that Jesus' words spoken on a hillside in Israel two thousand years ago still made them nervous today. The executives, media people, and workmen in my group echoed the verdict of James T. Fisher in *A Few Buttons Missing: The Case Book of a Psychiatrist*:

> If you were to take the sum total of all authoritative articles ever written by the most qualified of psychologists and psychiatrists on the subject of mental hygiene, if you were to combine them and refine them and cleave out the excess verbiage, if you were to take the whole of the meat and none of the parsley, and if you were to have these unadulterated bits of pure scientific knowledge concisely expressed by the most capable of living poets, you would have an awkward and incomplete summary of the Sermon on the Mount. And it would suffer immeasurably by comparison.

Because of what these studies did for those businessmen, I felt that it would not be presumptuous of me to put them into print. In doing so I acknowledge my debt to commentators who sat on my desk and guided me with their research. To name a few: Martyn Lloyd-Jones, a great preacher himself, has two volumes of sermons on Jesus' single Sermon on the Mount. Donald Carson served me well with his thoughtful and relevant exposition of Jesus' words. Undoubtedly the most important and most scholarly study of Matthew 5–7 published in the last half century is Robert Guelich's, and I profited greatly from his detailed explanations of the text. William Barclay's comments demonstrated again that scholarship does not have to be stuffy. His explanations and applications help the reader to love God with mind, heart, and soul.

I owe thanks or blame to Robert DeVries, an old friend, for urging me to publish these studies, and I am indebted to Paul Hillman, a new friend, for helping me turn the spoken word into the printed word. I also owe a special debt of gratitude to my administrative assistant at Denver Seminary, Lori Seath. Not only has she contributed to this book, but she has contributed even more to my life and ministry.

In writing about Jesus' Sermon on the Mount, I have the uneasy feeling that I am shining a flashlight on the sun. I comfort myself in knowing that when preachers have been at their finest, that is all they have ever done.

COMPANY GOALS

■

After World War I, General Pershing planned a series of victory parades through many European capitals. He needed 27,000 soldiers to march in those parades, and each participant was to possess two qualities. Each soldier was to have an unblemished military record, and he was to stand, at least, one meter, eighty-six centimeters tall.

Forty American soldiers, guarding an ammunition dump about one hundred miles from Paris, read with interest the notice about Pershing's victory marches. What is more, each man in the company met the first qualification. None of them had ever been court-martialed.

The second condition, however, puzzled them. They did not know how high one meter, eighty-six centimeters was. The corporal asked the sergeant, and the sergeant didn't know. Then the corporal said, "Well, Sarge, I know that I'm taller than you are." After that it began. Since nobody in camp knew how tall one meter, eighty-six centimeters was, the soldiers began to compare themselves with one another. They stood back to back like children in a kindergarten until they knew the tallest through the shortest men in the company.

Slim, the tallest, kidded his buddies about taking a look at the girls in the capitals and sending back picture postcards. And Shorty knew that if he marched in the parade, everyone else would, too.

When a captain from headquarters arrived to find out if anybody qualified, the soldiers told him their problem, "We don't know how tall one meter, eighty-six centimeters is." So he translated the meter and centimeters into feet and inches and made a mark on the mess hall wall.

Some of the men looked at that mark and turned away, knowing they could not measure up to it. Others stood up against the wall, but they fell short of the mark by an inch or more. Finally Slim stretched himself as tall as possible, but he fell one-quarter of an inch short. Not one of them came to the six feet, one and one-fifth inches that one meter, eighty-six centimeters represents.

Pershing eventually found qualified men who marched in his victory parades, but the point of the story is that when we have an absolute standard it is futile to measure ourselves against other men and women. We must stand up to the mark.

Some folks interpret the Sermon on the Mount as Christ's mark on the wall. This is what we must measure up to in order to gain acceptance with God. If we determine to work our way to heaven, then the Sermon on the Mount describes how we must live. "If you simply live up to the Ten Commandments," these people say, "you'll do all right with God." This popular interpretation has two fatal flaws.

First, it contradicts the rest of the Bible. The New Testament declares many times over that we are justified because of God's grace; that is, we do not have a right relationship with God because we are well behaved, clever, or religious. So if you decide to get to heaven by keeping the Sermon on the Mount, it's like making up your own exam without consulting the teacher. God doesn't have a do-it-yourself plan for getting to heaven. Second, keeping the Sermon on the Mount to get to heaven is the impossible dream. No one can live the standards set in the Sermon on the Mount. So if you choose it as your mark on the wall, you will have shot yourself in the heart. You will condemn yourself to hell.

Although you may feel you are doing better than some others in keeping the Sermon on the Mount, God doesn't grade on the curve. He will grade you on the basis of an absolute standard. The old spiritual said it well, "God wants one hundred percent and ninety-nine and a half ain't going to do."

But if you choose the Sermon on the Mount as the standard, your mark on the wall, you'll fall short by more than one-half of an inch or so. Even the best of people—Pharisees, religious types, moralists—fall as short as an ant measuring itself against the Empire State Building.

A second interpretation of Christ's teaching in the Sermon on the Mount tries to counteract the error of the first view. This approach asserts that Jesus wanted to convince His hearers that they could not possibly measure up to God's righteousness.

In this understanding of the Sermon, Jesus did more than establish the mark; He told us how impossible the standard is to reach. We should not commit adultery or kill, but also we should not lust or harbor anger. By getting at the heart of the matter, the motives behind our actions, He demonstrated that no one could possibly please God on the basis of human merit.

It is true, of course, that the Sermon on the Mount as a standard condemns us. But why would Jesus spend His time making that point to His disciples—to those who were already believers? Why preach an evangelistic sermon to the choir? If Jesus was addressing insiders and not folks on the outside trying to get into the kingdom, then this second view about setting up an unreachable standard misses the point. The disciples were already part of His kingdom; what would be the purpose of telling them how impossible it is to attain God's righteousness on their own?

The first two views about the Sermon focus on individuals. A third approach applies it to nations. It resembles a political platform for governments to adopt. In this interpretation, Jesus wasn't discussing personal morality or individual ethics. Instead He offered a blueprint for a better world built upon His teachings. In other words, if the nations of the world followed the Sermon on the Mount, the kingdom of heaven would be established on the earth.

One noted figure who read the Sermon on the Mount this way was

Leo Tolstoy. After Tolstoy had a conversion experience, he became enamored with some of the teachings of Jesus, and he was particularly impressed with the Sermon on the Mount. Tolstoy felt that governments needed to submit to the guidance of Jesus. Courts should stop administering oaths to witnesses because of Christ's teaching about not swearing. Since a line in the Sermon says that we are to resist evil, Tolstoy wanted to do away with police forces and armies. If people did not fight against evil, somehow they would usher in God's kingdom.

Tolstoy tried personally to live according to the concepts in the Sermon on the Mount, but when he attempted to get the Russian government to join his crusade, they hounded and persecuted him. In fact, Russian leaders thought he was evil, and they resisted him.

Even if Tolstoy were partially right, the world would not improve much even if nations decided to adopt the Sermon on the Mount as their constitution. Men and women are depraved—individuals and governments. All of us suffer from curvature of the soul. Setting up higher standards of behavior doesn't mean citizens will behave that way. Every nation has better laws than its people keep.

This change-the-world approach to the Sermon gained popularity in the United States at the turn of the century. The progressive idealism in politics was baptized into the Christian faith uncorrected. Every day and in every way the world was to get better and better. The Sermon on the Mount was a manifesto for great political programs. That philosophy has few supporters today. Two world wars blasted it out of contention, and not many politicians or religious leaders would seriously defend that proposition today. Not only does this view resemble blue sky, but also we should dismiss it because it does not fit the context of the Sermon on the Mount. Jesus was not addressing a first-century United Nations meeting; He was not urging political leaders to adopt a new ethic.

A fourth group of interpreters have seen the Sermon on the Mount as a lifestyle for the disciples who were to enter the kingdom that Jesus was about to set up on the earth. This takes the context somewhat more seriously. Jesus did preach about the kingdom, proclaiming, "Repent for the kingdom of heaven is near" (Matthew 4:17). Adherents of this view assert that the Sermon on the Mount was an instruction manual for the two or three years before this kingdom would be ushered in. When that kingdom was rejected by the Jewish leaders, the Sermon on the Mount was no longer operative until the establishment of a future kingdom. The Sermon becomes the ethic for Christ's followers in the kingdom to come. This view is not without its problems.

Jesus said at the end of the Beatitudes that blessing will come as a result of being persecuted as righteous people. If this happens in the millennium, God's golden age, who are the persecutors? In Matthew 6, Jesus spoke of want and worry. Would these be part of His kingdom? To relegate the Sermon's principles to the sweet by and by as an ethic for how people are to behave in a future ideal age is to miss the Sermon's thrust. Christ's Sermon may make us nervous, but there is little in the context or the Sermon itself that allows us to relegate it to some future time. Matthew wrote his gospel after the death and resurrection of Jesus to the churches in the first century and to Christians who follow in their train.

If we traverse the globe on foot, the first view of the Sermon sees it as an instruction book on how to swim an ocean. The second tells us the swim is impossible; we will drown. The third contends that if people in every nation will take the Sermon seriously we can swim the ocean together. The fourth looks forward to a better day when it will be easier to swim across the ocean than it is now. None of these views charts the right course.

In his book *The Quest for the Historical Jesus*, Albert Schweitzer described the Sermon on the Mount as an interim ethic. Jesus was giving His followers an ethic to follow until His kingdom was established on earth, and this was how they were to behave until that event occurred. Albert Schweitzer may have been on to something. The Sermon details how Christ's disciples were to live from the time He gave it until the time He will return to establish His earthly kingdom. This is the fifth and perhaps the best view.

The Old Testament prophets looked forward to a political kingdom in which the Messiah, God's King, would rule over the earth. Without this background, Matthew and the Sermon on the Mount become difficult to interpret. Jesus came to the Jewish people as recorded in the book of Matthew and declared that He was going to establish His kingdom. Now the Sermon on the Mount was the ethic that His disciples were to follow between the time of His promise of that coming kingdom and its actual establishment on the earth.

The mountain discourse was given to the citizens of a kingdom who, in a sense, were destined to live in exile until their Leader returned to set up His kingdom on the earth. They remain loyal to their King; but since exiles do not have land to call their own, they look forward to the King's return and the establishment of a homeland.

The Sermon then is for all loyal followers of Jesus Christ. It is the manner of conduct He expects from them in a foreign environment as they anticipate the time He will return and set up His kingdom.

The message on the mount is not the standard by which we can and will have a relationship to the King. Neither is it the unreachable line on the wall nor a constitution for nations. Nor is it merely something for the future.

The principles of the Sermon on the Mount, and particularly the Beatitudes, are goals to dominate us now, here on earth. They are not ideals. Ideals are unreachable and often frustrate us because they demand perfection to reach them. Christ didn't set up impossible ideals; He established goals, markers, and muscle-builders along the way. We may not be able to swim an ocean, but we can dog-paddle a stream, backstroke a river, or sidestroke a lake. We even can crawl-stroke a sea from island to island. Yet reaching a goal is not the end; it only gives us more strength to swim another stroke.

In understanding the Sermon on the Mount, proponents of views one and three convert goals into realizable ideals for pleasing God and ruling nations. Champions of view two turn goals into impossible ideals; backers of view four change present goals into future ideals. All these advocates of different views miss the point; God is more interested in the process than the pinnacle itself. Going after the goal becomes its own reward.

If we were to ask an Olympic swimmer to describe the ideal swimmer, she might say that the ideal swimmer has perfect motion—breathing in sync with every stroke without wasted energy. The perfect swimmer turns quickly, getting the maximum push at the end of the pool. She would be quick to say that no swimmer could ever reach the ideal in every race. An ideal is helpful, but it doesn't motivate an athlete. A goal, on the other hand, is something toward which a swimmer can strive. At times a goal may seem unattainable, but it is not so far off that an athlete cannot work toward it.

If a child in grade school desired to enter the Olympics, the youngster's goal might be to break a world mark set at the last Olympics. It is out there, something toward which that child is going to work. Now at first that goal may seem like an ideal, especially as the youngster learns to swim and paddles from one end of the pool and back. He or she doesn't come close to the record. Yet as that individual continues to practice through high school and college, the goal has a way of flavoring the swimmer's attitudes and actions—disciplines needed to break that Olympic record. The person does not become a perfect swimmer; that's an ideal. But he or she can achieve Olympic standards; that's an attainable goal.

The problem with an ideal is that it causes us to give up. We decide to postpone reaching the ideal until we get to a sinless heaven. Reaching the ideal through the sheer act of dying, however, is not what Jesus sets before us.

An ideal is what we will be when God makes us all that we should be. A goal is different; we can work toward it now, and our actions and attitudes are affected in the process.

Now, admittedly, when we first look at a goal, we may regard it as an impossible ideal. Like the goal of weighing 156 if we are 295 pounds. Yet it's there; and because it's there, we work toward it. We allow it to influence our eating and dominate our thinking; the goal affects our conduct.

Jesus was setting goals in the Beatitudes and the whole Sermon on the Mount, not impossible ideals. He wants His disciples to strive toward these goals to master a new kind of life. Although we may initially feel like a fourth-grader splashing in the pool, as we press toward the goals they begin to permeate and change our lives.

NEW EMPLOYEES

∎

When a minister preaches at a church service being broadcast on the radio, he speaks primarily to the people in the pews—some committed, others not. He also has a radio audience. The minister is aware of them, but he speaks primarily to those in front of him. Here and there, he may speak to his radio listeners, particularly, at the end of the sermon.

Jesus was speaking authoritatively to His disciples, but the word *disciples* does not always mean the twelve apostles. It refers to those who are learning, and many people surrounded Jesus to learn. Some were true disciples; others went away after a while. His words were too tough for them.

In addition to the committed and fringe disciples, the crowds gathered around. After the crowds heard His teaching, they were amazed because in contrast to their teachers of law He spoke with authority (Matthew 7:28).

Jesus was primarily talking to His dedicated disciples, but He was aware of those disciples on the spiritual periphery. He also seemed to address the crowds at the end of the sermon when He spoke of narrow and wide gates, trees and their fruit, and wise and foolish builders. So Jesus spoke to three groups: dedicated disciples, uncommitted disciples, and the crowd.

SERMON NOTES

Jesus addressed at least three groups of people in the Sermon on the Mount. If you were in Christ's audience that day, with which group would you most closely identify?

In the Sermon on the Mount, Jesus was speaking to His disciples. Where would you place yourself on a "disciple" scale?

WORDS FROM THE TOP

∎

Before Jesus began His Sermon, He went up on the mountainside and sat down. Christ's sitting down may not strike us as being very important, but in the world of the first century, the teacher's position was important. Jewish rabbis might teach while strolling through the market or standing up; but if they wanted to teach authoritatively, they sat down. For example, when the Pope speaks authoritatively, he speaks ex cathedra. That means "out of the chair." He speaks with full authority when he does that.

Seminaries often try to get folks to endow a chair—of theology, of missions, of evangelism. One of our seminary constituents wrote, "You want to endow a chair; you are asking for five hundred thousand dollars; I can get you chairs a lot cheaper than that." Well, it's not the furniture, it's the authority associated with the chair.

What is more, many of the versions say that He opened His mouth and began to speak to them. It seems almost obvious; how do you teach if you don't open your mouth? It is almost redundant. But, again, Jewish writings always describe teachers of authority this way.

Sitting and speaking, Jesus told His followers about the principles of His kingdom.

SERMON NOTES

What is the significance of Matthew's mentioning that when Jesus preached, He sat down? What significance does that have for you?

COMPANY MOTTO

∎

F or I tell you that unless your righteousness surpasses that of the
Pharisees and the teachers of the law, you will certainly not enter
the kingdom of heaven" (Matthew 5:20).

The Pharisees and the teachers of the law prayed, fasted, tithed,
and lived according to the rules; but Jesus was not saying that we have
to do better than that. He was saying that their righteousness was external. They thought that religious performance made them acceptable to God.

When we stand before God, we've got to do better than that. God
requires an inner righteousness, not an outer righteousness. And so
Jesus was really saying in the key verse of the Sermon on the Mount
that our righteousness has got to be of a different quality.

Putting it another way, Jesus said who we are is more important
than what we do. Righteous acts must come from righteous attitudes.
That is what the Sermon on the Mount is all about.

SERMON NOTES

In your own words, state the motto of the "company of Christ."

Matthew 5:20 states, "Unless your righteousness surpasses that of
the Pharisees . . . ." The Pharisees seemed to have a corner on the

righteousness market. In what way must our righteousness be different from that of the Pharisees? How is it possible for us to surpass them?

What does this motto mean and how is it reflected in our daily lives?

Does being a Christian mean that we keep a set of rules? That we ignore the rules?

SEAL OF APPROVAL

■

The editors of *Psychology Today* once published a questionnaire designed to answer the questions: What is happiness? And how do we obtain it? They invited their readers to respond and a couple of months later the editors put together an article based on the survey.

They discovered that pursuing happiness for many was like pursuing a black cat in a dark room at midnight when one is not even sure that the cat is there. One man, for example, when asked about his happiness said, "I don't know. I filled out the questionnaire. I think I'm happy; please verify."

The article also pointed out that there were very few factors that directly correlated with happiness. For example, whether or not one had much money did not have much to do with happiness.

People on the lower end of the economic scale often felt the pressure of not having money, living a thirty-one-day month on a twenty-one-day check. For them money could solve all problems and bring happiness. As a result, winning the lottery was a favorite dream.

The survey revealed that the rich were not happy either. The bluebird of happiness might land on a large home, a big pool, or a big deck, the things of affluence, but deep inside the rich were still unhappy.

The editors received answers from every part of the country, but geography had nothing to do with happiness. Sexual preference did not make much difference either.

The editors found no correlation between pleasure and happiness. We can understand the finding. Some of us have gone to a concert hall and listened to great and very pleasurable music, yet we went out into the cold night and suddenly felt an emptiness inside.

Many people confuse pleasure and happiness. People take narcotics, sniff cocaine, and put heroine in their veins for the high, the tremendous sense of pleasure. The kick is so great that people want to repeat it. Other folks find pleasure by going to the corner bar or by downing a few in the easy chair. But people caught by drugs or alcohol are not happy.

Igor the poet expressed it when he said, "Pleasure is frail, like a dew drop. While it lasts, it dies." And Robert Burns, the Scottish poet, compared pleasure to snow falling in a river. It is white for a moment, but then it melts forever.

The results of *Psychology Today*'s survey shows that we may afford pleasures and enjoy them, but enjoyment does not necessarily equal happiness.

A cartoon pictured a middle-class husband lecturing to his wife. He was seated on the sofa with a blackboard. He had written an equation on the blackboard: "The mortgage is paid; we're fully insured; the kids are okay; we're healthy; and we have each other. It all equals happiness."

And his wife said, "Walter, would you run through that just one more time?" The bottom line is not necessarily happiness.

Perhaps our denseness about happiness is why Jesus seems to grab us by the lapels at the beginning of the Sermon on the Mount and repeat the word *blessed* eight times. In our English translation *blessed* may not jump out at us; it sounds a little too religious. That's why some of the modern translations use the word *happy* instead of *blessed*. This may be okay if we are using it the way the Bible uses the word *happy*.

Our English word *happy* comes from the French and from the Middle English and has to do with something that is accidental, something that happens by chance. We say that if perhaps something happens, we will be happy. That's not the way the Greek word *makarios*, which is translated "blessed" or "happy," is used.

In secular Greek the island of Cyprus was called the "makarios" isle, the blest isle. The idea was that those who lived on Cyprus never had to leave its shores in order to have all they needed to be content. They had natural resources and minerals. They had a beautiful place to live, with fruit and flowers. The island was self-contained. No one had to search for the needs and wants of life.

Another meaning besides "self-containment" comes out of the Old Testament. God blessed men and women, and they, in turn, blessed God. When God blessed them, He was giving His approval. When they blessed Him, they were appreciating Him. If they were blessed by God, they stood approved before Him. Blessed = approval

When we are blessed by God, we are in a sense self-contained; that is, our happiness does not come from circumstances, or by accidents, or through diligent searches. It comes because we stand approved before the Creator of the universe. In some way or another, we all seek approval from someone, but not all seek God's favor.

If what matters most to us in life is the approval of our loved ones or the approval of our colleagues, then these Beatitudes are not going to do us any good. They deal with how we can stand approved before God. And in knowing that our Creator approves, we will experience true contentment and joy.

To be blessed means to sense the joy, or happiness, that comes from knowing that we stand approved before God. That's why eight times over Jesus spoke about that kind of blessedness, or happiness, that comes out of approval.

SERMON NOTES

If you were asked, "What is happiness?" how would you respond?

Contentment

Name some things that society sometimes claims will bring us happiness. List three things you have felt might bring you happiness.

Can you explain the difference between "happy" as we use it today and "blessed" as it was used in the Bible? Do you know many people who are "blessed" by God? How can you tell?

Do you believe you are blessed by God? Why?

COMPANY SPIRIT

∎

The religion of the Pharisees is one that is always with us. People who have grown up in religious families understand the Pharisees' system. After all, decent, moral parents give their children rules of behavior, and they have a system of rewards and punishments. The rewards can be very subtle—a smile or word of praise. The punishment can be parental disapproval or more forceful applications. But such children know the standards and rules. What is more, if children are part of a religious family, they do religious things. Parents take them to church; they may start as early as the first week after birth. It is not uncommon to see parents bring a newborn out so that all of the religious folks can see the child. Many children's earliest memories are those of Sunday school, church, and religious activities.

In some traditions children of eight or nine respond to an invitation and walk an aisle. In other traditions, children go through confirmation. When they take their first communion, it is the big time. Children know that parents and relatives approve of such activities. So religious behaviors are spelled out, and a child's self-concept comes from that.

How people feel about themselves is determined to some degree by how other people feel about them. If parents say, "Isn't that wonderful; Johnny accepted Christ when he was four" or "Mary just went through her first communion; she has a lovely first communion dress," a child quickly feels good doing religious things. Going to church gives a child a warm glow. If these children skip church to watch television, they often feel guilty.

One of three things can happen to children growing up in a religious home. First, they may struggle through to faith and values of their own.

My daughter, Vicki, went off to the University of Texas; and after she graduated, I kiddingly asked her what I got out of her education. I had put her through school, and I wanted to know what happened down there at the university. She surprised me with her answer. She said, "Well, Daddy, I went off to the University of Texas and I had your faith and your values. When I got out of the university, I had my own faith and my own values. They happen to be very much the same, but they are mine."

Second, some children may rebel. They have learned the behaviors and have adopted the practices, and they agree with them to a degree. But when they get into high school or college, they kick the traces.

Many parents can tell the story of children who stopped going to church and became atheists after their first year of college. It may seem that such children have lost their faith, but they may never have developed a faith of their own. What children discover at the university is that God doesn't have any grandchildren.

Sometimes a child's faith is handed down like a grandfather's watch. It may be a family treasure, but it is not the child's own. If he or she rebels, it is not against the faith but against standards and patterns that are not his or her own. Behaviors have been externalized, but never internalized.

Third, some children may live by the standards but not have faith inside. This is practice without faith. They go through all of the religious practices and feel good because mom and dad approve.

These children become faithful church attenders as adults, but they don't understand sin in the biblical sense. They are taken up with Mickey Mouse morals. Religion is the fatal five, the sordid six, or the nasty nine. They have strong convictions about those things they don't do themselves. If a person pushes one of their hot buttons, they will drum him out of the church. Nothing bugs these people more than to find someone enjoying what they condemn.

This is not a diatribe against growing up in a religious family; a religious heritage can be wonderful, particularly in learning the Scriptures. But if it ends in self-righteousness rather than a righteousness through faith, it is a tragedy.

Jesus was bothered by self-righteous people—those who really felt they had it all together religiously. They were the folks who knew the rules. They knew the commandments and what righteousness was, and they could live up to it. The severest words Jesus spoke were against folks like these.

The Pharisees were people with outward standards, and Jesus said our righteousness had to exceed theirs (Matthew 5:20). Now, they were deeply religious people, those willing to make themselves miserable for the cause. They fasted on Mondays and Thursdays, denying themselves even necessary food. To make themselves so uncomfortable, they had to be earnest about their religion. There were 250 commands to keep and 365 prohibitions to observe, and the Pharisees tried to be straight as a ruler.

That system of religion was the prevalent one about which Jesus spoke in the first century. But He wasn't saying unless we have 290 commandments and 500 prohibitions, we can't get into heaven. Upping the ante won't help. No, Jesus was saying that one kind of righteousness came from keeping the rules and another kind came from inside. And inward righteousness was what should characterize kingdom citizens. Jesus was talking about people who have found their own faith—those changed inside.

C. S. Lewis, who came the long way around from atheism to theism to finally trusting Christ, concluded that new Christians think God is going to come in and fix the faucets and putty the windows.

Instead He does a whole reconstruction job. He tears the walls down and starts at the foundation to build a new structure.

Many times the toughest people to reach are people who live good lives. They've got a nice foundation, the walls are up, and they don't want anyone messing with their lives.

If people have the religion of the Pharisees, it is usually characterized by what they don't do. One community is like this—no smoking, drinking, gambling, or carousing. Crosses and stars of David are everywhere. It is the cemetery. Christ's religion is not about death but life.

Jesus was not playing with rules or starting out with negatives. He was saying that something has to happen deep inside to get God's approval, and that does not come from keeping rules. We may keep rules and religious ceremonies and still have true religion, but that is not what causes it.

A man who has worked with alcoholics for over twenty years has wrestled with why some people abstain from liquor for several years and then one day fall off the wagon, yet others quit and never return to the bottle. He said some people become abstainers; others fall in love with sobriety. Abstainers are always in danger of going back; for them quitting is a matter of reform. For lovers of sobriety it is a matter of the spirit.

The difference between abstaining from drinking and loving sobriety is the same as the difference between being religious and loving God. And that's what Jesus is driving at. He is talking about a religion that is on the inside—a quality of life that comes out of a relationship with Him. So blessedness is getting approval from God by a vital and alive relationship with Jesus Christ.

We may feel uncomfortable when we consider the attitudes that should characterize kingdom citizens. That is why people ultimately crucified Christ. The prostitutes and the pimps did not get Him; it was the religious people. Nothing is more uncomfortable than to discover what we thought was going to pass muster doesn't even get us in the front door.

My wife teaches children piano, and I usually sit in my study listening to them. I am amazed at what she is able to do. I am also astounded at the difference between a person who plays the piano and a musician. Some folks play notes, and they hit the right keys for Chopin's *Fantasy Impromptu*; but they don't really play Chopin. Another kind of musician catches the spirit of Chopin. Something goes on inside the performer; and when he or she plays, people pay money to hear the glorious notes. The pianist has captured the spirit of Chopin.

One does not suggest to the spirited player that he or she forget the notes. Notes matter, but hitting the notes isn't what it means to be a musician. Somehow the musician has to have spirit; without it the notes do very little.

Paraphrasing the words of Jesus: unless our musical ability exceeds that of the good note player, we'll never make it as musicians. And that is what Jesus is after. He's not primarily concerned about the notes; he is concerned about the spirit. The person of spirit is the blessed, the approved, man or woman.

SERMON NOTES

List the traits of the Pharisees that we consider to be "positive" traits and often strive to develop in ourselves. What traits of the Pharisees would you like to see in your children? Is it wrong to want to see these virtues develop in their lives or in ours?

Can the discipline you received from your parents confuse you at this point? How? What is Jesus saying about rule-keeping?

Parents teach us to obey the rules. It does not help us love God.

Some of us grew up in homes that had a number of rules for us to keep. Are rules necessarily wrong? Explain.

No, Rules can keep us from danger.

An alcoholic is used as an example to illustrate the difference between acting "religious" and loving God. Can you think of another example of this difference between being religious and being truly devoted to God?

Baker. Some turn out good pastries, some turn out pastries filled with love.

Why do you think religious people, rather than crooks, pimps, or prostitutes, crucified Christ? Is there any part of you that would not welcome Jesus if He came to teach the Sermon on the Mount today? Why or why not?

Because Jesus was teaching something different than what they knew.

How might Jesus' teaching make some religious leaders in our society uncomfortable?

Many leaders preach what makes them feel good, not what Jesus teaches.

The Pharisee was the standard of religious success in Jesus' time. In our own time, in your own town, who seems to be the standard of religious success? How about in your church?

Forrest
Carol Tiede
Lon Log
Brand Judy

Have you ever set standards of religious "success" for yourself or for others? What were they? My success would be to have an extremely close relationship w/ God.

What does the chapter say is the essence of what Jesus wants from us in the way we live? To be filled with the spirit.

BANKRUPTING THE COMPANY

∎

Candidates for president always promise that the next four years will be better than any past years—not only for a few but for everybody. If we just give them enough time, they will lead us to the golden land of prosperity. And not only that, they will give us world peace, beating swords into plowshares, transforming nuclear weapons into farm machines. They will make education number one because they care about the needs of our children. If farmers are having a tough time, a candidate promises if elected to keep prices for grain high. Smart political candidates in the kingdoms of this earth don't campaign by being poor in spirit. That is because they are campaigning in a society that believes leadership, happiness, and success have nothing to do with being poor in spirit.

Blessed and happy people are those who have it all together—the record-shattering athlete, the best-selling author, or the Nobel prize-winning scientist. We don't think of folks like this as poor in spirit.

So when Jesus begins the Sermon on the Mount by proclaiming that the poor in spirit are blessed, He seems to be talking nonsense in our society. It is indeed a paradox. It is like saying, "Blessed are the dependent." Somehow we just don't think that's true.

We can begin to understand what Jesus was saying by explaining what He was not saying. He was not saying, "Blessed are the poor spirited." Wimps of the world and flunkers of personality tests should not unite behind Christ's words. He's not promoting passivity or asking people to imitate Dickens's Uriah Heep, who kept saying, "I'm a 'umble man."

Abraham, Moses, Daniel, and Paul were not poor spirited, uninvolved, letting life happen to them. They could make it through the day without calling their psychiatrists.

Poor in spirit does not mean poor financially, either. Slum dwellers merit no special favor with God. That's a myth folks would like to believe, but poor and rich stand equally before God.

Being poor in spirit has to do with our relationship with God. Of the two words for *poor* in the Greek language, the one used here meant absolute poverty. The Greeks distinguished between those who lived hand-to-mouth and those who had nothing at all. The first group lived day-by-day with nothing left over for a rainy day; the second group found every day to be rainy. It wasn't that they didn't have anything left over; it's that they didn't have anything at all.

In essence, Jesus was saying, "Blessed are the beggars in spirit," those spiritually humble. The concept was the opposite of pride and self-righteousness. Yet we have strange ideas about what humility is. We often confuse humility with modesty, and as a result we confuse pride with conceit.

We think humble people have the social grace of modesty. They are the aw-shucks football runners who give all the credit to the line. That may be a nice way to handle touchdowns and life, but these players may not be humble people. The opposite of modesty is conceit, and the opposite of pride is humility.

In the Bible humility is a Godward virtue, and pride a Godward vice. Pride or humility may affect our relationship to others, but the two are most descriptive of who we are before God.

In Luke 18 Jesus told the story of the tax collector and the Pharisee. The Pharisee thanked God that he lived differently than extortionists, adulterers, and tax collectors. He fasted twice a week and gave a tenth of his income to God. What the Pharisee said was true; he was leading an exemplary life.

The Pharisee did not make his living by driving his neighbor to the wall. No contracts with fine print! He shook hands on a deal, and that was it. His word was his bond. And in a day that was as sexually loose as our own, he had not sacrificed his life on a wayside altar. By any conventional standards, ancient or modern, he was a success. He gave a tenth of his net worth every year, not just his income; he was willing to lower his standard of living for God. And his religion had done him good. The people in his community looked up to him. When people of that day wanted a standard of religious success, they turned to the Pharisee.

Apparently throwing reason to the wind, Jesus said the tax collector, not the Pharisee, went down to his house justified. The tax collector was a scoundrel in the ancient world. If we think that he was really a good guy in disguise who admitted his limitations, we don't understand the place of the tax collector in the society of his day. He ranked with the pimps and prostitutes of our time.

To make a living, the tax collector bought the right to tax from the Roman government. Because Rome didn't care how much they charged, tax collectors could take in as much as the traffic would bear. Everyone doing business had to stop by the tax collector.

No government publication explained the tax rates. No board of examiners looked over his shoulder, and no one operated without operating with him. We would compare his tactics to those of the Mafia. Anything extra he could squeeze out of people he could keep. Extortion was built into the job. He had hold of the jugular vein, and no one could do anything to get free. He was a traitor to his own people, the Jews, and a pipeline to the Romans.

Tax collectors were the scum of society. When this man prayed, "God, have mercy on me, a sinner," some said to themselves, "He ought to be praying that." If we want a first-rate sinner, we've got one in the tax collector.

When measured by the standards of that society, the Pharisee, without argument, was on top of the heap. Yet Jesus astounded everyone by declaring the tax collector justified. The people then must have said, "That's weird. What's coming off?"

By anyone's standard, the Pharisee was better than the tax collector. Society was better off because he was there. If they both were running for election today, we would be out campaigning for the Pharisee. We would do everything to keep the tax collector out.

And if both of those men wanted the hand of one of our daughters in marriage, we'd be glad to have a Pharisee as a son-in-law—noble, upstanding, good references, a personality that was ten feet tall. But if she dragged that tax collector in, we'd say, "Good night! You can't be that hard up to get married."

What is going on in this story? We would probably say that the Pharisee's problem was conceit. He was certainly the better person, but he should not pray that way in public. We don't stand up and begin a Bible study by saying, "Thank you, I'm here today because I am better than all these other men." It may be true, but we've got to be more modest.

Pious people don't talk like the Pharisee. It just doesn't sit right. He should say, "Aw, shucks, you know, I made the best of what I was."

We think his problem was conceit. We don't like conceit because it is a way of bragging. But that man wasn't put down because of conceit; it was his pride. He was in prayer, in God's presence, and he thought that what mattered in the community mattered in heaven. He assumed God and people were concerned about the same things and that he could pass because he was better than most others in the city.

When Luke introduced the story of the Pharisee and tax collector, he said that Jesus told the story to some who were "confident of their own righteousness and looked down on everybody else" (18:9). One wrong way to decide if we are righteous is to look at other people.

The Pharisee was saying, "Lord, You know that I thank You that I'm not as they are. You made me better, but You had pretty good material to work with. If You didn't have my kind of cloth, You couldn't have made my kind of suit." In the presence of God he thought he was something, but he was nothing. Either humility or pride describes a man or woman before God. And when we really live before God, we become aware of our tremendous need of humility.

We may dismiss the tax collector's humility. We may say it was easy for him; after all, he had plenty to be humble about. There is some truth to that. That's why Jesus said that it was easier for prostitutes, pimps, and tax collectors than those of wealth, education, and moral standards to enter the kingdom. The former, at least, sense their tremendous need.

Of course, a tax collector can be proud and say, "I thank God I'm not like the Pharisee. I may live a wretched life, but at least I'm open and honest about who I am. I may not pray long prayers and go to church regularly, but I'm not a hypocrite." Some people think hypocrisy is the paramount sin. They could use a short course in guile to cover up the pollution in their lives!

We can make a virtue out of anything if we twist the truth enough, but the point is that the tax collector saw his desperate situation and cried out for God's mercy. That's poverty of spirit, bankruptcy of the soul. It is not how we stand in relationship to other people that matters, it is how we stand before God.

Mt. Everest is approximately five miles above sea level and the Philippine Trench, five miles below. If a diver could look from the lowest spot on earth to the highest, the ten-mile view would be enormously different from what a person can normally see.

But if we could stand on the sun and look at the earth, we would probably say it was as smooth as a billiard ball. With that perspective, we would not see the ten-mile difference between Mt. Everest and the Philippine Trench. The differences that matter on the planet don't matter if we are in outer space.

Some people are Mt. Everest people, and others are as low as the Philippine Trench—great differences from a human viewpoint. But from God's perspective, these differences are inconsequential. It is our sense of bankruptcy that counts.

Two people may each owe ten million dollars. For repayment, one may have one thousand dollars and another, one dollar. One is a thousand times better off than the other; but if they owe ten million dollars, they are both bankrupt.

Jesus was talking about bankruptcy, that deep sense of needing God. If we don't need God, we won't come to Him. And if we don't come to God, we won't be in the kingdom.

It's one thing to write about being poor in spirit; it's another thing to convince someone of its importance. I know religious people will confess that they are sinners, but they're just being modest. In our society, as a seminary professor, I probably pass muster externally, but the Sermon on the Mount gets me on the inside. I know down inside what I want to be and ought to be, but I know I'm neither.

In his book *Loving God*, Charles Colson noted that when we look at our sins *en masse*, they don't seem to bother us. It is like knowing that we have a national debt of over one trillion dollars; we don't get bothered by that. That's the president's problem.

Somehow we must make our sin more personal. We can worry over owing five thousand dollars much more than we can worry about owing a trillion dollars. When we see individual maggots, we realize how maggoty maggots are.

My mother died when I was a boy, and my dad raised me. He really gave his life for me. One time in college I asked him why he didn't get married again, and my father said, "Well, I wasn't sure that I could marry someone that would care for you as a mother, and I just didn't want to take that chance."

When he got older, he came to live with us. He became senile and began to lose track of time. He'd walk around the house at night and knock on the bedroom doors. He was a child, and I became a parent to him.

One day we were home, and he wanted to go outside. I got him ready; but it was a cold day, and he quickly came back inside. Then he went out and came back in again. After about the third time out and in, I became very irritated. And I said, "Look, either go out or stay in."

He wanted to go out again, but he had no sooner gotten out than he knocked on the door. I was furious. He looked at me a bit confused. He stood there in the door and didn't go either way, so I hauled off and swatted him. I could have punched him in the mouth, knocked him to the ground. When I hit him, he gave me that quizzical look that old people have. At that moment I could have killed him.

It is a horrible memory because of the ugliness inside me that day. With a glimpse like that, I realized the bankruptcy, the depravity of my life. I wish he were still here, but I couldn't honestly tell him that I didn't mean it. I meant it that day. We can excuse my behavior and say, "Old people get that way; they can be irritating." The truth is, I had a flash—the flash of a murderer.

What happens when we truly see our lives? If we wash it from our minds, we travel alone in our self-righteousness. If we have a sense of bankruptcy, that poverty of spirit, we throw ourselves at His feet and cry out for mercy and forgiveness.

We all need the grace of a forgiving God. Those who understand this make it into the kingdom. As Samuel Rutherford said, "Bow low, man, bow low, the door into the kingdom is low."

SERMON NOTES

Jesus starts out His sermon on what sounds like a negative note. What does He mean by "poor in spirit?" Explain the difference between being poor in spirit and having a low self-image.

In your own life, is poverty of spirit something that appeals to you? Why?

How do we confuse humility with modesty? Pride with conceit?

Why would Jesus say the absurd—that it is easier for disreputable people, such as prostitutes and tax collectors, to enter the kingdom of heaven than the "best" of society?

Is one more aware of spiritual bankruptcy when one says "All of us are sinners," or, "I lied to you yesterday"? Which is easier to admit? Why?

In your own words, write the Beatitude in terms that might communicate it effectively today.

BAD DEBT

∎

The Arabs have a proverb that says, "All sunshine makes a desert." Yet it is difficult for us to think of sending condolences to a successful business person whose office is perched on the top of the world. The second Beatitude, "Blessed are those who mourn, for they will be comforted," then is as paradoxical as the first and grows out of it. Christ was saying, "Happy are those who are sad." We would like to rewrite this. "Blessed are those who have no tears at all" makes more sense. How can the griefs of life bring the benefits of life? The principle of mourning is not easy to understand. If we mourn about the wrong thing, we are going to be miserable. Some people mourn because they don't have more money, don't have the right job, and don't have as many gifts as some. Others spend their lives mourning about the sick or the dead. None of it helps very much.

Growth in life can come when the rain falls, but Jesus was not talking about mourning over unfulfilled dreams or personal tragedies. The mourning here is about grief over sin. In this sense, the second Beatitude is the emotional expression of the first. The poor in spirit are those who sense their need of God and who mourn over their sins.

When we sense our need of Him and mourn about our sins, He comforts us. The Christian life is a cycle of sensing our fallenness, turning to Him, and then standing. The process starts when we realize how far we are from who we ought to be.

I have known some outstanding scholars with first-rate minds. These people are leaders in their fields. They got to be leaders because they have a sense of ignorance. People who figure they know it all don't get anywhere.

I have a friend who is a leading Old Testament scholar. He said to me several years ago, "I'm fifty-four years of age, and I haven't touched the hem of the garment in my field."

When I was ten, I was constantly reminded of my ignorance by my thirteen-year-old cousin. That is a miserable thing; God should never let that happen! Talk about a bad self-image! My cousin would say to me, "Tell me one thing that you know that I don't know. Tell me! Go ahead and think of something." I knew that I didn't have one card to play. He was three grades ahead of me. Sports, or whatever the subject, he knew more than I. I have learned a great deal since boyhood, and I might be able to keep pace with him now; but at best, we've both only taken on a few more facts.

Sooner or later we come to fields, whether it be medicine, law, or real estate, where our knowledge runs out. We are then in great shape because that's how we begin to learn.

Sometimes as I sit at my desk I get very discouraged about what I don't know. The process of mourning about ignorance is not unlike what should be happening in my spiritual life. In sensing my need of God and staying continually aware of it, I draw closer to Him. When I do, I get upset about my sin. The light of His presence shows up the gravy stains in my life. But because I know God forgives my sin, I'm comforted. I know I am a forgiven sinner.

We don't honor God by worrying about our sin. We need to go to Him and simply experience His grace and comfort. That is blessedness.

That is why H. G. Stafford wrote:

> My sin—oh, the bliss of this glorious tho't,
> My sin—not in part, but the whole

>   Is nailed to the cross and I bear it no more,
>   Praise the Lord, praise the Lord, O my soul!

Paderewski, the great Polish pianist and composer, had a young woman training with him. She was playing in a recital, and in the middle of her piece, she forgot the music. It sounded as if she was playing bed springs as she hit one wrong note after another. She stumbled through it, but at the end she just sat at the piano and wept. Paderewski went over and kissed her on the cheek. He hugged and comforted her. It wasn't that Paderewski no longer cared about her playing correctly. He knew that comforting the young girl in her failure would motivate her to try again; her frustration was a sign that she sensed her need of more study. And because of his comfort, she wanted more than ever to please him and become a brilliant concert pianist.

Blessed are the poor in spirit, for theirs, and only theirs, is the kingdom of heaven. Blessed are they that mourn, about their sin, about their failure, about their lack of faith, about the way they blow it, because they shall be comforted. And in being comforted they are blessed because they know God accepts them.

Fred Smith told about a couple who took in a messed-up young girl. She lived with them for a year and went through all kinds of problems. Every evening after supper they did something that ultimately made a difference in the girl's life. They had her repeat, "God does not love me because I am good. He loves me because I am precious, and I am precious because Christ died for me."

When that dawns on us—God does not love us because we are good, He loves us because we are precious, and we are precious because He died for us—we will have the poverty of spirit that allows us into the kingdom. Repentance is a recognition of our need. And when we sense that need, we can cast ourselves with reckless abandon at His feet. His grace will meet our need.

SERMON NOTES

Look up the word *mourn* in the dictionary—what is the definition? If you or someone close to you has ever been in mourning, what was the reason? What feelings did it involve? What actions did it involve?

Exodus 32:30–33:6, 1 Kings 13:1–32, and Nehemiah 8:1–12 all deal with people mourning. Which of these incidents is closest to what Jesus is talking about in this Beatitude?

What is the relationship between mourning as we experience it in the death of a loved one or the loss of a friendship, and the mourning we should experience over our sin? What do they have in common? How are they different?

What must happen inside of us before we are able to mourn over our sin? Does being "blessed" because we mourn mean that Christians must be sad and solemn all the time?

Can you think of an example in your life when you grieved over your lack of Christlikeness, over your sin? Can you describe that experience?

Why do you think the Beatitude "Blessed are those who mourn . . ." follows the Beatitude "Blessed are the poor in spirit . . ."? How is the second Beatitude the emotional expression of the first?

When we mourn over our sin and depravity, Jesus says we will be comforted. In what manner would you like God to comfort you? What would that feel like? Is it possible to have false comfort?

POWER BASE

■

While studying for my master's degree at Southern Methodist University, I had a bit part in a university play. The young woman who played the female lead was looking forward to a Broadway career, and she already understood the dog-eat-dog world of theater. Sometimes during the rehearsals we would sit in the blue room and talk. She had no use for Christianity, less for Christians, and even less for Jesus. She couldn't take seriously a man who went around babbling about the meek inheriting the earth. "You and I both know that the meek get ground into the earth," she would say.

What that young woman said to me on those occasions was similar to Nietzsche's philosophy. He said that when we look at the ethic of Jesus, bound up in the Beatitudes as part of the Sermon on the Mount, we are listening to the most seductive lie history has ever heard. When Nietzsche came to "Blessed are the meek, for they will inherit the earth," he rephrased it and said, "Assert yourself; it is the arrogant who take over the earth."

We may be for Jesus, but we're not up to defending the idea of the meek inheriting the earth. We're not sure we believe it. In fact, we doubt the idea at both ends. We are not particularly attracted to meekness, and we are uncertain about the meek inheriting the earth. The meek may get to heaven, but we know who gets the earth. The arrogant, the aggressive, the multinational corporations, the Mafia, the porno kings, the military dictators, they're the ones who take over the earth. Successful people claim that we must assert ourselves to get ahead. We must be take-charge people. As Leo Durocher said of

Mel Ott and the New York Giants in the 1940s, "Nice guys finish last."

If we handed out placards with the motto "The meek will inherit the earth," few business and political leaders, or religious ones, for that matter, would rush to hang them over their desks. Our uneasiness about meekness may spring from its meaning in English. The dictionary defines *meekness* as "deficient in courage," so we think it means to be weak. If we did a word association test, most people would describe a meek man as a Caspar Milquetoast—a person who strains himself in squishing a grape.

The word *meek* in Greek does not mean "meek and mild." Aristotle used the word for the "golden mean." It was the point between extreme anger and extreme angerlessness. A meek person in the Greek sense of the term was controlled and balanced, getting angry at the right things at the right time. Injustice in the world, not personal insults, mattered to this person.

A young soldier in the Peloponnesian Wars wrote to his fiancee about a gift he had for her. It was a white stallion. He described it as "the most magnificent animal I have ever seen. He responds obediently to the slightest command. He allows his master to direct him to his full potential." And then he wrote, "He is a meek horse." The soldier wasn't saying that the horse was shy or even that he was like an old plow horse that allows people to beat him. He was an animal with great spirit, but that spirit was submissive to the rider.

Tied up in the word *meek* is the concept of power under control, the idea of being submissive to someone greater than ourselves. When we look at meekness as weakness, we discover that the examples in the Bible contradict this view, too.

Moses was called the meekest man on earth (Numbers 12:3, KJV). That is a strange description. He started a revolution against the Egyptians and slew one of them in the process. And forty years later when he stood before Pharaoh, the head of Egypt would not have described Moses as meek. This man was able to lead two and one-half million rebellious people through the wilderness not because he was weak, shy, and retiring. In fact, he missed out on the Promised Land because he tried to get water from the rock by smashing it rather than touching it. He doesn't sound weak. How can the Bible describe him as the meekest man of his day? With controlled power and absolute submission to God, Moses was the definition of meekness.

Christ even called himself "meek and lowly" (Matthew 11:29, KJV). No moneychanger would have called Jesus that; He upended tables and drove the greedy-hearted from the temple.

Meekness is submission, power under control. The Greeks described some winds as meek in contrast to hurricanes, or winds out of control. Perhaps the idea of power under control is best translated by the English word *gentleness*.

We understand meekness as "gentleness" better as we see the relationship of the third Beatitude to the first two. In the first one, being poor in spirit means recognizing our personal bankruptcy, our inability to get out of debt to God. It's knowing that deep inside we are sinful people, desperately in need of God's grace and forgiveness. The second Beatitude is the emotional outgrowth of our sense of being poverty-stricken spiritually. As we catch a glimpse of who we really are, we mourn. As we mourn over our individual sins, God comforts us, displaying His grace and forgiveness. Out of our desperate condition should come a spirit of gentleness.

If one thinks that one is the center of the universe, like billions of others who think the same thing, the spirit of gentleness will never be ours. When we believe that everything ought to revolve around us, our views, our wishes, our businesses, our plans, we will keep bumping into others. If we live those kinds of lives, we will be arrogant and aggressive, always putting people down. We will also put up fronts, afraid to let others know about the unhappiness inside us. We will wear masks of supposed strength, hiding our true feelings and making ourselves look superior to other people.

Henry Drummond was right when he said that anger and irritation at other people for not giving us "straight A's" in our lives is probably responsible for more pain than any other kind of sin. How do we handle the slings and arrows of others? Jesus said that meekness is my response to who I am before God; and when I understand who I am, I will relate to others differently.

Carl Jung, the Swiss psychiatrist, said that we are fortunate that no one ever knows us completely. Of course, God does; and sometimes in our better moments, we can catch a glimpse of ourselves as He knows us. But if other people knew us as we really are, it would be tough, wouldn't it?

I sometimes get upset when people criticize me. Yet I also know that if those same people could hear my confessions to God in the morning, they would know they had not seen the half of who I am. If they knew what God knows about me, they would have an ironclad case.

When we live before God and see ourselves as He sees us, we confess the hidden sins, and that changes our attitudes. This confession keeps us from being angry and irritated when people attack us, because we know that if they could see our hearts, they would have a field day. Out of this changed attitude comes meekness, a sense of submission, a gentleness of spirit, and a deep knowledge of what God has forgiven in our lives.

Jesus said that "the meek will inherit the earth." This phrase comes from Psalm 37, where the idea of inheritance is repeated numerous times, and there it refers to inheriting land. It means the same in the Sermon on the Mount. When Jesus instructed His disciples to pray for His kingdom to come, He meant an earthly kingdom, a dwelling place for the meek, those submissive to God. They will not earn it or win it, but they will march triumphantly into it.

Inheritances are given through someone's death, and people simply receive them. When we pray for His kingdom to come, we are not dreaming the impossible. The whole Bible points forward to that day when Christ will return and set up His literal kingdom on earth. And those who are in submission to God, who know their sinfulness, who have admitted it, who have accepted God's forgiveness, to them the kingdom belongs.

But it is also true that the arrogant and the power seekers don't inherit the earth. Hitler followed Napoleon and countless others in his quest for world domination, but God was not on the side with the biggest cannons. Hitler ran into God in the form of a Russian winter and army, and the German people never became masters of the world. Throughout history nations such as Assyria, Babylonia, and Rome have seemed invincible, and if we judged them on a given Tuesday, we might believe it. But if we examine them not by the day but by the years, we discover that the arrogant and the power-mad do not inherit the earth.

What's true with nations is true in the animal world. The lions and tigers should be in control; the lambs should not be baaing anymore. If we were betting people, no doubt we would place our money on the eagle rather than the sparrow. Yet the lion, tiger, and eagle are endangered species. Plenty of sparrows and lambs!

The arrogant and powerful do not inherit the earth. The people in Moscow and Washington don't seem to understand this. They may wipe out a good part of the earth with nuclear weapons, but they will never control it.

The arrogant are not even those who win in personal relationships. No one wants a rude and self-seeking friend. Folks who surround such people want something from them; they don't want their friendship. Those hungry for power are lonely people. They think they possess the earth, but the earth possesses them. They always want more, and soon the envy and desire for more is controlling them. In restaurants, they fight over the best table. At airline counters, they become hostile if they can't get window seats. In the end, all they get is ulcers. They are miserable people. No one wants such people as friends.

The kind, the gentle, the gracious, at least enjoy the earth, whatever they have of it. When they see who they are before God, they know anything they receive is of grace. Hell is what they deserve. And knowing that, they keep power under control, living gentle and meek lives, knowing that one day God will give the earth to them.

SERMON NOTES

What normally comes to mind when you think of a "meek" person? How did Aristotle use the word *meek*? How would the ancient Greeks have described a "meek" person?

What picture comes to mind when you read about the white stallion, the "meek" horse? Can you picture other ways in which meekness can also be strength?

Moses was called the "meekest man on earth." Why? Can you think of other biblical characters who could be described as "meek"? Can you think of anyone you know who might fit this description? Why?

Define meekness. Can you think of another word for meekness?

Explain how this third Beatitude relates to the first two.

What encourages meekness in your life? What inhibits meekness in your life?

In your own words, state what Jesus meant when He said, "Blessed are the meek, for they will inherit the earth."

COMPANY MEALS

∎

Frederick Forsyth, the writer of books about international intrigue, says the greatest motivation in the world is hunger. The fourth Beatitude is about hunger. If we only had the first three Beatitudes about being poor in spirit, about being mourners, and about being meek, we could develop a bad self-image! If we ended up with just those three, we'd admit our sinfulness, our inability to grieve over it, and our cover-up of it before others. In the fourth Beatitude, the focus changes from our needs to our desires—to what we hunger and thirst for. Hunger is sacred, whether one speaks of food, pleasure, or power. Hunger drives us. Advertisers understand this; they know hunger moves merchandise. They motivate us to buy the product by playing upon our deepest desires. Subtly they promise what the product doesn't deliver.

Advertisers make us believe that the basic hungers and thirsts of life will be satisfied by junk food and soda pop. The advertisements for Las Vegas, Reno, and Atlantic City promise happy holidays and the deepest desires satisfied. After a few days of feasting from that table, people discover they have been eating large bites of cotton candy. Fun-seekers leave those places more hungry than when they arrived.

Christ has a different diet; it starts with hungering and thirsting after righteousness. People in the ancient Near East had meat once a week if they were fortunate. Many lived on the edge of starvation. They had a limited diet; they understood gnawings in their bellies. The Near Eastern sun can turn throats to sandpaper. Desert people felt the sweep of the wind and the hot sand in their faces. The people of Christ's time knew hunger and thirst.

When Christ talked about hungering and thirsting, He meant a deep desire to be righteous, which should come from a realization of need; and He pinpointed that need in the first three Beatitudes. Candy-biting and soda-swigging are not what He had in mind.

Yet I'm not sure that righteousness takes top billing on our desire list. Perhaps we're not really sure what righteousness is. If we've grown up in certain types of churches, we often think of righteousness in terms of negatives—rules and regulations that dampen life and its joys. In these churches, to be righteous is not to go to the places that we want to go and to have to go to the places we don't want to go. It's not doing fun things but those that seem like nonsense. It is the essence of the Pharisees' righteousness. It's negative.

If righteousness is negative, we're not sure that we really want it. Our response to righteousness, as we think we understand it, is like what an Anglican scholar wrote in reviewing a book on the moral authority of the church: "There isn't much in this book . . . that makes the reader want to be good."

It was Mark Twain who said, "Having spent considerable time with good people, I can understand why Jesus liked to be with tax collectors and sinners." Righteousness sometimes turns us off. So the question is, What do we mean by righteousness?

We could take off the *ness* in righteousness, but the *righteous* may not be much better to our ears, sounding like self-righteous. If we do some further cutting by removing *eous*, we end up with the word *right*. Righteousness then is the "desire to be right." As some theologians have put it, "It is uprightness because we are down-right." In other words, as we sense our falling short of what we ought and want to be, and what God made us to be, our desires become different. As we see our sin and admit it, we desire to be the kind of person God wants us to be. The great thing about Christ's words is that He did not say, "Blessed are those who are righteous." He said, "Blessed are those who hunger and thirst after righteousness."

When we put down a spouse or spout off to a friend, we may at first defend our words; but when we recognize our ungraciousness, we want to be different. We want to be *right-eous*, a straight ruler rather than a crooked stick. It is this desire that will bring satisfaction to our lives, but without wanting it, we will never get it.

As long as we keep defending our behavior by making excuses, we can't have Christ's filling. Hungering and thirsting to be right is basic to being filled. One doesn't kick hunger or thirst with one meal; hungering and thirsting is a sign of being alive. It is an ongoing process. As the Puritans claimed, "The man who feels not his need to be righteous is the man who needs it most desperately."

It is a mark of life, spiritual life, that one has a hunger and thirst for "right-ness." In certain parts of China, when they bury a person, they put some food, usually bread, and some water in the casket. The corpse never says, "Thank-you." If we dig up the corpse a few days after burial, the bread and water would still be there. Corpses never eat bread or drink water unless they do it at the same time they smell the flowers! What marks a corpse is its deadness; hungering, thirsting, and smelling are out the picture. Hunger is a sign of health and life.

If we do not have an appetite for righteousness, that is a red flag. Something is wrong. To see ourselves as God sees us and to recognize how far we have to go are the beginnings of hunger and thirst. God can fill us, but not with one meal.

We have all pulled away from Thanksgiving tables thinking we could never eat again, yet at five o'clock that afternoon we were back in the kitchens. Dining at God's table once will not take care of hungering and thirsting forever. We must have a constant appetite for "right-ness"; and with that consistent desire, God gives continual filling.

As the old hymn says, "Let not conscience make you linger, or of a fitness fondly dream, the only fitness God requires is that you sense your need of Him." When we sense our need, then we are blessed. The question is, How good do we want to be? If we hunger for righteousness, if we thirst for it, God will fill us, and fill us, and fill us again.

An old Scottish woman used to pray, "Oh God, make me as holy as a forgiven sinner can be." It is a good prayer. And those who pray it out of honesty and integrity, out of a sense of need, are the ones who are blessed. The meek, who live in submission and gentleness before God, will inherit the earth; they are God's kind of people. And blessed are those who hunger and thirst to be right before God. That constant, continual desire, will be continually filled.

SERMON NOTES

What kind of image does "hungering and thirsting" conjure up? How does hungering and thirsting compare with merely wanting something?

When you crave something, how does that feel? How does craving affect your actions?

What kinds of things do people "hunger and thirst" for in our culture? What feeds those desires and keeps us wanting more?

Christ tells us we should crave righteousness. Think about your life, your desires. Have you ever had a hunger for righteousness? What was happening in your life when that occurred?

Compare religious performance with the righteousness Jesus was referring to. How do we get to the point of "desiring to be right"?

Jesus might have said, "Blessed are the righteous." Why didn't he state the Beatitude that way?

When someone loses his appetite, what does that indicate about his physical condition? What might a lack of hunger or thirst for righteousness indicate about our spiritual health?

What is it that we need when we hunger and thirst physically? What does Jesus promise those who hunger and thirst after righteousness?

Explain what "be filled" means. How often will God fill us?

COMPENSATION PLAN

■

When John Wesley was a missionary in Georgia, Governor James Oglethorpe had a slave who stole a jug of wine and drank it. Oglethorpe wanted the man beaten, so Wesley went to Oglethorpe and pled for the slave. And the governor said, "I want vengeance. I never forgive." To which John Wesley said, "I hope to God, Sir, you never sin."

In Wesley's time, and especially in the ancient world, mercy was often despised. To the Greeks and Romans, mercy was a sign of weakness. They admired justice, courage, and discipline. As one of the Roman philosophers said, "Mercy is a disease of the soul." The ancient view of mercy was reflected in the culture. According to Aristotle, slaves were living tools and thus were treated in a very impersonal way. For no other reason than being tired of his slaves, an owner could send them to the arena as an evening meal for some red-jowled beasts. If a slave grew too old to work, he could be disposed of like a broken hammer or a rusty plow.

Babies were not treated much better than slaves. If a woman gave birth to a daughter or a crippled son, the father might expose the infant to the elements and allow it to die. And as far as enemies, the only good one was a dead one. It was absolutely unthinkable to have mercy toward an enemy.

In this culture of the ancient world, Jesus proclaimed, "Blessed are the merciful, for they will be shown mercy." We hear His words now and they have a softer sound to us. Mercy may have a good press, but that doesn't mean we are merciful in our culture. We may give some mercy to the underdog, but not to the equal dog or the top dog. We will have mercy on the dependent, but that is sometimes only a way of exercising power. We may have a better regard for mercy because of twenty centuries of Christian influence. But if we look carefully at Christ's words, they may be as unsettling to us as to the people in the first century. Before we can comprehend the fifth Beatitude, we need to understand what the Bible means by mercy.

Evidently the word *mercy* in the New Testament was a Greek translation of a Hebrew word. That Hebrew word is almost untranslatable into English. Perhaps the closest concept is that of sympathy, or empathy. According to William Barclay, the Hebrew word meant to get inside someone else's skin, to look at life from another perspective, to feel what another person was experiencing. But it was more than to feel; it was to act, to think, to will as someone else might in desperate circumstances.

Another way we might look at *mercy* is to compare it to *grace*. Grace and mercy are both reflections of God's love. Theologians say grace is unmerited favor, which means God gives us what we don't deserve. Grace is God's reaction to our sinfulness; mercy is His reaction to our misery.

Several years ago when I was speaking in Oklahoma City, a man there offered to buy me some shoes in appreciation for my ministry. I was a bit hesitant about the whole thing, but he took me to a shoe store and said to the clerk, "I want you to bring out three pairs of brown shoes and three pairs of black shoes. Show us your best shoes and don't let him see the price. He can choose the pair he likes best." Well, it was a good deal and so I responded. That was grace; I didn't deserve the shoes. I wasn't even barefoot!

The man who gave me the shoes didn't show pity on me; I had my own shoes. It was simply an act of kindness. Mercy, in contrast, is a response of grace to people's needs. Mercy is a response to misery;

mercy understands the hurt, feels the hurt, and moves out to cure the hurt.

We understand mercy if we have ever had small children. When my daughter Vicki was a toddler, she had a cold—fever, sore throat, stopped-up nose, the whole works. She was miserable and almost too sick to whimper. I picked her up and put her arms around my neck and held her tight. She cried. I got out the humidifier, rubbed her with Vicks, and did everything I could think of. She still couldn't sleep. I stayed up all night with her; I wanted to crawl in that crib and suffer for her.

Biblical mercy, however, is more than showing sympathy for a child. It is feeling for the kid down the street who is suffering because of a broken home but who also has shattered our garage windows three or four times. Mercy has not only the idea of sympathy or empathy but also the concept of thought and action.

In the fifth Beatitude, "Blessed are the merciful, for they will be shown mercy," Jesus set forth a principle of mercy. Some have understood the principle to be "do unto others as you would like others to do unto you, and they will do it." That is, we will receive what we give. The way we behave toward other people will determine how they will behave toward us. This view may be true, but it is only half-true. When we show mercy to others, they are not always merciful in return. Jesus Christ restored a Roman soldier's ear, but that didn't keep the Romans from crucifying Him. It is good to be merciful, but we may discover a number of Romans in society. The merciful are sometimes trampled underfoot.

A second way in which people have understood the fifth Beatitude is that "you should do unto others as you would like God to do unto you." In this case people view the Beatitude from the standpoint of how God will respond rather than how people will respond. And at first glance, that seems like a possibility. However, the Bible never teaches that we can earn God's mercy. God deals with us in grace. God isn't like an investment broker; we don't get grace the old fashioned way, by earning it. It is a gift. God gives it because of who He is, not because of what we do.

If we cannot earn mercy from people or God, what was Jesus saying? He was teaching that "we should do unto others as God in His grace and mercy has done unto us." We can't buy God's mercy; we are the objects of it. In this sense, the fifth Beatitude grows out of the other four. When we see our bankrupt condition in the first Beatitude, grieve over our sins in the second Beatitude, sense our dependence on him in the third Beatitude, hunger because of our desperate need in the fourth Beatitude, He responds in grace and mercy.

The first three Beatitudes deal with our condition; the fourth with our qualification, that is, all we need to be made right with God is the urgent sense that we have a need. If we have been made right with God, what is the evidence of it? The proof that we have obtained mercy is that we show mercy. So mercy does come as a result of mercy. Mercy toward others comes as a result of God's mercy toward us, which is constant and never-ending.

In Matthew 18:21, Peter asked Jesus, "Lord, how many times shall I forgive my brother when he sins against me? Up to seven times?" Peter's problem was that he wanted to know what the limits were on forgiveness. It's easy to take a cheap shot at Peter, but some of us have a tough time showing forgiveness even once.

The ancient rabbis felt that a person should show forgiveness three times. If someone transgressed a fourth time, forgiveness stopped. Peter took the rabbinical standard, doubled it, added one for perfection, and came up with seven times. Who will be a patsy after seven times? Peter's solution seemed quite gracious.

Peter viewed forgiveness like a mathematical formula. One could count it, weigh it, and measure it. It is like responding to the question "How many times should a person love?" with elaborate calculations. To ask such a question is to negate the question.

Jesus responded to Peter's question with the answer of seventy-seven times, or in other textual variations, seventy times seven. Jesus was simply playing on words and saying forgiveness is unlimited. Forgivers are forgetters, and to count to seven, an individual must remember the first six. Forgivers may recollect some incident, but they don't remember it with emotional overtones.

If someone borrowed fifty dollars from you and later paid the debt, you might remember the borrowing and reimbursement of the fifty dollars, but the debt is settled. You would have no emotional overtones in your memory. To forgive and forget doesn't mean that we don't recollect the past, but we're not in emotional bondage to it. According to Jesus, forgiveness must be unlimited; and when we forgive, we don't emotionally drag up the past.

How do we forgive or show mercy the way Jesus taught? Jesus explained through a story. A king wanted to settle accounts with a man who owed him ten thousand talents. This man may have been a tax collector for the king. Whatever he did for the king, it's obvious the man had sticky fingers. A common laborer in those days would have to work twenty years to make one talent. Rome only collected eight hundred talents a year in taxes from the five Jewish regions of Judea, Samaria, Galilee, Perea, and Idumea. This fellow was into the king for ten thousand talents, which might be as high as thirty million dollars in American money.

With this staggering debt, the man was brought to the king. The king ordered all the man's possessions sold and commanded that the man, his wife, and his children be sold into slavery. A slave sold for somewhere between two hundred to a thousand dollars in the ancient world. Under Roman law, debts could be settled this way.

The man begged for mercy from the king and promised to repay him, although he could not do it in a thousand lifetimes. He was like us before God. We recognize the debt we owe God and promise to reform, but we are stalling. The man was buying time, trying to keep himself and his family from being sold into slavery. The king took pity on the man and canceled his debt. He asked for time, but the king gave him a pardon.

The king acted in mercy, and the man left. He soon ran into an associate who owed him about thirty dollars. He choked him, demanding his money. The small-time debtor pleaded for mercy with the same words that the man had used before the king, but the man had him thrown in prison. It might be possible to repay thirty dollars, but a person can't do it in jail. The man obviously wanted strict justice and revenge more than money. He was going to follow the letter of the Roman law. If a debtor could not pay, he went to jail.

No pity, no mercy. The king dealt with the man mercifully, but the man demanded his rights with others. Word got back to the king about the man's behavior, and the king called him in again. He asked the man a very pointed question, "Shouldn't you have had mercy on your fellow servant just as I had on you?"

Then in anger the king turned the man over to the jailers until he paid back what he owed. At this point, the story concluded with a warning, "This is how my heavenly Father will treat each of you unless you forgive your brother from your heart." These last words were rather dark; Jesus sounds threatening. What does all this mean?

The man in the story heard of forgiveness and accepted it but never entered into it. He took it as a matter of course that the king would forgive him the thirty-million-dollar debt. A sense of being forgiven had never made its way to his inner life.

Christ's parable is a story of us all. We could never pay the debt we owe to God in a thousand lifetimes, and the final warning is to those who have never recognized their poverty of spirit. If they had, they would be forgiving others.

When we enter into God's mercy, we recognize our poverty of spirit, we mourn over our sin, we submit ourselves to Him, and we hunger and thirst for forgiveness. The proof that we have entered into it is that we show mercy to others. The king in the story did not ask the man for gratitude—only the evidence of mercy received in mercy shown.

If we know God's forgiveness, we will forgive. A forgiven person is a forgiving person. If we refuse to forgive, this betrays something about our relationship to God. The fifth Beatitude must be understood in its context. What Jesus is saying in the Sermon on the Mount and throughout the Bible is that the mercy of God and the forgiveness of sins are not theological doctrines to which we give only intellectual assent; they are the experiences of a poverty-stricken spirit, filled with mourning, meekness, and hunger.

Kenyon Scudder, a west coast prison warden, told the story of the small-town Oklahoma boy who had deeply embarrassed his family and community by ending up in prison. While he was in the penitentiary, he heard very little from his folks at home. They were illiterate, so writing was not easy. Yet he wasn't sure whether writing was their problem or if they had simply given up on him. When it came near the time for his release, he wrote his parents that he was coming through their town on the train. The train ran past his parent's backyard, so he told them to tie a white ribbon on the apple tree if they could forgive and accept him. If he did not see a ribbon, he would keep on going and be out of their lives forever. As expected, the man did not get a written response from his parents. He finally left prison and boarded a train for his hometown. As he got closer to the town, he was so overcome with emotion that he moved from his window seat. He had related his story to a nearby passenger and sighed, "I can't bear to look out the window. Will you look for me?" When they came to the town and passed his house, the passenger grabbed his leg and whispered, "The whole tree is white with ribbons."

If we are honest with ourselves, we have all felt like the Oklahoma boy in our relationship to our heavenly Father. I know I have. When I thought of how I had disappointed God, I was afraid to go home. I wanted to send a letter first, asking, "Will you forgive me for all the things I've done?" Finally, out of my desperate need, I journeyed home. Before I even saw my Father, I saw a tree in the shape of a cross. It was filled with white ribbons. Then He rushed out to meet me and hugged me long and hard. He put His arms around me and said, "That's okay, Son, I forgave you a long time ago." When we see the white ribbons hung for us, we hang out white ribbons wherever we go.

SERMON NOTES

How was *mercy* viewed in the ancient world? Is that different from the way we regard mercy today? Compare mercy with grace.

Is it easier to be merciful to those who look up to you or to those who are wealthy and powerful? Why?

Sometimes we are motivated to do good in order to get something. If we do good will we usually get something good in return? Where should our motivation to be merciful stem from?

Do you think mercy is an act or an attitude?

Sometimes our mercy to others is paid back with ungratefulness, or even cruelty. Have you experienced this in your life? Can you think of any examples from the Bible that illustrate this?

Why is this the fifth Beatitude? How does it grow out of the first four?

In Matthew 18:21, Peter thought he was being exceptionally generous with his suggestion that we forgive people *seven* times. Have you ever forgiven someone seven different times for what they've done to you? In your own words, explain Jesus' answer to Peter.

In the story about the man in debt to the king (Matthew 18:23–25), what is the significant fact about the debt the man owed? How does this relate to us as we stand before God?

What do you think kept the debtor in the story from forgiving his associate?

How do we become merciful people?

PURE WORK

∎

Ken Chafin, a Southern Baptist writer, surveyed Baptist seminary students' spirituality with the question, "What does it take to be a good Christian?" He got five different answers. First, a good Christian attends Sunday school and training union. Second, a good Christian goes to the worship services of the church. Third, a good Christian goes to prayer meeting. Fourth, a good Christian tithes and gives to the church. And fifth, a good Christian wins somebody else to Jesus. If you look at those things, at least four of the five have to do with the organization. They have to do with the ritual, with the ceremony. It's not that the ceremony is necessarily wrong, but you could do all of those things and only be a Christian for a week. That's the problem with religion; it sometimes doesn't get to the heart of the matter. People want to see each other; they don't necessarily want to see God.

Christ wants us to see God. He said, "Blessed are the pure in heart, for they will see God." The thought of either purity or of seeing God is a bit scary. When I was in second grade, just learning addition and subtraction, my older cousin showed me a school paper full of long division. I didn't understand short division, much less long division; but that one glimpse caused me dread for the next year. I confess the sixth Beatitude affects me like my apprehension about long division in the third grade.

I really don't know why the purity Beatitude bothers me, except that it is easy to confuse being pure in heart with being prudish. Sexual purity opponents have done a good job of making chastity defenders seem like fun spoilers—the dull and the drab of the earth. Was Jesus saying, "Blessed are the prudes, for they will see God" or even worse, "Blessed are the sinless, for they will see God"? Down inside I know that if that's what it takes to see God, then I don't have the hope of even a passing glance. If Jesus didn't mean "prudish" or "sinless," what did He mean? We quickly see that the focus of purity is the heart. Jesus was grappling with the kind of purity that comes from deep inside.

The key verse of the whole Sermon on the Mount is Matthew 5:20, in which Jesus declared that our righteousness must exceed that of the Pharisees. Living up to more commands or prohibitions than they did was not His point. The Pharisees had an external righteousness, but Jesus said that we must have an internal religion if we expect to see God. That is the heart of the matter.

In Matthew 15, we read the story of the Pharisees and religious leaders who traveled all the way from Jerusalem to Galilee merely to ask Christ why His disciples didn't wash their hands before meals. They didn't come to discuss hygiene but purification rituals. Just eating could be an elaborate religious ceremony, and the Pharisees had to wash their hands in a certain way. Those religious leaders believed that to see God they had to go through the proper rituals and ceremonies. One Jewish rabbi was arrested by the Romans and only given a couple of bread crusts and a cup of water for a meal. Instead of drinking the water, the rabbi used the water for ritual purification, saying he would rather die than go against the traditions of the fathers. History probably records more deaths for religious traditions than martyrdoms for Christ.

When I was growing up in New York City, some of my Catholic friends went to confession in anticipation of a wild weekend. They confessed not only past sins but also those they planned to commit. They were not taught that in church I'm sure, and the priest would not have approved of it had he known. My friends made religion external. Catholics do it; Protestants do it, too.

When we base our religion on rituals, we spend a great deal of time evaluating other people's performances. As long as we are out-performing them, we feel good. When we live on that kind of moral ladder, we are always looking at people on the rungs below. We want to feel that we are better than others. And when we do that, we are always looking at other people's sins. We decide which people are the extortioners, the unjust, and the adulterers, especially if none of those descriptions fit us. If people on down the ladder also measure others this way, the lowest measure becomes the standard. Somebody down the ladder is comparing himself or herself to the vilest of people. Adolf Hitler can comfort us because we can say that we are at least better than he. When we constantly compare ourselves with others, God marks us as self-righteous people. Jesus was not talking about ceremonies and rituals but about purity of heart.

When Christ spoke of the heart, He was talking about the core of the personality—the ego, the innermost part of a person. It was not just the emotions. When Tony Bennett sings "I left my heart in San Francisco," he means that he likes the city. He has a warm feeling about it. That is not the way the Bible uses *heart*. The heart includes emotions, but it is more than feelings. It is the totality of our being.

Our emotions come out of the heart (John 14:1), but so do our thoughts (Matthew 15:19). In fact, Jesus said in Matthew 15 that the heart can veil evil thoughts—those of murder, adultery, sexual immorality, theft, false testimony, and slander.

The heart is the seat of our emotions, our thoughts, and our wills. It is in the heart we decide to do good or to sin. So when we say, "Blessed are the pure in heart," we are saying "Blessed are those whose personalities are pure."

What does it mean to be pure? Originally, it meant something clean, such as clothing. It was later used to describe grain free of chaff or wine without water. Thus people with pure hearts do not have mixed motives. They are single-minded in their desire to see God.

The first three Beatitudes have to do with our state of being—poor in spirit, mourners over sin, and meek before Him. The poor in spirit recognize their utter need of God. Those who mourn express emotionally what it means to be poor in spirit. In sensing their utter need, they see their sins. Meekness is a submission before God, a recognition of dependence upon Him.

The fourth Beatitude grows out of the first three, for when we see our true condition, we hunger and thirst for God's righteousness, and He fills us. In coming to God and being filled, we are receiving His mercy as the fifth Beatitude indicates. We demonstrate that we have received that mercy by showing mercy to others.

And then in the sixth Beatitude, those who have gone through the hungering, the thirsting, and the filling process exhibit not only mercy but also purity of motive. A pure heart comes from receiving mercy.

But again, the process is a cycle; we are not once and for all pure. That's the way the Beatitudes work. They deliver us from two ditches—self-pity and self-praise. If we had only the first three Beatitudes, we might have a woe-is-me religion. Even if we escape this problem, a puffed-up-chest religion is lurking around the corner. If we follow the Beatitudes all the way, we see that we can't shape ourselves up through moral living or rigid rule-keeping. When we sense our need and are filled by God, we recognize that what happens has nothing to do with our being stalwart individuals, but everything to do with God's being merciful to the weak. Out of God's mercy grows our desire to be pure.

The cycle of our growth continues on and on. We never stop being needy people. Many years into his Christian life, Paul called himself the worst of sinners (1 Timothy 1:15). The more we become aware of our need, the more we become aware of Him; and the more we become aware of Him, the deeper grows our need and longing for His filling, His mercy, His very face. We never need less of Him.

A similar cycle happens in the music world. A youngster just learning piano may play through a Beethoven sonata and come away feeling pretty good about it. But a man like Van Cliburn, who practices ten hours a day, can sight-read that sonata and make it seem perfect to the untrained ear. But he goes over it again and again, because the closer he gets to perfection, the greater his distance from perfection. The closer he gets to the goal, the more he realizes how many light years he is away from it.

As we come to know God, we discover that the closer we get to Him, the more aware we become of sin. Out of this awareness comes poverty of spirit, mourning over sin, dependence on Him, and hungering and thirsting for righteousness. As we receive mercy, the more mercy we show, and greater grows our desire to be pure. The purity is not sinless perfection but a cleansing that comes through the process of getting closer to God. As we go through this process, we truly see God.

By seeing God, I mean perceiving, understanding, and sensing the reality of Him. Jesus called the Pharisees blind leaders because they were blind to spiritual things, to God's reality (Matthew 15:14). Moses left Egypt, not fearing Pharaoh, because he saw Him who was invisible (Hebrews 11:27). The burning bush experience had given Moses an awareness and consciousness of God.

We see what we want to see, and who we are determines what we see. Two people go to a museum. One exudes, "That's art!" The other exclaims, "That's art?"

While the pure in heart perceive God, the unpure see other things. When I was a student in seminary, I worked in the post office. At

Christmas time, especially, they hired all kinds of extra workers. I can remember being with two men whose hearts were set on sexual immorality. I used to wonder what kind of vermin would indulge in child pornography, but then I worked next to two of them. In all of their jokes and comments, that's all they talked about. Who they were determined what they saw. Perverted sex was all they saw in life.

In this process of becoming pure, we will perceive and see God. We will enter into that reality. We are not sinless, and we are not like Pharisees who are thankful that they are not like other men. The process makes us aware of how much like other people we are, and it produces in us mercy instead of judgment. Although we may be aware of our likenesses with other people, our focus is on God. Instead of looking down the ladder, we are looking up at Him. This looking up begins a cleansing process deep down in the heart.

What is our greatest delight? Whom do we delight in most? Bragging about being better than another, or satisfying some overwhelming lust, are phantoms of delight. Those who delight in the pure are the only ones who will find pure delight.

SERMON NOTES

Define "seeing God." How does purity of heart lead us to see God? Explain why Jesus called the Pharisees "blind leaders."

How can religious practices help us to see God? Can they ever hinder us from seeing Him?

When Jesus spoke about the "pure in heart," what was He referring to? How much of a person does "the heart" involve?

Describe the symptoms of an impure heart. For example, we might indulge in immoral sexual fantasies. Can you name some other ways in which we betray an impure heart?

How does becoming pure in heart relate to the previous five Beatitudes? Is attaining purity of heart a process or a state we achieve?

How do we achieve purity of heart?

When Paul called himself the "worst of sinners" (1 Timothy 1:15), what did he mean? Was he saying he sinned more than anyone else?

As we come close to God, the more we see our sin and our need for God. Describe the opposite situation—if we drifted further from God. What would we experience?

Give an example from everyday life of how who we are determines what we see.

PERSONNEL PROBLEM

∎

Washington, D.C., is full of peace monuments; we erect them after every war. One cynic remarked that peace is a moment when nations take time to reload. Communists and capitalists use peace as propaganda; pacifists feel they have a corner on it. Yet we are not very good at peacemaking. When Jesus said "Blessed are the peacemakers" in the seventh Beatitude, He was not saying "Blessed are the peace lovers" or "Blessed are the peace eulogizers." We will understand Christ's meaning of peace better when we understand the Hebrew word *shalom*. *Shalom* is a positive word, not a negative one. When Jewish people say *shalom*, they are not talking about the absence of war; they are wishing all the best for someone.

Shalom is an active word, not a passive one. Some kinds of peace are passive. It is not uncommon for two people to fight and settle their argument with guns. Sometimes they end up killing each other. The two dead people have finally come to peace, but it is a very passive peace. A cemetery is filled with peaceful people. Sometimes couples live together in an armed truce, but that is not the peace of *shalom*. That's more like the détente between North and South Korea; that kind of peace often erupts in trouble.

When Jesus talked about peacemaking, He meant active involvement in bringing together people who were estranged. This is going out of our way to establish peace. The peacemaking Beatitude grows out of the purity Beatitude; people with pure motives want to be peacemakers. People with mixed motives like peace because they don't want to be disturbed, but they are sometimes troublemakers.

The first seven Beatitudes deal with people personally. These seven could probably be divided into two groups of three with the fourth one, the hungering-after-righteousness Beatitude, in the middle. That is, when God fills His people with righteousness, the poor in spirit are merciful; the sin-mourners have pure motives, and the meek become peacemakers. Meek people are particularly suited to make peace. They are humble of mind and dependent on God. They aren't arrogant, touchy, or demanding of their rights. Out of meekness can come true peace.

What sort of peace do peacemakers make? One kind is a peace between God and men. The good news of the gospel is that we don't have to do anything to make peace with God. That peace has been already made. God signed a peace treaty in the blood of His Son, saying that He is no longer angry. Our sins are forgiven, and all we have to do is sign the peace treaty. God is satisfied with the death of Jesus Christ to take away our sin and remove its penalty, and all we have to do is be satisfied with what satisfies God. God declares that the cross was enough to end the war. When we agree with God about that, the war is over.

Peacemakers make every effort to get out the good news that God is not angry, that peace has been made, and that the peace treaty has already been signed. At the end of World War II, the United States signed a peace treaty with the Japanese; yet in the South Pacific islands, a number of Japanese soldiers did not get the word. They kept fighting years after the war ended. In fact, it was only a few years ago that the last Japanese soldier from World War II may have been found. For years after the war ended, messengers repeatedly went out to isolated islands to bear the good news about the peace treaty, but a number of the soldiers shot at them. They wouldn't believe it, so they kept on fighting.

Isolated in their own selfish ways, many people are fighting God.

They won't agree with God that the war is over. Many of them never got the message. One of the kinds of peace that we can make is helping people understand and eventually sign the peace treaty with God.

In addition to peace with God, Jesus may be talking about peace within men and women. As the prophet said, "There is no peace . . . for the wicked" (Isaiah 48:22). Sigmund Freud unscrewed the tops of men's heads and said, "As I've looked into men's lives, I've never met one who is not thoroughly afraid." But no possibility of having peace inside exists without coming to peace with our Maker.

No peace will exist between nations unless peace reigns in each country. And no country will have peace unless peace resides in each community. And no community will have peace unless peace inhabits the church. And no church will have peace unless peace dwells within its people. And no people will have peace unless they surrender to the Prince of Peace.

So peacemakers are helping people find peace with themselves. Many people are walking civil wars because they have never settled the peace issue. If we know the God of peace, we will be people of peace; and this will mark us wherever we go. Instead of driving people apart, we will try to bring them together.

If we can bring people to righteousness, we can establish a communion between them. In fact, we'll find that principle in the Sermon on the Mount. Making peace with a brother is more important than going through religious ceremonies (5:23–24). In other words, we shouldn't bother coming to church if we are bothered with a brother, unless we settle the matter before the service. Peacemaking is of greater consequence than church-playing. Loving our enemies and praying for our persecutors is what peacemaking is all about (5:43–45). That's a tough task. But one way we destroy our enemies is to make them our friends. If we curse them, we put a division between them and us. If we get back at those who get back at us, we are building walls instead of bridges.

Peacemakers drain the moats; they bring people together. In recognition of their work, God gives them new names—sons of God. This is fitting because six separate times in the New Testament our Father is called a God of peace. In every one of Paul's letters, he wrote about the peace of God that comes from the God of peace. If God had stood on His rights and demanded what He deserved, we'd all be in hell. We defamed His name and disobeyed His commands, and He could have demanded His rights. Yet He made the first move; indeed He made all the moves. He sent His Son to make peace through His death. He is a God of peace, so His children as peacemakers are rightfully called sons of God.

The phrase "sons of God" deals with character rather than relationship. When the Bible talks about the children of God, it is dealing with the idea of a father's relationship to a child. But in "sons of God," Christ is denoting a quality of character. Hebrew doesn't have many adjectives, so one of the ways they devised adjectives was to talk about the son of something. Barnabas was called the "son of consolation"; Judas, the "son of perdition." Barnabas was consoling; Judas was doomed. In English when we call someone the "son of a gun," we are talking about the parent. We imply, of course, that the child is as explosive and loud as his mother or father. So if someone is called a "son of God" or a "daughter of God," he or she is displaying God's character.

Whenever we make peace by bringing people into a relationship with God or by bringing two people together, we look a lot like God. It's this family resemblance that marks us out as the sons of God.

Perhaps the prayer of St. Francis of Assisi said it best:

Lord, make me an instrument of Your peace. Where there is hatred, let me sow love; where there is injury, pardon; where there is doubt, faith; where there is despair, hope; where there is darkness, light; and where there is sadness, joy.

When we live out this prayer, people will call us sons of God. We can do nothing more God-like than to bring peace to those separated from God and from each other.

SERMON NOTES

The Hebrew word *shalom* is translated *peace*. What is the full meaning of the word?

Peacemakers can make peace in three different ways. Give examples of how people in a church can make peace in each of those ways.

How important is it that we make peace with those we have offended? Will our efforts at making peace always establish harmony?

Why do some people refuse to make peace?

Why does Jesus say that peacemakers will be called "sons of God"?

If peacemakers are called "sons of God," then fill in the following:

"The hostile shall be called _____."

"The angry shall be called _____."

"The irritable shall be called _____."

OCCUPATIONAL HAZARD

■

As E. M. Forster noted, "Every now and then people have preferred sorrow to joy." When the first-century Christians signed on, they must have indicated such a preference. Of the eleven disciples left after Judas's defection, ten died vicious and violent deaths. And the one who was spared, John, died a prisoner on the isle of Patmos. The apostle Paul was whipped five times with thirty-nine stripes, beaten with rods, stoned once, and repeatedly hounded and persecuted (2 Corinthians 11:23–27). Early Christians suffered in every avenue of life. We can only imagine what it was like for the Christian stonecutter who turned down the construction contract for a pagan temple. What about the tailor who refused to make garments for pagan priests? What about the couple who declined an invitation from friends to a heathen banquet?

Christianity split families apart. A wife would come to faith in Jesus Christ, and her husband would be furious. He felt he was put down by others in the city who knew he was a devout pagan. Children were often thrown out of their homes by parents who did not share their faith. Brothers were separated from brothers. This faith, designed to bring people together, often brought not peace, but a sword.

At first glance, the persecution of early Christians doesn't seem to make sense in light of the first seven Beatitudes. Why would anyone want to persecute the poor in spirit? People who see themselves as faded yellow photographs of what they ought to be hardly seem candidates for persecution. And those mourning about their inability to please God don't seem like rabble-rousers.

The meek, those submissive to God, probably don't lord it over others. In fact, broken-spirited, sin-grieving, dependent people hunger after righteousness rather than for power and fame. They are merciful, pure, and peace-loving people. It just doesn't add up that people with such sterling attributes are beaten to the ground.

Beatitude people should be applauded, not booed. We might expect one of the great hymns of the faith to be, "For he's a jolly good fellow, for he's a jolly good fellow, for he's a jolly good fellow; that nobody can deny." That's why when we come to the eighth Beatitude Jesus again takes us by surprise.

In this last Beatitude, Jesus said, "Blessed are those who are persecuted because of righteousness, for theirs is the kingdom of God." Then He elaborated, "Blessed are you when people insult you, persecute you and falsely say all kinds of evil against you because of me. Rejoice and be glad, because great is your reward in heaven, for in the same way they persecuted the prophets who were before you."

Jesus predicted that the kind of people who demonstrate the virtues of the first seven Beatitudes would be persecuted. He didn't say, "Blessed are you if you are persecuted." We all know religious people who seem to court persecution—those running around with their own stake and box of matches. People want to reject them. They are very zealous people, lapel-grabbers with a religion that probably never goes below the shirt pocket. They may think that they bear the offense of the Cross, but they are just plain offensive. They've got body odor, bad breath, and bad manners.

Jesus spoke about people being persecuted because of righteousness, not self-righteousness. People may be reviled and punished without being persecuted. They may be getting what they deserve. Punishment and persecution are not the same. Peter wrote that a Christian should not suffer as a murderer, as a thief, as any kind of criminal, or even as a meddler (1 Peter 4:15). Punishment is what just people give to those who are evil. Persecution is what evil people give to those who are good.

Persecution did not seem to be an option for the first Christians. It was part of the job description. Take Jesus himself as a case in point. If anyone lived in submission to the Father, it was He. If anyone displayed mercy and goodness, it was our Lord. Yet the historical records indicate that Christ's enemies schemed about how they could murder Him after He had performed miracles. Ultimately, the best man history ever saw was put on a Roman execution rack by religious and political authorities.

Are good people really persecuted? Maybe Christ, the disciples, the early Christians. But those were different times, weren't they? After all, Nero was not one's average ruler; his lions had a strange diet. The whole Roman world overdid its cruelty. People had to get used to a new religion. Couldn't the first few hundred years after Christ have been an historical fluke? Of course, thousands died for Christ, but that was so long ago.

If we live according to the Beatitudes, we will be persecuted. It still goes on today. Church historians estimate that more Christian men and women have died for their faith in the twentieth century than in any other comparable period in history. People have died in Uganda, in China, and in Russia. We had a Romanian woman on our seminary campus who, before she arrived, was hounded by the communists and forced to flee from her homeland with nothing. Her husband was murdered. She is a Beatitude kind of person who wanted nothing more than to bring other Romanians to faith in Christ. That is still her passion. From 1981 to 1985, the Peruvian government or rebels martyred thirty-five thousand Christians. Christian leaders in Central America have told me of three hundred pastors who were tortured and murdered for their faith in Jesus Christ.

If we live a Beatitude kind of life, will we be persecuted? Will we be reviled? Will people speak falsely against us? In the comfort of the United States, we may think we are exempt, but I know of people who have lost their jobs in major corporations because they refused to bend on what they believed right.

Why do people attack those who are living righteously? One reason is, they are different. They march to the beat of a different drummer. They have a different set of standards. And in a world that prizes conformity, difference is often looked upon as dangerous. Some people cannot tolerate those with different values and worldviews. What is more, Beatitude people become a kind of conscience in a community. It bothers those who have no integrity to live and work with people who play by the rules. What's-in-it-for-me people are put off by what-can-I-do-for-you people.

The reasons for persecution may be numerous, but Jesus said, "Blessed are those who are persecuted because of righteousness." A couple of times in my life people have reviled and lied about me. At first I was somewhat overwhelmed to discover what I thought was good, others considered evil; to find what I thought was mercy, others found objectionable; and to learn what I knew was right, others viewed as grounds for job dismissal. I went to God and filed a complaint, "Lord, they are on my back; Lord, they are persecuting me." Now I expected that the Lord would say, "My, how I pity you. I want you to know how terrible I feel about all of this." Instead God said, "Congratulations!"

What kind of nonsense is it when the Bible tells us to rejoice and be glad about persecution? If we are feeling the pain of rejection and persecution, God's reply of "Great!" seems like a callous put down. Yet He is not being flip; we should rejoice for two reasons.

We should rejoice if we suffer because of righteousness. We are in great company; the prophets took their licks, too.

Ever notice how people we admire, who are now dead, may have been reviled and persecuted when they were alive? I remember Martin Luther King, Jr. We now name streets after him and a holiday has been set aside in his honor. Yet throughout his life he was cursed and he was ultimately martyred. The greatest president of the United States, Abraham Lincoln, was a man who was mocked, scoffed at, and ultimately assassinated. He is a hero now, but he was not in the 1860s.

When we look at the prophets of the Old Testament, men who stand out above all the crowd, who receive our acclaim and our admiration, we find they were persecuted and despised while they lived. In fact, Jesus said to the people of His day, "You build tombs for the prophets, and it was your forefathers who killed them" (Luke 11:47). If we live according to righteousness, if we live for God, we are in great company—that of the prophets and the thousands that followed them.

During the Watergate scandal, President Nixon had an enemies list. People in Washington who found that they were on that list were highly complimented. It was an honor to know that the President hated you. Our enemies, not our friends, are a true test of who we are. If we walk a different path, some will speak evil of us. When that happens, we are in good company. Those who have stood above the crowd have been characterized by one thing—evil people scheme against them.

We can rejoice not only because we are in great company but also because we have a great reward. Jesus said our reward would be great in heaven. If anyone but Jesus had said this, we might think it an exaggeration. If we suffer for His sake, we will receive a significant bonus.

Sometimes the idea of rewards bothers people. At least one altruistic soul says, "I am righteous for the sake of righteousness; I don't want to live for rewards." What we must recognize, though, is the difference between rewards and incentives. Incentives have nothing to do with the act; but rewards, at least as the Bible uses them, are always the product of the act.

In one of Charles Schulz's *Peanuts* comic strips, Schroeder is playing the piano and announces to Lucy that he is learning all of Beethoven's sonatas. Lucy, leaning on the piano, says, "If you learn to play them all, what will you win?" Schroeder is upset and says, "I won't win anything." Lucy walks away and says, "What's the use of learning the sonatas if you don't win a prize?" Lucy was turned on by incentives.

My wife, a piano teacher, once tried to teach our children how to play. We gave them quarters for practicing. My son and daughter were mercenary, so they practiced. Unfortunately, quarters were all they got out of their piano studies. Giving quarters was an incentive, but it wasn't a reward. No relationship existed between the quarters and the piano playing.

The reward of practicing is playing the Beethoven sonata. A man is mercenary if he marries a woman for her money because money is not the proper reward for love. But if a man marries the woman he loves, that's the reward. It's a proper connection.

What do we get if we suffer because of righteousness? The answer is, Him. As we live the Beatitude life, we enter into an eternal relationship with God. We may not understand all that means, but Jesus tells us it is great. To really have God because God has us, is to have an eternity in which we are the objects of His grace, mercy, and special love. When we come into a relationship with God, whatever that involves, we can only describe it by the word *great*.

Some things are certain. When we go through the waters, they will not overwhelm us. When we go through the fires, they will not wipe us out. In the midst of the persecution, He is with us. If we are compassionate and blameless peacemakers, we should not be surprised if some people sing dirges rather than anthems. Even if we are sometimes persecuted, He didn't oversell the job. Good company. Great benefits.

SERMON NOTES

Why would anyone persecute a person for being righteous?

Explain the difference between being persecuted and being punished.

In what way might a Christian today be persecuted for acting righteously? Has it ever been tough for you to make a righteous decision for the sake of your faith? Can you give examples?

How should we respond to false accusations and other types of persecution? If we are to live at peace according to the previous Beatitude, shouldn't we avoid persecution at all cost?

Is it possible to needlessly invite persecution and destroy peace?

In this life, sometimes the consequences of a right life include persecution. How would you balance these *consequences* with what Jesus said was the *reward* of a righteous life?

MARKET DEFENSE

∎

E dward C. Bentley, the mystery writer, began his novel *Trent's Last Case* with an intriguing question. He asked, "Between that which matters and that which seems to matter, how will the world know that we have judged wisely?" That, it seems, is a foundational question of life. How do we judge between what matters and what seems to matter? To inhabitants of the marketplace, business matters. They get up very early and go to bed very late, and they give up what is valuable in order to build the bottom line. And yet few men come to the close of life, lie on a deathbed, and wish they had spent more time at the office. What matters and what seems to matter is often hard to distinguish.

To others what matters is power. They spend the money made in business to gain a position of power. Perhaps it's a seat in the House or Senate; or if they are multimillionaires, they run for president of the United States. What matters, they think, takes place in Washington, London, or Moscow. But many people who have served in political life realize eventually that power really didn't matter much at all. When all is said and done in the capitals of the world, infinitely more is said than done. And even those in power cannot control much of what happens.

How will the world know that we have judged wisely between what matters and what seems to matter? Jesus' disciples never asked the question, but He gave them a surprising answer anyway. He told them they mattered, but He said it in a curious way: "You are the salt of the earth" (Matthew 5:13).

The young carpenter/preacher, not much older than thirty, spoke those words to His disciples. Most of them were evidently His age or perhaps a little younger. They had yet to make their mark in business; they had not established a sphere of influence; they were not political leaders; they were not born of nobility. They were ordinarily ordinary; some were fishermen, others probably farmers, and one was a tax collector. None of them was particularly religious. And yet to those mostly uneducated men, some speaking with country accents, Jesus said, "You are the salt of the earth." And His "you" was emphatic.

In the ancient world salt was highly valued. The Greeks believed that it contained something almost divine. The Romans sometimes paid soldiers with salt. If a soldier did not carry out his duties, others said he was not worth his salt. And the association of value with salt is still with us. Even today if we know someone who embodies genuine quality or goodness, we say, "She is the salt of the earth."

The ancient world valued salt for several reasons. But the question is, which of those reasons did Jesus have in mind when He said, "You are the salt of the earth"?

Salt was valued as a seasoning agent. We say, "Pass the salt," because we recognize that salt has a way of bringing out the flavor in food. Even long ago Job asked, "Can flavorless food be eaten without salt?" (6:6). So perhaps Jesus meant that His disciples were to bring a flavor to life, a zest to living.

In like manner, we should season life. In a world with an overriding sense of futility, we should bring joy. Even though we are people who mourn, we also know the grace of God. That ought to bring holy laughter. Unfortunately, that has not always been true of the citizens of heaven.

Some time ago, a public relations firm in New York conducted a study of what outsiders thought about the church. The unchurched respondents had three major negative reactions. First, the church always asked for money; next, it was always sad; and finally, it always talked about death. That kind of salt doesn't have much flavor.

If Jesus was talking about the flavor-giving qualities of salt, He was saying to His disciples that they mattered in this world because only they made life palatable.

People in the first century also understood salt as a symbol of purity, perhaps because salt was glistening white. As far back into antiquity as we can go, the earliest pagans offered salt to the gods. And Leviticus says that an offering to God must be accompanied by salt; if there was no salt, the offering was not acceptable (2:13). So when Jesus said we are the salt of the earth, perhaps He was saying that we are of value because we can display pure motives before a decadent culture.

In a culture that has perfected the art of lying, we ought to be known for our honesty. When we give our word, people should be able to count on it. In a world in which a thousand billboards proclaim the excitement of sexual looseness, our lives should stand for sexual and moral purity. Perhaps that's what Jesus had in mind.

Salt also creates thirst. Even today Arabs take salt to force them to drink liquids and avoid the dehydration caused by the desert. Salt forces them to drink before they sense the need. If that's the case, then Jesus was saying that we are of worth because we cause people to thirst after God.

But Jesus probably had another quality of salt in mind—its ability to preserve. Farmers and fishermen who heard Jesus speak those words would have thought of the way they used salt most often—to preserve fish and other meat.

After catching fish in the Lake of Galilee, the fishermen sold them in the capital city of Jerusalem, many miles to the south. Transportation was slow and refrigeration nonexistent, so they would salt down the catch. When a farmer killed a cow, he would salt the meat, the only method of preservation.

In many parts of the Bible, the righteous are seen as a force that preserves a decaying society filled with the germs of its own disintegration. Christians are worth their salt because they keep that decay from spreading as rapidly as it might.

Paul described in Romans 1 what happens in a society that has no preserving influence; it is eventually destroyed. Paul could have been reading tomorrow morning's newspaper. What was unthinkable in our culture thirty years ago is now promoted as something right and wonderful. In such a world Christians are important because they can partially stop the rot.

The city of Sodom was synonymous with evil in the ancient world. Located near the Dead Sea, it was evidently a city of commerce, where people came and went, bought and sold, boasted and rotted all at the same time. If we had gone to the Chamber of Commerce and asked them what they really needed, they might have said a convention bureau to attract people and more money to the city. If we had gone to the city fathers and argued for a campaign to bring in permanent residents who were upright and honest, they probably would have treated us like a bad cold. They might have argued that such people don't spend money as fast as the convention crowd.

In the biblical story, we're told that if just ten righteous people could have been found in Sodom, the city would have been delivered. Unfortunately, they couldn't be found and the destruction of Sodom was inevitable.

The French culture of the early 1700s was in the process of decay. The king had a motto: "After me the deluge." He was absolutely right; that was a prophetic voice. The deluge came and France was ripped apart by the French Revolution.

Just twenty miles across the channel, the English culture had the same rot. Historians have described at length the moral corruption of English culture. And yet England did not go through a revolution. What spared it? Its mighty navy? Its suave diplomats? Its politicians? Its police force? No. The country was spared, as historian and president Woodrow Wilson insisted, because in 1703 a man called John Wesley was born in England.

In Wesley's early years his heart was "strangely warmed," and he became a citizen of the kingdom of God. He reached out and won others to Christ, and the historians believe that it was in large part the righteous Methodist movement, spread like salt throughout the land, that delivered England from a revolution.

The safety of a nation does not reside in its military genius, its armies, or even its atomic weapons; it comes from the character of its people. Throughout history, civilizations have fallen like decaying trees. The outward push may come from an enemy, but the country falls because of inward rot.

We are significant if we are Beatitude people, meek and pure peacemakers, though sometimes persecuted. We are like salt in a decaying society.

But Jesus implied that we should be aware of two things if we are going to be salt in the world. First, we must be in touch with our culture. One thing about salt is that it must come into contact with meat. If we leave it packaged, it does absolutely nothing.

Throughout history, religious types have often taken the salt out of society. With the monastic movement, monks with good motives withdrew from society to live holy lives separated from the evil of the culture. That was never, however, the biblical example. Jesus sent His disciples forth as sheep among wolves; a wolf pack is the most dangerous place in the world for sheep. We are to be in the world, but not of it. Both of these are commands.

Whenever the church becomes a salt warehouse, it has missed Jesus' basic lesson that salt must come in contact with meat. If we don't relate to non-Christians in their culture, we won't make much difference in society.

Second, we must retain our distinctiveness, that is, our saltiness. From chemistry we know that salt is sodium chloride, and sodium chloride as we know it cannot lose its saltiness. So what was Jesus talking about?

In ancient times two kinds of salt existed. One salt was relatively pure, but another was impure. The relatively pure salt was made through the evaporation of clean sea water. But most of the salt in Palestine was taken from the Dead Sea, which was filled with white minerals that resembled salt. Farmers piled the impure salt behind their houses and used it for fertilizing their fields because a small amount of salt benefited some soils. But when the rains came and pounded on that mound of salt, often the true salt, the sodium chloride, would be washed away. A useless, white sandy substance was left. Farmers couldn't even throw it out on their fields because it had a hardening effect on the soil. Instead they would throw it out in front of the house when they wanted a hard path, and men would walk on it.

If salt loses its distinctiveness, it is worthless. And that's true of those of us who are citizens of the kingdom and are called to be salt in society. If we lose our unique Christian qualities and become like society, we make no impact. We become the problem instead of the solution.

As Christians we matter because by being part of society and having the grace of God displayed in our lives, we preserve that society from evil. But we must come in contact with society and be distinct from it in order to make a difference. If we really belong to Him and are Beatitude people, we are salt to the society.

How shall the world know that we have judged wisely between what matters in the world and what seems to matter? We must first accept Jesus' judgment that we matter to Him. On the basis of that, we can decide wisely how to spend our lives. In pouring out our lives like salt, we will find our true value.

Jesus didn't call us to be sugar; He called us to be salt. Salt irritates sometimes, but it also preserves. He called us to make a difference. And to do that is significant. The world will know we have chosen wisely when the real values of life are revealed.

Between what matters and what seems to matter, we should know what counts because we count to God.

SERMON NOTES

Give some examples of how salt was used in Jesus' time. As Christians, how do we become salt in the modern world? For example:

How do we flavor our community as salt?

How do we exhibit purity in the world?

How can we be like salt to make people thirsty for God?

How can Christians be a preservative in a rotting society?

Why do you think this chapter is titled "Market Defense"?

John Wesley's life and ministry preserved England from a revolution. Discuss how Christians might preserve their countries from decay.

Edward C. Bentley wrote, "Between that which matters and that which seems to matter, how will the world know we have judged wisely?" How do we judge between what really matters and what only seems to matter?

Are you salt in the small plot of earth where God has placed you?

MARKET OFFENSE

∎

The sun is the light of the world. But at night, when the sun is busy brightening the other side of the earth, the moon becomes the light of the world. The moon, of course, is only reflected light. Whatever light it has comes from the sun. In much the same way, Christians are the light of the earth. While Christ is away, we reflect His light. In John 9:5, Jesus said to a dark world that He was its light. But in the Sermon on the Mount He says that we are the light of the world. Just after calling His disciples the salt of the earth, Jesus said, "You are the light of the world." The contrast is interesting. Salt is negative in that it keeps something bad from happening—it keeps food from decaying. Light is positive in that it causes something good to happen—it enables us to find our way in the dark. And Jesus said we are the light of the world. In some ways that's one of the highest compliments ever paid to the people of God.

Jesus was not saying that we will make a difference by sheer will power, but by being related to Him. He went on to make two points about light. First, you can't miss it. He expressed this by saying that a city set upon a hill cannot be hidden. Hill cities in the Holy Land were impressive sites. They were built there because it was cool; the sea breezes acted like air conditioning in an arid land. And they were built on hills because the location helped them to defend themselves against invaders. Fighting was a lot tougher going uphill than down-hill. The mark of Palestinian cities is that they are always in view. At night they glow in the distance.

When we are the light of the world, everyone will know it. We cannot reflect His light and remain obscure. We cannot hide His light. God doesn't call us into the secret service. Either secrecy will destroy the discipleship or the discipleship will destroy the secrecy. We cannot live light-filled lives in our society without standing out, without having people notice us. They may not like us, and they may persecute us; but they will know we are there.

Second, you use light to help people see. If we buy a new lamp, we don't cover it up; we put it where it will give light to everyone who enters the room. The lamp Jesus spoke of was probably made of clay with oil and a wick in it. A lamp being difficult to light and relight, people put it under a noncombustible measuring bushel of porous clay but only for safety and reduction of light when they went out or to bed. Otherwise they used a lamp for light because that was its purpose.

When speaking of salt, Jesus implied the culture was rotting. When speaking of light, He implied the world was covered with moral and spiritual darkness. The only way for people to see clearly what matters is for us to become light. In so doing we bring a moral and spiritual influence that enables people to see what is there, and to find their way to God.

Jesus said, "Let your light shine before men, that they may see your good deeds and praise your Father in heaven." Jesus did not say that someone will see our good deeds and admit what outstanding, marvelous people we are. God's light does not shine in our external righteousness; it displays itself when we live with an awareness of our need of God's grace. Out of our sense of need comes a merciful and peace-loving spirit. Like light, we simply shine.

When Stephen was being stoned, the record in the book of Acts declares that his face shone like that of angels. I doubt that Stephen ever attended a face-shining seminar. I'm confident that Stephen didn't even know that his face shone. People who live in the light are not conscious of their own light. People who only reflect light do not brag about how bright they are. There are no 1,000-watt Beatitude people. People living in the Beatitudes are more conscious of their own darkness, of His grace, and of His light than they are of how much light they reflect. But they do shine, and groping people who see them find their way to God.

Whether we are in business, politics, or some other life pursuit, what really matters is that we be light. And it is imperative that the light shines in the darkness.

Over the years I've had many friends say to me, "I'm in an office where there is not another Christian, and it's rough. The things that go on there are disgusting. I wish I could get out of it." I understand the tension. Our natural tendency is to withdraw under such circumstances. We like to draw as little attention as possible to our distinctive values. If someone gives us a "God Is Love" lapel pin, we wear it under our suit coat where no one will see it. That way we won't get any hassle. We know we should let our light shine, but we're concerned about being misunderstood.

But God needs our light where the world is the darkest. The blacker the night the greater the need for a light bulb. If the bulb does not shine, it's not because of the darkness. Darkness cannot put out a light. If the darkness increases until it is as black as a cave, it is still not dark enough to extinguish a light. No one yet has smothered a light by increasing the darkness. Darkness gets darker because the light fails. When we fail to reflect Christ's light, we let the darkness win.

Jesus did not call us to be magnificent chandeliers for people to admire. He called us to be a single bulb in a back hall to keep people from breaking their necks when they go to the bathroom in the middle of the night. He called us to make a difference in the darkness. Doing so makes us significant.

On June 5, 1910, American short-story writer O. Henry spoke his last words: "Turn up the lights—I don't want to go home in the dark."

As lights in the world, our mission is to make sure no one ever does.

SERMON NOTES

Explain the difference between light and salt. What should happen as a result of our being "the light of the world"?

When Jesus says, "you are the light of the world," is He telling us to *be* light or is He telling us we are light? What's the difference?

Beatitude people aren't really conscious of "shining." They shine with Christ's light naturally. Think of a man or woman you know today who shines as light. Describe how this person lights up his or her environment.

Some Christians work and live in very sinful environments. Should Christians leave such dark situations to better shine for God?

FULFILLMENT RATE

∎

I n one of his poems, Robert Browning asked the question, "Why with old truth needs new truth disagree?" It is a good question and one that implies that human beings often expect new ideas to replace old ones rather than enrich them. The people of Christ's day might have expected that Jesus would discard Old Testament truths. Matthew pictured Christ as a Healer of the sick and a Preacher of good news (4:23). This young carpenter had suddenly burst upon the scene and captured people's imaginations. People flocked to Him from every part of Israel. They wanted to hear what He had to say. When Jesus proclaimed the good news of the kingdom, people understood the words *good news* in a specific way. The original word translated into these two words was used by the Greeks to announce a victory. Because they believed that all victories came from the gods, good news meant a divine announcement of peace and happiness for the Greek nation. The Romans took the word and used it to speak of anything that had to do with the emperor. If a herald announced an emperor's birth, his enthronement, one of his decrees, or some battle he had won, the proclamation was called *good news.*

When Jesus announced the good news of the kingdom, the people recognized a declaration normally associated with the gods or a king. He enforced His announcement by healing the sick; and, as a result, He won the hearts of many people. These people must have wondered what was going to happen to the old system if Jesus planned to set up something new. If He erected a new kingdom, would He dismantle the old?

During the French Revolution, Robespierre and his confederates decided that the only way to establish something new was to tear down the old. They completely changed the calendar, renaming years, months, and days of the week. They even changed from a seven-day week to a ten-day week. They renamed the streets and boulevards of Paris. In all of this, they tried to destroy France's past to establish something new.

In the 1960s, a number of young radicals in the United States argued that the old ways, built-up over two hundred years, had to go if justice and equality were ever to be established. They wanted to lay new bricks instead of repairing the mortar on the old.

When Jesus heralded the kingdom, the people must have wondered what He would do with the Law and the Prophets. Would He turn His back on it? Of course, the conservatives were concerned that the past be kept; the radicals perhaps would like to have had the past removed. What was Christ's view? What did He mean by, "Do not think that I have come to abolish the Law or the Prophets; I have not come to abolish them but to fulfill them" (Matthew 5:17)?

Jesus declared these words with authority. The phrase "I have come" connoted authority and was a way Jesus often referred to himself. He was expressing who He is—the One who existed before the creation of the world, the One who knew His birthplace and when and where He was to die. As one old country man said, "If I knew where I was to die, I'd stay away from the place." Jesus, knowing where He was to die, set His face toward Jerusalem. Israel referred to the Messiah as "the Coming One" (Matthew 11:3). In using the phrase "I have come," Jesus identified himself as both Messiah and God.

Jesus also demonstrated His authority by the phrase "I tell you" (Matthew 5:18, 20, 22, 28, 32, 34, 39, 44). To the people of the first century who were used to listening to the rabbis speak, the phrase was something new. When the rabbis spoke, they gained their authority from the past. They would refer to the Old Testament laws, the traditions built on those laws, or to some previous rabbi's teaching. No record exists of any rabbi in all of Jewish history speaking out of his own authority.

With the phrases, "I have come" and "I tell you," Jesus authoritatively spoke about not abolishing the Law and the Prophets. But He didn't use just phrases. He gave two lessons—one in astronomy, the other in penmanship.

Jesus said that the Old Testament would be around as long as the universe, that is, "until heaven and earth disappear" (Matthew 5:18). Its Law and its Prophets will not be discarded like some old relic. Jesus was saying that the Old Testament and its teachings have His authority behind them, and they will continue until time is ended.

We may think that the Old Testament was some ancient book for Jews and not for Christians, yet the Old Testament was the Bible of the early church. When they met to worship, they had only the Old Testament. We can't understand the New Testament without the Old, and Christ's full authority is behind the Old Testament. If we claim to be citizens of the kingdom, if we pledge our allegiance to Jesus Christ, then we must give allegiance to the book that He honored.

After peering through a telescope at heaven and earth, Christ examined the written Law with a microscope. He said that "not the smallest letter, not the least stroke of a pen will by any means disappear from the Law until everything is accomplished" (Matthew 5:18). The smallest letter in the Hebrew alphabet was about the size of an apostrophe. The least stroke of a pen would be a small line that distinguished Hebrew letters. It would be like the top and bottom lines on the capital *I* that distinguish it from a lowercase *l*. Christ's lesson about letters was His emphatic way of saying that all of the Law and all of its teachings will continue.

Christ put His full authority behind the Old Testament with His words and examples, but what did He mean by "not abolishing the Law"? Some elements seem to have been abolished. God gave Israel a whole menu of foods that they could not eat. They could not eat pork, rabbit, shrimp, or eel. Yet, according to Mark, Jesus declared all foods clean by saying, "nothing outside a man can make him 'unclean' " (7:14–19).

Whole chapters of Leviticus are devoted to telling people how to sacrifice animals and grains to God. Very specific, very detailed. Today most of us do not feel we should make a trip to Jerusalem and offer a sacrifice. Even if we did, the Jewish altar and temple do not exist. Why did Jesus talk about not doing away with the Law? What about many of the other regulations of the Old Testament? Many of them we do not and cannot follow today.

Some find the answer to Christ's denial of abolishment by dividing the Law into three parts—civil, ceremonial, and moral. The first two had to do with Israel's government and religion, and the last with the Ten Commandments. In this view Christ was referring only to the Commandments. Because Israel was no longer under the direct supervision of God, the civil laws didn't apply. The ceremonial laws about sacrifices would no longer be binding after Christ's death. The moral law of God existed in the Old Testament and would be repeated in the New Testament, so Christ did not come to abolish the moral law. This view seems satisfactory initially, but it is not without problems.

Why do the Old and New Testaments never make the distinction between the three types of law? The Law was simply given and God's people were to obey it. God never said, in effect, obeying traffic lights and attending church were less important than not killing someone. The whole force of God's righteousness seemed to be behind all three types of law. After all, Jesus was very specific. He talked about minute pen marks not disappearing, and He seemed to be including not only all the Law but all the Prophets. The phrase, "Law and Prophets," was a way of denoting the whole Old Testament.

The interpretation of Christ's words must revolve around the meaning of *fulfill* (Matthew 5:17). If we understand the word as meaning "to fill full," then what Christ was saying becomes clearer. The Law and Prophets were pencil sketches, and Jesus Christ was the painting. All of the details of those pencil sketches would be fulfilled in that painting. The painting filled those sketches full.

In Matthew 11:13, Jesus declared, "For all the Prophets and the Law prophesied until John." What did the Law and Prophets do until the time of John the Baptist? The Law and Prophets anticipated Christ.

How did Christ specifically fulfill the Law and Prophets? Christ directly fulfilled many Old Testament prophecies. Micah 5:2 said Christ would be born in Bethlehem, and that was where He was born. Christ also indirectly fulfilled a number of prophecies. In Matthew 2:15, Christ's parents fled to Egypt to escape Herod. When they later left Egypt, Matthew explained that this was a fulfillment of Hosea 11:1, "Out of Egypt I called my son." Hosea was writing about Israel that had left Egypt for the Promised Land, but the broad outlines of Israel's history pointed forward to Christ. One example was Israel's forty years in the wilderness. Moses told Israel that God tested them to show "that man does not live on bread alone but on every word that comes from the mouth of the LORD" (Deuteronomy 8:2–3). Christ spent forty days in the desert; and when Satan tempted Him, He quoted Moses' words (Matthew 4:4). So the experience of Israel pointed to Christ's experience.

The relationship of the Old Testament to Christ is like the link between the details in Leonardo da Vinci's *Last Supper* and Christ. Christ is the central figure in the painting, but subtle touches also draw the viewer's attention to Christ. The beams in the ceiling all focus on Him; the hands of the disciples point toward Him. Some Old Testament writers directly described Christ's life; others used "beams and hands."

Perhaps the event that filled the Old Testament more full than any other was Christ's death. The Law prescribed a whole system of sacrifices to deal with sin. For fifteen hundred years, day after day, week after week, and especially year after year, the people brought their sacrifices. These offerings signified that sin brings punishment and only death and blood could release someone from that punishment. Those thousands of dead animals pointed forward to a sacrifice. That's why John the Baptist exclaimed, "Look, the Lamb of God, who takes away the sin of the world" (John 1:29).

Such events from Christ's life as His birth, temptation, and crucifixion give full meaning to the Old Testament, but He also filled full the Law and Prophets with His words. In the last part of Matthew 5, Christ took the laws about murder, adultery, divorce, oaths, retribution, and neighborly love and enriched their meaning. These laws were like empty jars, and He filled them full. He showed that the laws were not dealing with just external standards but also internal values.

Whether we study the furnishings of the temple, probe the messianic passages in the Psalms, or delve into the details of Isaiah 53, we see Christ. Just as the fetus is fulfilled in the adult human, so the Law and the Prophets are fulfilled in Christ's works and words. He is the fulfillment of the Old Testament.

In the ancient world craftsmen often fitted together stones of different colors to make a picture, or mosaic. One of the earliest mosaics is the "Standard of Ur," which is dated about 2500 B.C. In this mosaic the artisan used pink sandstone and lapis lazuli, which is blue stone. He cemented stones on both sides of a two-foot piece of wood. On one side he pictured an army going to battle; on the other, using the same materials, he depicted a king or noble. These two mosaics on one piece of wood were used like a banner or flag; the decorated wood was an emblem of the kingdom of Ur. If a person saw only the side with soldiers, he or she had a distorted view. The kingdom had soldiers, but it also had a leader. When we read the Old Testament, we may see only endless details; but when we take those details and arrange them properly, we see the King.

SERMON NOTES

Imagine Jesus coming to the world now for the first time instead of in the first century. What kind of kingdom would we expect Him to establish? How would we expect Him to deal with the "kingdoms" that now exist?

Jesus said He came to "fulfill" the Law of the Old Testament, yet many Old Testament laws no longer apply to us as Christians today. Why don't the ceremonial laws apply to us? And the civil laws? Do the moral laws apply to us today? Why or why not?

How does Christ "fulfill" the Prophets?

Explain how Christ gave new meaning to the sacrifice offerings of the Old Testament. Describe how He "filled full" the laws about murder, adultery, divorce, and similar commandments.

Does Jesus' teaching in the New Testament make the Old Testament obsolete and unnecessary to study? How might understanding the Old Testament affect your comprehension of the New Testament?

Name some specific benefits you might gain from integrating more knowledge of the Old Testament into your Bible study.

JOB EVALUATION

∎

"If any man seeks for greatness," wrote Horace Mann, "let him forget greatness and ask for truth, and he will find both." Even if we agree that seeking after truth is a worthy journey, we must still answer the question, "What is truth?" Christ identified some of His truth with the words *these commands*, for He said, "Whoever practices and teaches these commands will be called great in the kingdom of heaven" (Matthew 5:19). In contrast, He warned, "Anyone who breaks one of the least of these commandments will be called least in the kingdom of heaven" (v. 19). What commands did Christ have in mind? The Pharisees might have thought He was referring to the Law and Prophets; they had been doing their best to keep the commands of the Old Testament. Unfortunately, they were seeking greatness rather than truth, and their observances of Old Testament commandments were shallow and external.

Christ came not to abolish the Law and Prophets, but He wanted to supply a complete understanding of them. Therefore, the words *these commands* must refer to more than just Old Testament revelation; they must include Christ's interpretation of it. It was only through a true understanding of the Old Testament that the hearers of Christ's sermon could surpass the righteousness of the Pharisees. The Pharisees were actually least in God's kingdom because they were violating the spirit of His commands. Although the commands have the backdrop of the Old Testament, they are best understood as the commands of the Sermon on the Mount.

Christ had challenged His listeners to be salt and light. In the last part of Matthew 5, Christ gave a number of commands in explaining the true spirit of various laws. In essence, He was saying in the Sermon on the Mount, "I am the fulfillment of the Old Testament; and now as a King establishing a kingdom predicted in the past, I am giving commands. Your standing in the kingdom will depend on your obeying and teaching these commands."

Despite what Christ said about the relationship between our keeping His commands and our standing in the kingdom, we are tempted to minimize His commands. We want the truth on our side, but we don't always want to side with the truth. We may feel this way for two reasons. One is that we don't keep the spirit of the Law, so we avoid our responsibility by concluding that Christ didn't really mean what He said. Christ will teach about murder, adultery, and divorce in the last part of Matthew 5; and like the Pharisees, we will initially applaud His words. But when He gets to the heart of the matter, we will not like what He has to say about anger, lust, and selfishness. We'll rationalize that. He really didn't mean that anger was the source of murder, and that anger, as far as God is concerned, has the same penalty as murder. We get angry at that type of teaching and reduce its meaning. That is why Christ warned against breaking the least of the commandments and teaching others to do so. He didn't want us to downplay His words.

Another reason we diminish the importance of Christ's commands is that we are Beatitude people trying to show mercy, and we don't know how to balance grace and truth. People who adhere to truth often lack grace; they toss out the truth like hand grenades. And people who promote grace often do so at the expense of truth. So when many of us teach, and I know this tension in myself, we want to teach in a gracious way. Yet in so doing, we sometimes minimize Christ's commands.

I know how difficult it is to teach on divorce when some of my listeners are divorced people. Divorce is painful enough, and I don't want to cause more pain. I find myself wanting to sidestep the truth. I want to be gracious; I don't want to be severe. But Jesus keeps saying, "If you are going to represent Me, you must interpret My truth correctly." And in what manner I interpret that truth will determine whether grace and truth kiss each other.

If I were a physician, I know it would be difficult to tell someone that he had terminal cancer. I wouldn't want to do that; I'd rather tell him that he had a hacking cough or his suspicious lumps were benign. But if I know he has cancer and I try to understate that, I have not been faithful to him as a physician. Misrepresenting the truth about cancer can destroy him.

"Truth without charity," wrote Joshua Swartz, the seventeenth-century German clergyman, "is often intolerant and even persecuting, as charity without truth is weak in concession and untrustworthy in judgment. But charity, loyal to truth and rejoicing in it, has the wisdom of the serpent with the harmlessness of the dove."

When we are Beatitude people, bankrupt of spirit, mourning over sin, and in submission to Him, we will hunger after righteousness. He will fill us; and out of His mercy toward us will flow mercy to others. As we receive mercy, greater will grow our longing to be pure. In the process of becoming pure, we will truly see God, who is all truth. As His truth becomes our truth, we will share that truth with grace because we genuinely know the God of both truth and grace. That gracious imparting of truth to others will make us great in His kingdom. But the whole process of knowing and sharing truth starts with God. As Matthew Henry noted, "Nothing can make a man truly great but . . . partaking of God's holiness."

Democritus, the Greek philosopher, pictured truth as lying on the bottom of a clear pool of water. Some people see it immediately; others position themselves to see their own reflection. Pharisees followed the letter of the Law because it mirrored themselves. Beatitude people see below the surface of truth. They understand the spirit of Christ's commands, and they practice and teach them.

What we do with God's truth is all important. In His kingdom, it will determine whether we are creatures great or small.

SERMON NOTES

Why do you think the Pharisees thought "these commands" referred to the Law and the Prophets?

Sometimes we minimize some of Christ's commands in our lives. Do you find this true for yourself? Are all of His commands equally important?

What happens when we try to show mercy to people without a healthy balance between grace and truth? Why are these two so difficult to balance?

Divorce is a delicate topic to teach about. There is that tension between wanting to be gracious and loving and yet being accountable for interpreting Christ's Word correctly. Name other situations where this tension might exist.

How do we achieve that point of balance where we hold the truth of the gospel with grace? How does being a "Beatitude person" help you with this?

When we're able to graciously impart Christ's commands to others, Jesus says we will be *great* in heaven. Do you think it's proper to want to be "great"?

WORK RULES

■

To teach my son mathematics, I might begin with addition. I'd start with easy figures: 7 plus 5 is 12, and 5 more is 17.

After we get that column added, my son might say, "That's it; I guess I've got it."

"No, there's more to it," I say. "We will have to go to some larger numbers." So we add 225 and 325 and 621.

"That's 1,161," my son exclaims.

"No, that comes to 1,171," I patiently state. "You forgot to carry the 1 from the first column."

"Well look, it's just 1," he complains.

"No, it's 10," I counter.

"If we're dealing with 1,000, what's give or take 10?"

"If we're talking about your allowance, ten is a lot; it's five weeks worth. If we're talking about miles, it will take you several hours to walk it."

"You are picky, picky, picky," he says. "I'm better at it than my sister; she'd miss it by 30."

"It doesn't matter that you're better than your sister. You've got to get it right."

"Whenever I come across 225 and 325 and 621, I'll remember that it's 1,171," he jokes.

"Sorry. That won't do; it isn't just getting the bottom line correct. You've got to do it intuitively. You've got to learn the process, not just the result."

"Look, you're really discouraging me; I don't think I have the ability to add up a column of figures. Why do you have to insist on the right answer?"

"That's just the way it is with arithmetic. I can't change it. I'll work with you. I'll help you. I'll try to get you to understand how it works. But you've got to get the correct answer."

What happens in learning mathematics also happens in learning to pitch a baseball. If I am completely ignorant about baseball and want to learn to pitch, I may get a knowledgeable friend and go out to a ball field. The friend shows me how to grip the ball to throw a fastball or a curve. Then he takes me to the pitcher's mound. He says, "You see that white thing about sixty feet away; that's home plate. When you throw the ball, you've got to get it over home plate."

And so I wind up and throw the ball. My first pitch goes wild to the left. My friend throws the ball back. The next pitch goes to the right, but it's only half a foot off. And I say, "Getting closer!"

And he says, "You're getting closer, but you've got to get it over the plate."

I throw five more pitches, and they all miss. I laugh. "Widen the plate a bit. Maybe double it."

"No, you can't double the plate. You've got to get it over as it is."

"Look," I reply, "I'm not sure I can do that. What does it matter? If we had a nice wide plate, I could get it over."

"Sorry, that's the way the game is. I can't make the plate wider. I can give you some more pointers, but you've got to get it over the plate."

"Boy, you're really being arbitrary, aren't you? Insisting that I get it over the plate."

"No, it's not arbitrary. If you miss the plate four times in a row, the batter goes to first base. I don't care how well you throw fast balls or curve balls. If you don't get it over the plate, you can't be a pitcher."

"Why couldn't you ease up and suit the game to my ability?"

"No, you've got to suit your ability to the game. I can work with you, but I can't change the standard."

In the mathematics and baseball illustrations, we see the problems of a teacher working with a student. Jesus was a master teacher, and He wanted to get across to the people of His day what it took to be righteous. He said, "For I tell you that unless your righteousness surpasses that of the Pharisees and the teachers of the law, you will certainly not enter the kingdom of heaven" (Matthew 5:20).

Jesus had to explain "righteousness" to two different groups. One group was the Pharisees. They knew how to throw fast balls and curve balls, and they could add a column. They didn't always get throwing or adding right, but they got them right more often than other people did. Therefore, they were looked at as the standard of righteousness of their day. Jesus wanted to show them that no matter how righteous they were, they were short of the righteousness required to enter the kingdom of heaven.

He was also talking to His disciples. He said that how they responded to God's commands would determine their place in the kingdom. The disciples were to hunger and thirst after righteousness. Christ wanted them to know what righteousness is.

The Sermon on the Mount offers an interesting combination of goals and grace. The Pharisees understood the goal, or thought they did. If all we have is the goal, we do one of two things with it, especially when the goal is righteousness.

First, we will fudge it. It's righteousness, give or take ten, fifteen, or fifty. Or we make home plate two-feet wide. Second, we will become dismayed. Goals by themselves can throw us for a loop, discourage us, make us feel bankrupt. That's not bad if it makes us recognize that we still don't understand arithmetic and motivates us to ask for more help. If I go back to my friend and ask him to watch the way I throw, that's a good sign. Unfulfilled goals can drive us back to grace.

And grace is somebody coming alongside and giving us the ability we don't have on our own.

If, on the other hand, we have all grace and no goals, we don't ever get any place. We don't understand what is required of us and what grace should do in our lives.

We can't fudge goals we don't have. We can't give ourselves credit for getting close. We can't make up the goals in arithmetic to match our ability. Or even our feelings. We can't urge an umpire to take the motives of the pitcher into consideration, or to be less strict on the rookie than on the veteran. We can't do that; if we fudge, we destroy the standard.

In the Sermon on the Mount, Jesus has been talking about the characteristics of the people who inherit His kingdom. He said they are folks who are bankrupt in spirit. They mourn over their inability to be righteous and that causes them to be meek, to be dependent on God. They hunger and thirst for a righteousness they don't have. And out of that hungering, grace comes, and God fills them. Such people are merciful; they become pure in heart; they become peacemakers. Jesus went on to say that these people stand in such contrast to society that they are like salt on decaying meat. They are like a well-lit city on a hill at midnight. We can't miss them.

Jesus' preaching led the people to wonder if these were revolutionary thoughts. Was Jesus bringing in a new standard? Was He doing away with the Law and the Prophets they had followed for seventeen hundred years? Jesus said, "No, I want you to know that I am related to the Law and Prophets in such a way that all it taught is fulfilled in me."

The history of the Old Testament led to the history of Christ's life. The ceremonies pointed to Him. The animals offered on the altar pointed to Him. The food laws pointed to Him. The Old Testament was the pencil sketch, and He was the portrait. He fulfilled it. He also fulfilled the Law in that He filled it full of meaning. For the Pharisees, those jolly good fellows who thought they could be righteous on their own, He wanted them to know that the standard was greater than anything they realized in the Law. For the disciples, who would hunger and thirst after righteousness, He wanted them to know what kind of righteousness to seek.

The people of Christ's day, like most in our day, thought they could keep the Law by simply keeping its letter. We can't blame them for that. That is the way law operates in a society. When I pay my income tax, the tax collector doesn't give a rip about whether or not I do it with good feeling. He doesn't care if I am a patriot or if I am loyal to the president. My motives don't matter. All that matters is that if I owe seventeen hundred dollars I pay seventeen hundred dollars. If I do, he's off my back for a year. I don't have to check a square that says, "I'm a patriot."

A wife may decide on a given day to murder her husband. She may feel like doing it, but the law will never bring the case to court. She may think about it; she may wish that she had the opportunity. But until she takes the axe to him, the law can't go after her. A man may want to rape a woman. He may play with that in his mind, fantasize about what it would be like, but he'll never go to jail for thinking about rape. It's only when he commits the act that he goes to prison. The district attorney cannot make a case on what a person thinks.

The people of Christ's day, like those in our day, didn't get convicted for their motives, so their main concern was the letter of the law. But God was concerned with the heart of the matter, and what matters is the heart.

When Grover Cleveland neared the end of his life, he lamented, "I have tried so hard to do the right." We may sometimes share Cleveland's thoughts; but as we think about what Jesus had to say about righteousness, we have to conclude that we will never be able to add up the figures or get the ball over the plate. But if we sense that bankruptcy, we are in good shape. Jesus said, "Blessed are the poor in spirit, for theirs is the kingdom of God." We can settle matters with God through Jesus Christ.

The law should drive us back to grace; the goals should drive us back to God. And knowing the goals, we see our need of grace; and understanding grace, we discover what it means to hunger and thirst for the kind of righteousness that God gives those who trust Him. That righteousness is not just conforming our behavior to the letter, but conforming our hearts to the Spirit.

SERMON NOTES

In light of the Beatitudes, why is Matthew 5:20 the key verse of the Sermon on the Mount?

Why do you think Christ makes this extreme demand of us, His disciples?

Surpassing the righteousness of the Pharisees was unthinkable to the people living in Jesus' time. Read Romans 3:21 and Philippians 3:8. How can our righteousness surpass that of the Pharisees?

The illustrations of learning arithmetic and learning to pitch a base-ball demonstrate the need for both process and end results. When people think about righteousness and focus only on process or re-sults, they make mistakes. What was the mistake of the Pharisees who emphasized results? What could be the mistake of a Christian who only emphasizes process?

OUT OF CONTROL

■

"A reservoir of rage exists in each person, waiting to burst out," wrote Dr. R. J. Beaber of UCLA. "We fantasize about killing or humiliating our boss or the guy who took our parking space. It is only by growing up in a civilized society of law that we learn the idea of proportionate response." In the Sermon on the Mount, Christ demonstrated that the proportionate response of the Law may cover up the purposeful rage of the heart. He said our righteousness must exceed that of the Pharisees, who pass muster in their society by keeping the letter of the Law. Instead, their hearts are evil.

Jesus represented six illustrations to show what the Law of the Old Testament was really about. The rest of Matthew 5 gives those illustrations. If we're going to understand the illustrations, however, we must be aware of at least four things.

First, we must read them in context. We will miss what Jesus was driving at if we look only at individual paragraphs or sentences in the Sermon on the Mount.

Second, we must keep in mind that Jesus preached in Palestine, and Near Eastern preachers and teachers loved to tell stories. They were their stock-in-trade. What is a bit frustrating is that they often told stories without explaining them. Jesus' parables are stories, but they don't work in the same way we use illustrations. We turn to illustrations to explain something abstract. The Near Eastern speaker just tells stories and allows the listeners to figure out the point for themselves. The listener comes to the lesson intuitively.

Third, not only are the stories unexplained, they sometimes

contain radical statements. Jesus said we have to hate our families before we can be His disciples (Luke 14:26). That's strong stuff. But He was not saying we must cherish animosity toward those closest and dearest to us; He was establishing the point that our devotion to Him will make our relationships to our families seem like hate. The contrast is hyperbole.

Finally, Jesus wanted to pound home the principle that the Law is not simply the letter; it is the spirit. An individual keeps the Law in the heart; outward conformity has little to do with true law-keeping. If we don't understand that principle, we simply turn the Sermon on the Mount into another set of laws.

The first of the six illustrations that Jesus gave about the Law came from the sixth commandment—"Do not murder." That was a safe place to begin because the Pharisees, the disciples, and most of the crowd could say, "I've never killed anyone, so I'm comfortable with that. That's good." It's always comfortable to have the preacher talk about other people.

So Jesus began by saying, "You have heard that it was said to the people long ago, do not murder, and anyone who murders will be subject to the judgment" (Matthew 5:21). The listeners didn't have printed Old Testaments, much less New Testaments, so Scripture was always read to them. In the synagogues the Law was divided into seven sections, and seven different men stood up and read parts of it. Then somebody else read a passage from the Prophets, and finally another person got up and interpreted it. So Jesus spoke about what they had heard—"Do not murder. Anyone who murders will be subject to judgment."

Actually the Ten Commandments did not talk about judgment, but the Jewish teachers combined Numbers 35:30–31 with the commandment. The Numbers passage prescribed the conviction process and the punishment. In adding consequences to the commandment, the teachers changed its emphasis from a moral law to a civil offense. They focused on the punishment rather than on the deed.

Jesus continued His teaching about murder with an illustration. He said if the Jewish teachers concentrated on the legal side of murder, that is, on the judgment about it by magistrates, they should also legislate that anger be dealt with in the local courts. Anger as the motive for murder deserves its day in court.

The word Christ used for anger was the one for slow, meditative anger, the anger we nurse to keep it alive. It was the kind of anger that plots to get even, to get back. It is like P. G. Wodehouse's character who "spoke with a good deal of animation about skinning you with a blunt knife."

Anger lies at the heart of murder, and Jesus argued that it ought to be dealt with if teachers were going to talk about civil courts. The motive leads to the deed. And then He said, "Anyone who says to his brother, Raca, is answerable to the Sanhedrin," the supreme court of that day. The term *raca* was an Aramaic word, which might be translated in English as "blockhead," "stupid," or "idiot." He was not talking about a word spoken in jest but a hate-filled put-down, a denigration, the expression of anger and perhaps murderous intent.

He said, "Anyone who says, 'You fool!' will be in danger of the fire of hell." To call someone a fool, or dull thinker, was not some easy-come, easy-go slang slinging; it was a way of saying a person lived as if there were no God, a morally and spiritually corrupt person. Using the word *raca* was an attack on a person's mental ability, but using *fool* assaulted a person's moral integrity.

If a murderer deserves to go to hell, then the fire-breathers and the mudslingers merit hell as well. The act of murder may have physical consequences and in that sense be worse than the thought of murder; but as far as God is concerned, the latter groups are as guilty as a murderer who beats someone to death. God deals with motives; He knows whether or not we have righteousness on the inside.

Somebody may want to get off the hook by arguing that Jesus himself got angry. That is true. One time He was furious about the Pharisees' legalism (Mark 3:5). The religious leaders were incensed that Jesus had healed a man on the Sabbath, and Jesus became deeply upset at them because their stupid religion kept them from realizing that good was being done. Later on, He called the Pharisees hypocrites and fools (Matthew 13:13–33). That was a statement of fact. They were morally bankrupt. He was making a judicial statement. When Jesus was angry, it was because of injustice and sin; His anger was not a personal attack. At times anger can be the fruit of righteousness. For example, dope peddlers should make us angry. We should be furious at pornographers, who pervert God's good gift of sex, or at those who unjustly treat others who cannot fight back.

Jesus was not talking about anger that leads to reform, but that which ends up in murder. We usually get angry at personal affronts— "You insulted me, and I want that made right. You understand!"

When Jesus was falsely arrested, taken to a kangaroo court, spit upon by the soldiers, crowned with thorns, mocked by the people, and nailed to a cross, He didn't say a word. When He was reviled, He did not revile again. When He hung on the cross He said from parched lips, "Father, forgive them, for they do not know what they are doing" (Luke 23:34). So anger against injustice is not the same as anger against petty slights. The crucifixion was not a petty slight, but Jesus treated it that way. If He could do that with hell-invented torture, how much more should we with minor tensions.

Anger against injustice sometimes gets perverted. It starts out as anger for a cause, and then it becomes a personal thing—like blowing up an abortion clinic. We can be against abortion without being against abortioners. If our righteousness degenerates into personal anger, we come under the judgment of God's law. That law deals with the spirit as well as the letter. We keep God's law not merely by outward conformity, but from the heart. And since that's true, Jesus said we need to do everything we can, as quickly as we can, to make matters right when anger destroys relationships. He used two illustrations to get this across.

First, He said that gifts to the church are not as important as reconciliation with a friend. We often try to cover up an offense in one place by doing good in another. Embezzlers may put an extra offering in the collection plate. Jesus said that church going will not cloak a ruptured relationship with a friend. Offering God a gift does not camouflage a wrong.

If I have something against a friend and she doesn't know about it, I can settle that before God. But if we both know about it, we must make it right. Then I can come back and offer a gift. Putting money in the collection plate, going to church, singing hymns, reading the Bible, and having devotions don't cover up a fractured relationship with another person. That must be settled before sacrificial service. That's what righteousness is—dealing with what we know is wrong.

Reconciliation is important because if the hostile feelings and thoughts I have toward a brother are left unresolved, I cannot worship God. As the psalmist put it, "If I had cherished sin in my heart, the Lord would not have listened" (Psalm 66:18). It is better to leave church early and keep God waiting, and then come back, than to think we can conceal a ruptured relationship with religious exercise.

I've been in congregations where people refused to talk to one another. They sang hymns, prayed, and gave money, but they despised people who worshiped with them in the church. God doesn't give us good marks for our external conformity. When we know something is wrong, if we are really interested in righteousness, we must settle these disputes with others.

Christ's second illustration takes the matter of reconciliation a step further. We are to settle conflicts not only before we go to church but also before we end up in court.

In the Greco-Roman world, the law allowed for citizens' arrest. If someone picked another's pocket, he or she was guilty of breaking and entering. If a person stole clothes from the public bath, a common crime, or a slave from another person, any citizen could arrest the thief and drag him or her into court without calling the police. At the court the judge would pass sentence and turn the criminal over to the jailer. The convicted thief would be taken to what we would call a debtors' prison. Robbers were kept in this prison until they reimbursed the victim for the goods stolen. But prison was a tough place to make money. Jesus said that a person should work out a settlement before a judge gets involved. He was stressing the urgency of rectifying a squabble.

If a matter is not handled quickly, anger can become open hostility, and problems left to fester will only get worse. More important, if we die with unsettled contentions, what will it be like to stand before a God of love and holiness? Thus, for practical and theological reasons, controversies should be settled immediately.

Dame Sybil Thorndike, the British Shakespearean actress, was married for many years to the distinguished actor Sir Lewis Casson. After his death, she was asked if she had ever thought of divorce. She replied, "Never. But murder often!"

Keeping the sixth commandment is more than not committing the act of murder. God is interested in our motives. He never lets us get away with murder. He knows our mind.

Why did Christ say that "anyone who says to his brother, 'Raca,' is answerable to the Sanhedrin?" What did He mean? How might He make that same point to us today?

Discuss why keeping the sixth commandment involves more than not committing murder. How can mudslinging merit the same punishment as murder? Does this seem fair?

Is anger in our daily lives always wrong? Explain the difference between the examples we read of Jesus' anger and the anger He is confronting in us.

Do you experience more righteous anger or unrighteous anger in your life? How do you know the difference?

How could Christ go through the abuse that led Him to the cross and remain without anger? What do you think you would have done under the same circumstances?

While Christ calls us to reconciliation, it isn't as easy as it sounds. What needs to happen in our lives before we can reconcile with others?

How important are the Beatitudes to this process?

Is there someone with whom you have had a difference or dispute? What steps should you take right now to get that matter settled?

COMPOUND INTEREST

∎

One young college student perhaps spoke for many in our generation when he said, "Look, just because some old man spent a night on a mountain and came down and said, 'You shall not commit adultery,' why should I let that spoil my fun?" When Hugh Hefner first published *Playboy* magazine in the 1950s, it was a national scandal. Times have changed; the magazine no longer seems very risqué. It has become nearly as acceptable in our society as *Time* or *Newsweek*. Hugh Hefner's Playboy Clubs in the United States have all shut down because the "bunnies" seem tame as rabbits. Hefner spun out his philosophy that all sex is just good, clean fun. People should be able to enjoy it with anyone they please, at any time they please, anywhere they please. Anyone objecting to this philosophy received the dreaded label "puritan," someone who lived to take the joy out of life. Adultery isn't wrong; it's merely a puritan hang-up.

Even more striking is that Hefner's philosophy of unrestrained hedonism has a great many adherents in the academic and religious worlds. Ethics teachers argue adultery is not wrong as long as it is done by consenting adults and nobody gets hurt. Under these circumstances, sexual looseness is nobody's business and certainly not something to alarm us.

Worse yet, some religious people try to baptize Hefner's freewheeling philosophy into the Christian faith. They maintain that Jesus came to teach us to love, and as long as two people really love each other, whether married or single, whether in an illicit affair or a proper affair, love covers everything. After all, isn't love really the religion of Jesus? These religious leaders not only advocate a destructive philosophy but are trying to get Jesus to approve acts that He would not have endorsed at all.

In *The Merchant of Venice*, Shakespeare put it this way:

> In religion,
> What damned error, some sober brow
> Will bless it and approve it with a text,
> Hiding the grossness with fair ornament?

In the Sermon on the Mount Jesus addressed the sins of our age, and He talked about adultery. As a Near Eastern preacher, Jesus set the points of His teachings in sharp contrast to each other, with no middle ground.

Jesus was developing an argument, and we must see the argument in its context. In the Sermon on the Mount He was calling people to a relationship with Him that will affect their relationship with others.

The adultery passage cannot be understood apart from the preceding verses. Jesus began His Sermon by saying that those who sense a poverty in spirit, a mourning over their sin, and a deep dependence on God will hunger and thirst for righteousness. God will fill them with righteousness, and they will show it in a merciful attitude, a pure heart, and a desire to make peace. Even though they may be persecuted, they will be salt and light in a putrified and dark world. Their hunger for righteousness must exceed that of the Pharisees, and it will if they understand that God provides internal rather than external righteousness.

To prove His point about God's filling, Christ gave six cases to demonstrate the priority of the internal over the external, or relationships over rules. The first case was murder and anger, and He showed that the motive for murder condemns us as much as the act. If murder is a capital crime, then anger, and its offspring name-calling, which leads to murder, ought to have their day in court, too. To put it in another way, if we cure anger, murder won't be a problem. Christ used two stories to illustrate why it is important to deal with anger. His gift-giving and court-threatening stories show that repairing relationships is both essential and urgent. Anger is the symptom of a broken relationship, but the outgrowth of our inward righteousness should be positive relationships.

Christ's second case was about adultery and lust. Here again, He showed that the hungerer's righteousness is superior to the Pharisee's righteousness because it is driven by the spirit rather than the letter of the Law. The hungerer's righteousness starts in the heart; it focuses on relationships rather than on rules.

As long as a religious leader had never met a woman at some Mediterranean motel, he could heartily agree with Christ's repeating of the seventh commandment, "Do not commit adultery." But Christ didn't stop at adultery. He said, "Anyone who looks at a woman lustfully has already committed adultery with her in the heart" (Matthew 5:28). Adultery is not just an act; it has to do with the heart. When Jesus talked about looking at a woman lustfully, He was not simply talking about sexual desire. That was given to us by God and is portrayed in the Bible as a good gift. Admittedly the gift is often labeled, "Handle with care," but sexual desire comes from God.

By the word *lust*, Jesus did not refer to sexual desire or the normal attraction between men and women. The word *lust* is the same word in Greek that is sometimes translated "coveting." It is desire that focuses on a woman with the view of possessing her or of having an immoral relationship with her. It is a look with a purpose. To put it another way, it is "I would if I could." Only convention, her husband, or the fear of getting caught stops it. The stress of lust is in its purpose. Anyone who purposes in the heart to commit adultery has already committed it in God's eyes.

After Christ's explanation of adultery, He warned that if the right eye, or another part of the body, causes a person to sin, radical surgery on these parts would be better than to have the whole body thrown into hell. Christ used hyperbole to make His point. Adulterous desires corrupt relationships; therefore, we ought to deal with them drastically.

To interpret Christ's words about mutilation literally can be almost humorous. Suppose I'm having a struggle with lust. I poke out my right eye, but no evidence shows that one-eyed people are less lustful than two-eyed people. I'll chop off my right hand, but no studies verify that one-handed people are less lustful than two-handed people. I could gouge out my left eye, but sexual fantasies will still play on the cinema of my mind. Even if I'm blind, I could go the whole way—amputate both arms and both legs—but torsos are not exempt from lust.

The problem isn't body parts. Jesus used absurdity to show that adultery, like all sin, is serious enough for men and women to end up in hell. We ought to deal drastically with anything that leads us to that. If our magazine reading or our cable TV watching causes us to lust, then we need to cancel our subscriptions. If we find ourselves in compromising positions, we should run as Joseph did from Potiphar's wife.

Lustful desires corrupt relationships. It may destroy the relationship with a friend if a person lusts after the friend's spouse. In general, lust on either person's part will shatter the relationship between two people, whether adultery takes place or not. Because lust is a matter of the heart it should be dealt with drastically and quickly. The impure in heart don't want anything to do with God, and God wants us to have a relationship with Him.

William Byrd, an eighteenth-century Virginia farmer and surveyor, kept a personal diary. He recorded his struggle with lust or, as he called it, the "combustible matter." He kept putting water on the fires, but they continued to spring up. In one entry he wrote: "I neglected to say my prayers, which I should not have done, because I ought to beg pardon for the lust I had for another man's wife. . . . Endeavored to pick up a woman, but could not, thank God."

Thank God, He gives us new desires. We can hunger and thirst after Him.

SERMON NOTES

Jesus teaches that anger is at the core of murder. Christ's second case, adultery, is also merely a symptom of a deeper problem. What is the deeper problem and how does it operate in us?

We heartily agree that the results of anger and lust are wrong—murder and adultery—acts we may not think we're guilty of. But Christ says we *are* guilty of these things. Do you agree? Do you see evidence of this in yourself?

Define lust as Christ sees it. Is sexual attraction the same as lust? Is lust always sexual?

Is it normal for lust to occur in relationships between men and women? Does lust enhance or detract from the relationship? Does it necessarily make a difference at all?

How do you think God wants you to deal with lust?

Why does Jesus use absurdity and exaggeration to demonstrate the seriousness of sin?

It is suggested that we take action if magazine reading or TV watching causes us to lust. Is such extreme action really necessary? What would people think of us if we pursued such measures?

Explain how Jesus' teaching on lust fits into the teaching of the Beatitudes. Which Beatitude speaks to this issue best?

Does everyone, including devout Christians, struggle with lust or anger? Will we reach a point where we are free from these struggles?

Will becoming Beatitude people change the nature or outcome of our struggles?

SEVERANCE AGREEMENT

■

"You can make divorce as easy to obtain as a dog license, but you can't burn away the sense of shame and waste," wrote A. Alvarez in his book *Life after Marriage*. The Pharisees knew all about licenses, but they knew little about commitment and love. Jesus continued His explanation of the letter and spirit of the Law by citing a third case. Having lectured on murder and anger, adultery and lust, He then addressed divorce and selfishness. In Deuteronomy 24:1–5, Moses explained the divorce law. In essence, a man with a proper certificate could divorce a woman if he found something indecent about her, but he could not remarry her if she was divorced by a second husband. Because women were treated like property in the ancient world, Moses gave the law requiring a divorce certificate as protection for women. A woman was regarded as no different from a saddle. If a man tired of his wife, he could simply dismiss her. To guard her rights, Moses set forth three principles in the law. First, a man could only divorce a woman for a serious cause. The word *indecent* in Deuteronomy 24:1 is used of human defecation; so Moses was referring to something filthy or vile—a serious matter.

Second, the man must give the woman a written certificate of divorce. Rabbis indicated that this certificate must be given before two witnesses so they could examine whether a man's accusations were serious. A written bill of divorcement gave a potential second husband a guarantee that he could legally marry a divorced woman. Without this, blood wars could develop between the first husband and a second suitor.

Third, a man could not take back a twice-divorced wife. Marriage was not a revolving door that allowed a man to leave his wife and take her again. Marriage is too sacred for that. So Moses gave his divorce law not to loosen divorce restrictions but to tighten them. He was not saying anything goes. In teaching that divorce must be taken seriously, legally transacted, and not trivialized, Moses was actually moving back to the original design of marriage.

By New Testament times the focus of Deuteronomy 24 had changed from protecting a woman to finding all the possible grounds for divorcing her. That is where legalism leads—to the letter of the law. The rabbis concentrated on one word: *indecent.* Since it was broad, they had a field day with it. One rabbi interpreted it as meaning loss of attractiveness. In this case, a man could divorce his wife if he no longer felt warm toward her. Rabbi Hillel and his followers said *indecent* could refer to a woman burning a man's dinner or speaking disrespectfully of him. Other rabbi schools took a narrower view and limited the meaning to some moral indiscretion, such as a woman tempting a man by letting down her hair or uncovering her arms or legs, both considered indecent in the first century.

When people follow the letter of the law, they are always looking for loopholes. Jesus came into all of this garbage of the first century and declared that no mercy or purity existed in outward conformity. A man could follow the Law exactly, yet show his wife no mercy, and cause her to live an impure or adulterous life. To understand the spirit of the law, we must comprehend God's original design for marriage. Christ didn't elaborate about this in Matthew 5, but He did in Matthew 19.

In Matthew 19, the Pharisees asked Jesus, "Is it lawful for a man to divorce his wife for any and every reason?" (v. 3). This was a trick question. If Jesus answered no, He went against the rabbis because they thought some reasons existed for divorce. If He replied yes, He went against all the rabbis because none of them thought every reason was valid.

Jesus answered their question by going to Genesis 2 instead of Deuteronomy 24. He said that marriage was an act of God, not a legal contract or even a union of mutual love. Society did not invent marriage; they received it. Marriage was not only an act of God, but also a union of a man and woman. Marriage was not like a business partnership, which might easily break up when times get rough. It was like the union of the head and torso; it was a dynamic, integral relationship. As the bow and the violin are one instrument. As the lock and the key are one unit. As the hand and the arm are parts of a single body. Therefore, we cannot break it. That was God's original design. That's what God intended. That's what is involved in the Genesis statement.

The Pharisees avoided what Jesus was saying about the creation and union of marriage. They wanted to talk about Deuteronomy 24, so they asked, "Why then . . . did Moses command that a man give his wife a certificate of divorce and send her away?" Moses never commanded anything; the Pharisees had upped the ante. Moses had simply provided protection for women who were treated as property, but the Pharisees implied that a man had no choice. They weren't concerned about relationships; they were caught up in legalisms.

Jesus answered their second question, but not in the way they expected. Moses gave the law because of men's hard hearts, not because God approved of divorce. In the oppressive ancient world, God was showing His mercy to women. Divorce was not in God's original design; His standard was one man with one woman for life. Only fornication, that is, sexual looseness, can break the bond between two people. If a man and woman are in a one-flesh relationship, sex with someone else by either spouse breaks the union and God's ideal. But if sex outside marriage is not involved and a man sends his wife away, he commits adultery in marrying again, and he forces his first wife to commit adultery. Several people will be forced into relationships outside the will of God. Adultery then takes on all kinds of forms. To avoid the multiplying of adulteries is to practice the spirit of the law; it is to understand Christ's teaching about man's hardness of heart and God's original design for marriage.

Christ was asserting that at the heart of marriage stands commitment, not love. In the Bible, marriage is for the tough-minded. The disciples responded to this emphasis on commitment by throwing up their hands, "If this is the situation between a husband and wife, it is better not to marry" (Matthew 19:10). At least the disciples recognized that dogged attention to the relationship is the heart of marriage. Marriage is not for as long as love shall last; it is as long as life shall last. It is a promise given and a promise received. Running out of romance provides no reason for running out of a marriage.

The very first divorce in the world must have broken God's heart; unfortunately, it did not have the same effect on mankind. Men have now been casting these commitments aside for thousands of years. In recent times, women have joined the freedom march. The results of divorce have been devastating. As Jo Coudert observed in *Advice from a Failure*, "The divorced person is like a man with a black patch over one eye. He looks rather dashing but the fact is that he has been through a maiming experience."

Divorce is a serious matter. As someone else said, "It is the psychological equivalent of a triple coronary by-pass." It is not about pens but scalpels, not about ink on a page but incisions on a heart. What concerns God the most centers on the heart. Although divorce destroys God's original intention for marriage, it is not the unpardonable sin. When we sense an impoverishment of spirit, a feeling of guilt, we ought to hunger after God's grace and forgiveness. We may not be able to restore the marriage bond, but we can renew our union with Him.

SERMON NOTES

Rabbis in New Testament times chose to interpret the Bible for their own benefit. They interpreted the word "indecent" in order to change the grounds for divorce. Do people still interpret the Bible loosely to justify divorce? Do you know of any examples?

The statement is made, "No mercy or purity exists in outward conformity." What does this have to do with divorce?

Describe how the Pharisees, caught up in legalism, implied rules that God never gave—what did this legalism stem from?

Christians sometimes feel divorce is the only answer to their bad marriage. They give all kinds of reasons why their divorce is the exception to Jesus' rule. Explain what Jesus noted as the root problem of divorce.

Divorce is difficult to understand. Is it easier to understand Moses' provisions for divorce after we understand God's design for marriage? In your own words, how did Jesus describe marriage?

Compare the type of marriage Christ proposes and the marriages you have witnessed over the last five to ten years. Do you see any marriages similar to the one Jesus desires for people? What makes them different? How can you tell? Does it seem easy to have that type of marriage?

What stands at the heart of Christian marriage? Is love all that is required?

Why did the disciples throw up their hands and say, "If this is the situation between a husband and wife it is better not to marry"?

What new concepts about divorce and marriage has this study shown you?

Divorce comes easily in our society. It happens so often, we have come to expect the side-effects of divorce to be less severe. Society's acceptance of divorced people has increased, but has its affects on the divorced *person* changed?

Some churches and organizations treat divorce as *the* unpardonable sin. Do you agree? Explain.

What should our response be to a divorced person? Suppose you are the divorced person. Where do you go from here in relation to God?

PROMISSORY NOTE

I attended a religious university in the South that had a lot of rules; and as part of admission, every student agreed to abide by them. The school had a rule against card playing. They said playing cards was sinful, but they really were against the deck of cards used for poker or bridge. Using those cards was wrong because they were associated with gambling and wasting time; so if students used them on campus, the school authorities would expel them. But the students could play Rook. Even though the game is similar to bridge it was allowed because it used different cards. I had a roommate who almost flunked out of school because he played so much Rook. But if he had ever played bridge, he would have been kicked out of college.

The morality, or righteousness, of the behavior at that university had to do with external values, not internal. It had to do with keeping rules. A student could, in effect, take an oath not to play cards, but as long as he didn't deal aces, kings, or queens, he kept the rule. Using cards with other pictures on them didn't matter, even though playing those card games could have caused him to flunk out of school. That's what happens when righteousness becomes only a system of rule keeping. We make distinctions so that we can do one thing and not the other. Whether or not you believe card playing is a moral issue is not the point. If you believe it is, you destroy the spirit of the card-playing rule with devious interpretations of it.

In the Sermon on the Mount, Jesus wanted us to understand that God is not primarily concerned with right behavior, but with a change of heart and right attitudes. The righteousness of which He spoke does not come through rule-keeping.

The righteousness of God requires a complete change of viewpoint, a complete change on the inside. That's why He began with what we call the Beatitudes. He began by saying blessed, or approved, are those who are destitute in spirit, for theirs is the kingdom of heaven. Just as we might say "Good appetite promotes good health," Jesus was saying "A great sense of inner need promotes righteousness." But we can't leave it there. People with good appetites starve to death.

But if we turn to God to meet our need, to satisfy our hunger and thirst for righteousness, we will be filled. We are not filled with a new set of rules to follow nor a bunch of religious regulations, but with mercy. Having received mercy, we become merciful. Concerned now about motives, we become pure of heart; and the pure of heart see God. And out of that purity, we become peacemakers and in that way bear the resemblance of our Father in heaven.

We might think that folks who are merciful, pure of heart, and peacemakers, would always be welcome. But Jesus said that such people are out of step with society. As salt, Beatitude people preserve society from decay. As light, they shine in the darkness and lead men and women to God.

All of this emphasizes what is crucial in the Sermon on the Mount. Jesus was not giving us a whole new set of laws. He was not saying, "The Old Testament was tough, but it wasn't tough enough. If we don't get this law-and-order bunch together, we've got problems; so let's make the laws tougher." He was not dealing with laws at all. He was dealing with the inner righteousness that God provides, that catches the mind and heart and makes a difference in life. He was not saying that Beatitude people don't keep the rules, but that rule-keeping is not their focus. Keeping rules never makes us righteous.

A world of difference exists between behavior that simply keeps a set of rules and righteousness that comes from the inside. Did Jesus point to the most religious people of His day and say, "You've got to do better than that?" No, not quite. He was really saying, "You've got to *be* better than that. You've got to have a completely different kind of righteousness than they have."

The Pharisees thought they could handle righteousness on their own. But Jesus said in the Beatitudes that righteousness begins when we see our need of God. When we feel this bankruptcy of spirit, it will drive us back to Him for the righteousness we don't have on our own.

The kind of righteousness Jesus demands develops from an inward change that God produces. It involves a new starting point, a new beginning, a whole new orientation to life. If we fail to understand that, we fail to understand the New Testament. And people who come to the Sermon on the Mount with this misunderstanding keep trying to make it into a new set of rules. They want to define it so they can keep it.

The Sermon on the Mount is about inner righteousness worked out in life. It doesn't apply to the world nor to the political establishment; it applies to people in whom God has worked. In the last part of Matthew 5, Jesus applied this fulfilling of the law to six areas. Having looked at murder, adultery, and divorce, He came to the fourth area: oaths.

Jesus used this fourth case to again underline the principle that righteousness is not outward conformity to rules and ceremonies, but an inner response of a heart that is merciful and pure and seeks to make peace. He reminded the Pharisees that people had said long ago, "Do not break your oath, but keep the oaths you have made to the Lord" (Matthew 5:33).

No Old Testament passage specifically prohibits oath breaking, but several passages speak about oaths. A person was not to swear falsely by God's name (Leviticus 19:12) or misuse His name (Exodus 20:7). But as a safeguard against frivolous vows, oaths could be taken in

God's name (Deuteronomy 10:20). The Old Testament was clear that an oath was a way to emphasize the truth and importance of what one said. It set a statement or promise apart in a special way—just as marriage vows mean that a husband and wife have solemnly sworn to love, honor, and cherish each other until death parts them. The purpose of wedding vows is not to keep a couple from lying to one another. No. Vows sworn to one another before God demonstrate the importance of what they are promising one another. It is to say that this is very significant to us.

In Hebrews 6:13–17, the writer recalled God's oath to Abraham. God swore by himself to make clear that His promise of blessing to Abraham would extend to future generations. God took an oath, not because He lies, but to confirm to Abraham in the most solemn way possible that the promise He made about land and descendants would be fulfilled. So when God takes an oath, He's underlining His words, placing them in italics, putting exclamation points after them. The purpose of an oath was to show the solemnness and to reinforce the importance of what was said.

There were two kinds of oaths. An assertive oath said, "I did it" or, "I didn't do it." A promissory oath said, "You can count on me. I give you my word." In the Old Testament the oath marked out the most solemn assurances that people gave to one another. It was used to stress a strong commitment.

By New Testament times, the legalists had focused on the "name of the Lord" in the oath. God's name, not commitment, concerned the religious leaders. And so an oath that was uttered to underline truth, came to undermine truth. They got to the point of saying that the only speech that had to be true was an oath. Then they went a step further. They decided, "But not all oaths matter." Only those that are in God's name, only those in which a person crosses the heart, swears to God, and hopes to die. Those are the ones that really matter. As a result, that whole culture, with its fine tuning of oaths, became a society of liars. Lying under oath became a fine art.

The *Mishna*, a Jewish commentary on the Law, had sections on both oaths and vows, explaining both assertive statements and promises for the future, the ones to keep and the ones not to keep. The Pharisees got it down to prepositions. If they swore *toward* Jerusalem, the oath didn't matter. Jesus mocked all of that. In Matthew 23:16–22, He mocked all of their oaths: swearing by the gold of the temple instead of the temple, swearing by the gift on the altar instead of the altar, and swearing by heaven instead of God's throne.

These nitpicking Pharisees were in the same category as people today who reason that bridge is sinful but Rook is okay. Their distinctions are all ridiculous. If anger was the real issue of murder, lust the real issue of adultery, selfishness the real issue of divorce, then deceit is the real issue of oaths. Jesus responded in two ways to the deviousness of the Pharisees.

First, Jesus dealt with it biblically. To the people who said they didn't have to keep their oaths as long as they didn't swear by God or by what is sacred, He said, "That's ridiculous, unbiblical, and illogical." If a person is swearing by heaven, earth, or the city of Jerusalem, they are swearing by God. The Old Testament says that heaven is God's throne (Psalm 123:1), that the earth is His footstool (Isaiah 66:1), and that Jerusalem is the city of the Lord (Isaiah 60:14).

A Pharisee not only swore by geography but also by his head and even his beard. Such oaths didn't matter. God is the Creator of man, so all oaths bring Him in. In other words, we can't get rid of God. Everything we swear by involves God. All of the universe, not just His name, belongs to Him.

The second thing He said was more shocking. Since the Pharisees couldn't leave God out of their oaths, we might expect Jesus to warn them to make sure to keep their oaths. But He didn't. Instead

He instructed them not to swear at all. In Matthew 5:37 He told them to let their "yes be yes" and their "no, no." Anything else came from the Evil One.

In a world that uses oaths to assure that we speak the truth, we need to have an inward truthfulness that doesn't depend on oaths at all. When I give my yes, it is yes; and when I give my no, it is no. Oath or no oath, when one says something, others can count on it. Men and women who are truthful will be truthful whether they are under oath or not. So we ought not swear in order to say, "Now I am telling the truth."

A society that has a hard time telling the truth signs tightly worded contracts and demands oaths: "Do you swear to tell the whole truth and nothing but the truth, so help you God?" But contracts and oaths cannot guarantee truth. People will lie despite formal agreements or pledges.

Jesus was not talking about rules, about what oaths to take or not to take, about how to frame an oath, about whether we should swear to God, or put one hand on the Bible when we testify. If we are truthful people, we don't need oaths to guarantee our truthfulness. Anything beyond a simple yes or no comes because the Evil One encourages deceit.

Because Jesus said not to swear at all, the Quakers believe they ought not take an oath in court, so the government allows them to affirm. They do this out of good motives and for sincere reasons, but affirming something is not much different from taking an oath. This is the same old hair-splitting legalism.

Jesus wasn't against oath taking. He allowed himself to be put under an oath by the high priest (Matthew 26:63–64). Paul put himself under an oath on two separate occasions to emphasize the importance of what he was saying (Galatians 1:20; 2 Corinthians 1:23).

Jesus wasn't addressing whether or not we should take oaths. He was talking about whether or not we are truthful. If we hire high-priced lawyers to build loopholes into our contracts, we are not truthful. When two people have a clear understanding between them, the contract shouldn't matter. In our society we have to sign contracts, and we had better read the small print closely because people write contracts to their own advantage. But not Beatitude people. It can't be true of us. When we give our word, that is all we have to give.

We don't tell the truth because we have taken an oath; we tell the truth because we are truthful. Our yes is yes; our no is no. When we begin picking at the loose threads in a contract to go back on our word, we have become like the Pharisees. There is a wickedness to that, and it comes from the Evil One. As salt and light, we say, "I know what it says, and I realize that I can get out of it because of the wording, but I gave you my word. You can count on it." Then we are light in darkness. We are salt in a decaying society. We are like God when we keep our word.

Something is desperately wrong in a society when a man guilty of murder gets off because the sergeant put down the wrong date on the warrant. Something is wrong when people get off on technicalities. But we don't rely on technicalities. We rely on truthfulness. We mean what we say. We try to say what we mean. Jesus calls us to integrity. We tell the whole truth and nothing but the truth without oaths and without affirmations. So help us God.

SERMON NOTES

While rules in general are set up to protect us, when used in the wrong way they become destructive and oppressive. All of us have a tendency to insist on rule-keeping—why?

When might rule-keeping interfere with God's will for us?

As a parent, or from your childhood, can you cite examples of productive/destructive rule-keeping?

What about God's rules for us? Does He expect us to enforce them in the lives of other people?

Is God primarily concerned with right behavior? Why?

OVERTIME

∎

I bn Saud, the king of Saudi Arabia from 1932–1953, once had a woman come to him and demand the death of a man who had killed her husband. The man had been picking dates from a palm tree when he accidentally fell, hitting the woman's husband and fatally injuring him. Although the king tried to persuade the woman not to pursue her rights, she insisted on them. Finally, the king said, "It is your right to ask for this man's life, but it is my right to decree how he shall die. You shall take this man with you immediately, and he shall be tied to the foot of a palm tree. Then you yourself shall climb to the top of the tree and cast yourself down upon him from that height. In that way you will take his life as he took your husband's." The woman quickly changed her mind, realizing that in following the letter of the law and demanding her rights, she might lose her right to life.

In demanding our rights, we often do lose our right to real life, the kind that comes to those who hunger and thirst after righteousness. It is the Beatitude life that comes out of a relationship with Him and with this comes a new relationship with other people. It is a relationship that comes out of meekness, mercy, and purity of heart. It is a relationship that seeks to make peace.

When we live that kind of life, we can expect to be persecuted. People will revile us, speak evil against us, and put us down. Our new goal will make us go the opposite way down a one-way street. We'll be bucking the traffic, and that annoys people.

Instead of keeping laws to be righteous, we will have an inward kind of righteousness. Instead of outward conformity to laws, we will have an inner response to the spirit of the Law. People who live that way are the salt of the earth and the light of the world. And their light draws others to God. Unless we have that kind of righteousness we have no hope of getting into heaven, because our righteousness must exceed that of the scribes and Pharisees.

Jesus says that His righteousness has nothing to do with rule-keeping; it has to do with relationships. And a right relationship with God shows in the way we relate to people.

Like all good preachers, Jesus used examples to drive home His point. He presented six case studies to show that His kind of righteousness has nothing to do with rule-keeping.

In the first He centered on the law against murder. He said our concern ought not be whether or not we kill someone—that's where the law starts. Our concern ought to be for relationships—we are to guard relationships and not allow anything to come between ourselves and others.

The second had to do with adultery. We can pass laws against adultery, but Jesus said the real problem is lust in our hearts. One ought to deal drastically with anything that corrupts a relationship with another person, with another man's wife or another wife's husband.

Then He talked about divorce. He said we won't solve the problem with stricter divorce laws. They only force people to live together in an armed truce. To solve the problem of divorce, we must go back to God's initial desire for marriage—for a couple to become one flesh, creating a spiritual union as dynamic as the union of the body. When we keep that in focus, the laws about divorce become immaterial. They never even come up.

Then Jesus talked about oaths. He said, "Don't swear," but He didn't say, "Don't take an oath in court." For Christians, oaths should be unnecessary. Our yes means yes, and our no means no. An oath will not make us tell more of the truth. Placing one hand on the Bible and raising the other in a pledge to God will not make someone more truthful than to simply say yes or no. The spirit of truth makes one truthful; taking an oath does not.

In the fifth illustration Jesus dealt with the law of retaliation. "You have heard that it was said, 'Eye for eye, and tooth for tooth' " (Matthew 5:38). The Old Testament repeated that principle of law at least three times: Exodus 21:24; Leviticus 4:20; and Deuteronomy 19:16–21. The Deuteronomy passage is most important for our consideration.

Some say the Old Testament Law was savage and bloodthirsty, but that is not true. Actually it was the beginning of mercy. And it is the foundational law of all civilization.

Although it allows retaliation, it limits it by setting restrictions. If a person knocks out my tooth, I get his. And if I poke out his eye, he gets mine. Retaliation as we know it sets out to get more than that. We want to up the ante. But this law limited retaliation. People could only get back what they lost.

In addition to being merciful, the law limited retaliation to the offended. It didn't allow the whole family to get into the act. When wronged, we tend to line up forces of family and friends to retaliate. If a person cuts off my ear, I want to cut off his head. And if I cut off his head, his brother will kill me, and if he kills me, my brother will kill his brother, and pretty soon we have a clan war. The battle between the Hatfields and the McCoys did not start as a family feud. It started with two individuals.

Without the law of retaliation, revenge goes from the individual to the family to the clan to the tribe and ultimately to whole nations. So what seems to some like a blood-hungry law was actually a way of limiting violence and bloodshed.

In the Law, retaliation was not an individual decision, nor was it something one individual could demand from another. It was a principle of justice that was decided by a judge in a court of law.

What is given as a principle of fairness, however, sometimes gets twisted into a law that prescribes vengeance. If a person knocks out my tooth and I know the law, I think I have the right and even the obligation to knock out his tooth.

As it worked out in Israel, the law seldom if ever was applied literally. If I knock out someone's tooth, what good does it do me to get a tooth in return? Both individuals lose a tooth that way. So in court a judge decides that a tooth is worth a thousand bushels of wheat. Or if a person pokes out my eye, the judge may decide that I should be paid four bulls, three cows, two lambs, and next year's crop. The judge tries to determine what a tooth and an eye are worth.

We use this principle in our modern courts. When I seek damages for an injured leg, the court determines the value of my loss and makes the guilty person pay me. But in our culture we have laws that go beyond awarding damages. We make claims for mental pain, inconvenience, and embarrassment. These laws allow more than retaliation. "He took my tooth, so I'm going to get twenty-five times that." When lawyers urge us to contact them if we've been hurt in an accident, they are saying that someone ought to pay for all our grief. So we use the principle of retribution to be vindictive. We're not happy with getting even; we want to get ahead.

When Jesus said, "Do not resist an evil person," He was talking about legal ways to get retribution for what happened to us. We see that in two ways.

First, it is given in relation to the law of retaliation, which is a law of the courts. When Jesus said, "Do not resist the evil person," He meant, "Don't go to court." Don't decide to sue the daylights out of the other person to get your rights. That opposes the law of retaliation. Jesus was referring to Deuteronomy 19:18, which gave people the right to retaliate and to make a false witness pay for what he did to them. He was contradicting it by telling us to give up that right. We are not to retaliate, not to take the evil person to court and apply the law of retaliation. Instead of standing on our rights, we are to deal with others with generosity of spirit, the kind that God has shown us.

To drive home that principle, Jesus gave four illustrations. In the first one, He instructed us to turn the other cheek if someone strikes us on the right one. Approximately ninety percent of the people in the world are right handed. If we punch someone with our right hand, we will hit him on the left cheek. If we try to hit him on the right cheek with our right fist, we won't do anything to him. We can't do anything to him. If I am going to strike his right cheek, I am going to do it with the back of my hand, and in Israel that was an insult. To strike a man on his right cheek, or to give him the back of your hand, was worse than injuring him. The insult was worse than injury. If a man struck you with the back of his hand instead of punching you in the mouth, you could collect twice the damages. It was considered an affront, a put down. We use similar euphemisms today. The Irish often say, "The back of my hand to you," which means, "You are scum."

If a man reviles you, speaks evil against you, or slaps you on the face, Jesus said not to retaliate. Although you have a right to take him to court, do not do it. Turn the other cheek.

If he insults me once, he can insult me again. If he makes me feel stupid in front of my friends, I allow him to do it again. I give up my right to retaliate: I am to have a generous spirit.

In John 18:22–23, Jesus followed His own advice. When He stood before the High Priest, someone in the crowd punched Him. Jesus didn't say, "Try the other cheek." He said, "Why did you slap me? If I spoke evil, show me where I spoke evil. If I spoke truth, show me where I spoke truth."

This demonstrates that Jesus was not speaking literally. He was talking about insults, not muggers in the subway. When people hurl insults at us, we are to respond in grace.

In the second illustration Jesus spoke about injustice. He said, "If someone wants to sue you and take your tunic, let him have your cloak as well" (Matthew 5:40). The tunic was the undergarment that a man in the Near East wore. It was like a form-fitting body shirt and worn like a long robe. The cloak was like an afghan and worn like an overcoat. The cloak was protected by law. Exodus 22:26–27 decreed that if someone took a man's cloak for security in a business deal, the person had to give it back at night because it was used as a blanket in winter and as a pillow in summer. A fellow needed his cloak at night.

But that was not true of the tunic. It had no such protection. A man's tunic was fair game in a lawsuit. Getting a judgment for a man's cloak was more trouble than it was worth. The winner would spend all his time picking it up every morning and returning it every night. But the tunic was a different matter. People frequently took tunics as security.

But Jesus said to give up rights even to cloaks. Although they're protected by law, we're to give them up to settle disputes. The attitude should be, "If you're upset with me and my tunic will make you happy, it's yours. And here's my cloak as well." That's the spirit of generosity.

Our seminary had a business deal with a firm in town that promised to do a job for a certain price. Two things happened. First, they did not do a good job. Second, they charged us almost a thousand dollars more than we had agreed on.

I checked with people in the industry to find out if the firm had any right to do that, and they didn't. So we sent a check for the amount we had agreed on, even though they hadn't done the job well. They responded by billing us for the other thousand dollars. But I knew my rights. I was ready to go to court. I had my case all ready. It wasn't the money, of course, it was the principle. Usually the principle is the money. In this case it was a little of both.

I didn't like being taken advantage of. But the other people on my team advised me to do the generous thing and send the firm the money. They put things in perspective for me by asking, "What if that person, believing he deserves the money, heard you speak? Would he believe anything you said?" So we sent them the check for the other thousand dollars. I gave in and gave up my rights. Interestingly, about nine months later they sent a check to the seminary for close to the same amount we had overpaid them.

In the third illustration Jesus talked about duty and imposition. "If someone forces you to go one mile, go with him two miles" (Matthew 5:41). That too, was a matter of law. When the Persians delivered mail, they made long trips on foot. So mail carriers were allowed to make Persian citizens carry the mail one mile. The Romans liked the idea, so they adopted it. A Roman soldier or official could compel a Roman citizen or inhabitant living under Roman protection to carry his burden one mile.

The word translated *forces* in this passage is used in only one other place. When Jesus fell beneath the load of the cross, the historian said, "They met a man from Cyrene, named Simon, and they forced him to carry the cross" (Matthew 27:32). The Romans had a legal right to make him do it.

The army exercised the privilege frequently. If a soldier got tired of carrying his pack, he could say to a person, "All right, buddy, you carry it." And that person would have to stop what he was doing and carry it. He didn't say, "Let's make an appointment. I'll meet you here tomorrow and carry it then." It was an imposition, but it was a duty. The Jews hated it. And they hated Romans for making them carry their loads.

The Jews held to the letter of the law on this. They measured the mile in steps. One thousand exactly. And they counted every one. When they got to one thousand they stopped, put down the pack, and left the Roman to carry his own load or find another victim.

But then Jesus came along and told them to offer to carry it an extra mile. And to do it with generosity, with a spirit that says "I am not going to count the steps." They were to give up their rights.

In other words, the first mile we do for Caesar, but the second mile, when we do our duty with kindness and generosity, we do for God. And so I say, "I am not going to be held down to just doing my duty. I am not going to chafe under the imposition. I am going to do it with a generous spirit." That is how we are to do our duty, how we are to live as disciples of Christ.

The fourth illustration has to do with requests for help. It deals with what is moral. Jesus said, "Give to the one who asks you, and do not turn away from the one who wants to borrow from you" (Matthew 5:42). This has to do with the law of lending, and it too comes out of the Old Testament. As Deuteronomy 15:7–11 indicates, debts were canceled every seven years. The borrowers loved it. The lenders weren't quite so enthusiastic.

If I were a lender and someone came to me for a loan in the sixth year, I would think twice before giving it to him. If he didn't pay it off quickly, the loan would turn into a gift. The closer the seventh year got, the more tightfisted businessmen became. But Jesus said they were not to allow the seventh year to govern them. Whenever a brother had a need, they were to give generously, openhandedly. After all, these people were not asking for home-improvement loans. They needed money for food.

Jesus wasn't talking about every panhandler who sticks his hand out, and He certainly wasn't talking about lending money for business ventures; they didn't do that kind of thing in the ancient world. He was talking about people in need. Our only consideration should be whether we can help. If so, we are to give generously, without thought of repayment.

In each of these illustrations the overriding principle is that we are not to seek our own rights. When we are insulted, we have the right to retaliate; but we are not to exercise it. If we are treated unjustly, we have a right to our possessions; but we are to give them up. If we are imposed upon, we have a right to set limits, but we are not to insist on that right. When someone has a need, we have a right to our money, but we are not to be tightfisted with it. Instead of being right, we are to be generous.

When we are generous with others, we reflect our Father in heaven. He said, "Let your light so shine that man may see your good works, and in doing so they will see God" (Matthew 5:16). Generosity that doesn't retaliate, doesn't seek what is ours, reflects God. The only people who can live that way are those who know the grace of God. We recognize that in God's grace we don't get what we deserve.

Several years ago, a church I'm familiar with was on the verge of a split. During a business meeting, a man stood up and said, "Look, all I'm asking for is my rights, and I demand my rights."

Another man responded, "If you get your rights, if you get what you deserve, you'll go to hell. Every drop of water this side of hell is the grace of God."

That's the key to understanding the Sermon on the Mount. God has dealt with us in grace, and we are to reflect His grace in all our dealings with others.

SERMON NOTES

When we work "overtime" for the company of Christ, how do we feel? How do we act?

Do you ever feel God owes you something for your work for Him?

From the six case studies Jesus used, what have you learned about righteousness versus rule-keeping?

Why would some say that the Law was savage and bloodthirsty? How is the Law the beginning of mercy?

Explain the phrase, "Do not resist an evil person." Does that mean we should let thieves, murderers, and terrorists have their way in society?

How are we to deal with those who do evil to us? Can we retaliate? Elaborate on the four ways Jesus teaches us to deal with others who treat us wrongly.

Does the spirit of generosity toward those who hurt you encourage someone to wrong you again? Why risk it?

How do these principles of Jesus compare with the ethics in our society? Can you give some examples of situations you have found yourself in where you applied one of these four methods that demonstrates generosity of spirit?

RECONCILED ACCOUNTS

■

Ramon Narvaez, the nineteenth-century prime minister of Spain, was dying and was asked by a priest, "Does your Excellency forgive all your enemies?"

"I do not have to forgive my enemies," replied Narvaez. "I have had them all shot."

We often shoot our enemies. To act otherwise is foolhardy; it's better to get them before they get us. Even if we don't fire at them, we rarely treat them kindly. To love an enemy would be an extraordinary feat. That would take a different sort of person with a different kind of righteousness. Jesus said that type of righteousness is internal. It grows out of a relationship with God and into a relationship with other people. It's not legalistic, and it's not something we can define.

Matthew 5:43–48 is the sixth case in point of this kind of righteousness. "You have heard that it was said, 'Love your neighbor and hate your enemy.' But I tell you: Love your enemies and pray for those who persecute you, that you may be sons of your Father in heaven" (vv. 43–44).

The Old Testament Law said we are to love our neighbors (Leviticus 19:18). From the negative perspective it says, "Do not seek revenge or bear a grudge against one of your people." But it adds a positive dimension: "Love your neighbor as yourself." Those who wore their righteousness like a three-piece suit wanted to take a close look at the word *neighbor*. Whom exactly did it mean? The person next door? Across the street? Across town? Across the state? Across the country? Across the ocean? Where do we draw the line?

Those folks figured it out. They decided where to draw the line. A neighbor was someone close. To those outside their immediate circle they could be indifferent. And there was a whole mass of people they regarded as enemies and were free to hate. They reasoned that people who weren't their neighbors must be enemies, so they could despise them. In a nice, neat, theological way they divided the crowd and almost dignified their hate.

But Jesus said the Old Testament Law did not teach that! He said we are to love our enemies and pray for those who persecute us. Other translations add the phrases, love your enemy, bless those who curse you, do good to those who hate you, and pray for those who hurt you. The middle two phrases aren't in the best manuscripts, but they are certainly in the spirit of what Jesus was saying. If we are His disciples, if we love Him, we will also love our enemies.

To understand what Jesus meant when He talked about loving our enemies, we need to consider several words in the Greek language translated *love*. One is probably closer to our word *lust*, and is not used in the New Testament. Another refers to the love of friends, and still another to the love of country. But apparently none were strong enough or sturdy enough for the New Testament writers when they talked about God's love for us or our love for others.

The word the New Testament writers used for this divine kind of love is the Greek word *agape*. Outside the New Testament, in classical Greek literature, it is only used five or six times; and it is a weak, anemic word. It could be translated "goodwill." Evidently the biblical writers took this word *agape*, baptized it into the Christian faith, filled it full of new meaning, and gave it strength.

In the New Testament *agape* is used to speak of God's love for us and the kind of love we are to have for others. One of the characteristics of *agape* love was that it was not primarily a love of the emotions; it was a set of mind, an act of will. It was directed and active benevolence, an attitude that said, "I will do what is best for the other person whether I am dealing with friend or foe."

Immanuel Kant, the philosopher, read these words about loving our enemies and dismissed them as absurd. He insisted it was impossible for people to love their enemies. If we are talking about the feeling kind of love, Kant was right. We can't control our feelings that way. We can't light emotion as we would a match and blow it out as if it were a candle. If we are talking about emotional love, the command is beyond us.

But Jesus was talking about *agape* love, a set of the mind. Putting it another way, I am to deal with every person, whether friend or foe, as if I like them. I seek their highest good, not because I feel like it but because I make it the attitude of my mind. It is directed benevolence. With other loves, I feel and then act. With this kind of love I act, and sometimes as a result, I feel. Therefore I can love my enemy.

If we wait until we have warm, friendly feelings toward our enemies before we pray for them or act benevolently toward them, we will all die first. But when we act with our enemies' best interests in mind, regardless of how we feel, we reflect our Father who is in heaven.

Augustine rephrased Jesus' words when he said, "To love those who love you is human; to hate those who love you is demonic; but to love those who hate you is divine." When we love our enemies as well as our friends, we reflect the character of God.

One way to love our enemies is to pray for them. In doing so, we find that it is difficult to go into the presence of God and pray for His will to be done in a person's life and come out bearing anger and hostility toward him. To pray for somebody makes a difference in the way we see and act toward that person. To pray for another person is godlike. To seek the best for our enemies in the presence of God is to discover benevolence toward that person.

We are to bear a family resemblance to our Father in heaven, and one quality that characterizes Him is His indiscriminate benevolence—the way He acts toward His friends and His enemies. God causes His sun to shine on the evil and the good. He sends rain on the righteous and the unrighteous, because it's His nature to do so.

It would be convenient, I guess, to drive through the country and know that fields rich in grain belonged to Christians and that the dry, shriveled crops belonged to non-Christians. But God doesn't work that way. When He sends rain, it falls on believers and blasphemers. When God makes His sun shine, the atheist gets as warm as the Christian. God deals with enemies and friends alike. When we deal with both enemies and friends with their highest good in mind, we are like God.

But God's benevolence and kindness are often misunderstood by unbelievers. God's goodness is designed to lead them to repentance. But many folks misinterpret it as God's indifference toward their sin. If God blesses them with growing grain, a warm body, and a full wallet while they are living in rebellion toward Him, they think God doesn't take their sin very seriously.

An atheist in a small town wrote to the editor of the local paper one fall. "I have conducted an experiment," he wrote. "I have a field by the Baptist church. When the Baptists came to worship, I plowed it. I planted it on a Wednesday night when they were at prayer meeting. And I brought in the harvest while they were having a revival meeting. But I want to report that the field produced as much as any other field I have." The editor printed the letter and added this comment: "What the reader does not understand is that God does not settle his accounts on a Saturday night." Many unbelievers do not understand that. Because they have been blessed, they become indifferent to God, not realizing that in His goodness, He deals with enemies and friends alike.

When He says we are to love our enemies and pray for those who persecute us that we may be the sons of our Father in heaven, He is not urging us to do those things to become God's children. We do them because we are God's children. It is a family likeness. We see family likenesses in children's physical appearance and in their behavior patterns. We say of a son, "He's a chip off the old block." Of a daughter we say, "She's the spittin' image of her mother."

When we treat friends and enemies with equal benevolence, when we seek their highest good, we show that we are in God's family.

If we love those who love us, what reward will we get? If we greet only our relatives, how are we different from anyone else? Even the tax collectors do that. The tax collectors were the scum of society in the ancient world. Around April 15th we're not too fond of them either, but in the ancient world they were considered traitors.

Speaking today, Jesus might use the Mafia as His example. One thing that marks the Mafia is that they are good family men. In fact, family is all-important to them. They look out for their own, and they wipe out those who threaten them. They love family and kill enemies. If we love only those who love us, how are we different from the tax collectors or members of the Mafia?

When Jesus spoke of greeting someone, He didn't mean a simple "Hello." To greet someone in the Middle East is to wish the best to them. Their greetings are all bound up in blessing. Blessing on you, blessing on your children, blessing on your children's children. Even the pagans did that. In fact, their greetings were known for that. They were often long and elaborate. If we bless only the people we like, Jesus said we are no different from the pagans.

Jesus was saying that their ceiling ought to be our floor. Their love ends with family and friends, but that should be only the beginning of our love. We start where they stop. The high end of their friendliness scale is the low end of ours.

The reason we do this is to reflect our Father's love to the world. We love our enemies not primarily to make them our friends, but to show them God's love.

Someone once castigated Abraham Lincoln for his benevolent attitude toward southerners, whom the critic considered enemies. Lincoln replied, "What better way to destroy an enemy than to make him a friend." Good response. But that is not why we do it. While it may happen in the process, that is not our motivation. Nor do we do it because we believe that we can draw enough goodness out of their hearts to transform them. That is both simplistic and unbiblical.

The truth is, we can love our enemies and they may spit in our faces. They may see our love as weakness and take advantage of us.

We do it to reflect the love of our Father in heaven, who has made us His light in the world. When people see us loving those who do not love us and seeking the best for those who have made themselves our enemies, they see something godlike. And that is the basis of evangelism. Often I have seen people come to faith in Jesus Christ because they saw a Christian who stood out from others, and they wanted to know what made the difference. They heard the melody of the person's life and wanted to learn the lyrics.

The conclusion of it all is found in the last line of Matthew 5: "Be perfect, therefore, as your heavenly Father is perfect." The word used here for perfect does not mean sinlessly perfect. No place in the New Testament does the meaning come close to that. The word was used of a sacrifice offered to God. It had to be perfect, that is, without blemish. It is used and translated most often as *maturity*, as opposed to what is childish. It was used to speak of a teacher, as opposed to the student. It's the sense of being well-rounded or complete, of fulfilling the function for which it was made. If we say, "That is a perfect tomato for a salad," we are not passing judgment on the character of the tomato. We are speaking of its ability to perform a function, to add flavor and appeal to a salad.

When Willie Mays was reinstated into baseball by the commissioner, a sports writer said of him, "He was probably the perfect ball player." He did not mean that Willie Mays never struck out, never dropped a fly ball. He meant that Willie Mays was well-rounded. He could hit, run, catch, steal, and he knew the strategy of the game.

That was how Jesus used the word *perfect.* We are to be perfect as our heavenly Father is perfect—in the context of love.

Inasmuch as we deal lovingly with people, we are well-rounded and complete. As God does not discriminate in showing love, neither do we. We are never more like God than when we act in love toward another human being.

Sometimes as I read this section of the Sermon on the Mount, I feel the poverty of my life. I feel a kind of bankruptcy because this is the kind of person I ought to be and want to be. But I am very conscious that I am not. And that realization drives me back to poverty of spirit, which is the basis of our relationship with God.

The Beatitudes begin by saying "Blessed are the poor in spirit, for theirs is the kingdom of God." This section of the Sermon on the Mount fulfills its purpose if it drives us back to God for the inner righteousness of thought and motive only He can give.

We cannot live such lives in our own power. One can't simply decide, "From here on out I am going to love my enemies." I may indeed become upright. But my uprightness will be like that of the Pharisees and the teachers of the Law. It passes muster with people, but I will never get into heaven with it.

We can only live in relationship to God. And in that relationship, God works in us to establish the same kinds of relationships with others—a relationship with God that does not allow us to be satisfied by keeping the letter of the Law externally, but gives us an internal desire to keep the spirit of the Law.

Alfred, Lord Tennyson, in writing about archbishop Thomas Cranmer, said, "To do him a wrong was to beget a kindness from him. For his heart was so rich . . . that if you sowed therein the seeds of hate, they blossomed love."

Like Cranmer, we must understand the heart of God. One enemy is too many.

SERMON NOTES

How you define "neighbor" has great impact on how you live your life. When Jesus said, "Love your neighbor as yourself," whom do you think He meant by "neighbor"?

Define the word *agape* and what it means to us as Christians. What are some of the characteristics of *agape* love?

Immanuel Kant argued that it is impossible for us to love our enemies. Do you agree with him? Why might he have thought that way?

What would we *pray* for our enemies? Who benefits most from our prayers?

What are some of the ways that our *agape* love might be interpreted by our enemies?

When Jesus said we are to be perfect as God is perfect, did He mean we are to be sinless? If not, what did He mean?

Reflect on how our relationship to God defines our relationships with others. How does this section of the Sermon on the Mount take us back to the beginning—to the Beatitudes?

PART 2

■

THE SOLID ROCK
CONSTRUCTION COMPANY

THE BLUEPRINT

■

Addison Mizner, a famous architect and builder of the early twentieth century, designed many houses for the rich of south Florida. Even though he had almost no professional training, and one time built a two-story house without a stairway, he had a knack for beautiful homes and was pursued by the moneyed elite. On one occasion a client, William Gray Warden, inquired about getting a copy of the blueprints for his new Palm Beach estate to unveil before friends. Mizner retorted, "Why, the house isn't built yet! Construction first, blueprints afterward."

In many ways Mizner's rejoinder is as much a comment on life as on building philosophy. We are often more interested in the product than the process. Like the Pharisees of the first century, exterior finish is more important than interior. Wandering about from house to house, we check out filigrees but not foundations. Sometimes we need to take a second look. A man's house may be his castle, but not all houses are castles. Some are rotting and crumbling underneath because they were not well designed or constructed. In building lives or houses, we must follow the blueprints; but the architect's drawing is only a guide. No house or life is built without design changes. Yet, if the blueprint is there, we have a goal.

My expertise is not in building houses but sermons, yet I know the importance of a plan. After all, good sermons are nothing more than spiritual blueprints. When I was eleven years of age, I went to Calvary Baptist Church in New York and heard Dr. Harry Ironside, pastor of Moody Church in Chicago, speak. After citing the factual details of his sermon in my diary, I wrote this editorial comment: "Some men speak for twenty minutes and it seems like an hour, others speak for an hour and it seems like twenty minutes. What makes the difference?"

I have pursued that question throughout my life, and I suppose that I have listened to or read five thousand sermons in my search. That is one of the reasons I am drawn to Jesus' Sermon on the Mount. What did Jesus say in the Sermon and how did He say it? Those who study preaching, like myself, agree that a good sermon has three basic ingredients.

First, it must have a sense of unity. Things that ordinarily might be separated come together in a oneness that either did not exist or was not recognized before. United States coins have the Latin inscription *e pluribus unum*, "one out of many." A good sermon is a simple truth that comes from many truths. It has unity. This criterion did not come from some back room experts who said, "Let's say that a good sermon has to have unity." It comes from the fact that whenever we see separate things we try to put them together. We go out at night, look up into the sky, and say, "There's the Big Dipper." What we really see are stars a million light years apart, but our desire for unity brings them together. We see them as a whole. The need for unity is a law of the listener's mind. If a good sermon doesn't have unity, it bothers us. In fact, it ultimately bores us. In houses, sermons, and lives, the pieces fit together.

Second, a sermon has to have order. A sermon is a unit that is preached in time. For us to understand the overall sense of unity, each part of the sermon has to come to us when we need it. It must answer the questions lurking in our minds at just the right time.

Third, a good sermon has a sense of progress, a sense of movement. We have the feeling that the preacher is going somewhere. And we have the comfortable feeling that when he gets there he will stop. He won't keep talking just to fill time.

Unity, order, and progress. I have found all three in the Sermon on the Mount. In fact, one of the reasons I keep reviewing the flow of thought in this book is so readers will see the unity, order, and progress of Jesus' sermon. People who don't see these make ridiculous judgments about its parts. To understand it we have to see it as a whole, in its completeness.

But how do we get unity, order, and progress? To accomplish this a sermon must have a single, central idea. A good sermon is an idea that is expanded and enlarged. Or, looking at it another way, we can compress a sermon into a central thought to give it unity and order. Progress comes as we develop the central thought.

The central subject Jesus developed in the Sermon on the Mount was: how can anyone have a righteousness that passes muster with God? What He tells us about that subject is that such righteousness has nothing to do with rules and regulations; it has to do with relationships—a relationship first with God and out of that a relationship with other people. That idea is central to the Sermon. Jesus strikes that note early. "Unless your righteousness surpasses that of the Pharisees and the teachers of the law, you will certainly not enter the kingdom of heaven" (Matthew 5:20).

The Pharisees were the major league religionists of their day. For them, religion consisted of rules and regulations, responsibilities and duties. But the heart of the problem for many of them was that their religion had no heart. Jesus was saying that if we are going to have a righteousness that meets with God's approval, it has to grow out of a relationship with God and it must focus on others.

Jesus began in Matthew 5 by giving us the Beatitudes, which are attitudes that characterize people who enter the kingdom of heaven. Those who are Beatitude people will be salt and light in a rotten and dark world because their faith will be based on a relationship rather than rules. As they enter deeper into that relationship with God, they will come to understand the truth. To help them understand the truth, Jesus gave six case studies—murder and anger, adultery and lust, divorce and selfishness, oaths and deceit, retaliation and rights, hate and love. In all these cases, Jesus set forth principles that flow from inner righteousness.

In Matthew 6:1 Jesus stated the principle that governs the next eighteen verses. "Be careful not to do your 'acts of righteousness' before men, to be seen by them. If you do, you will have no reward from your Father in heaven." The three acts of righteousness that demonstrate our relationship with the Father focus on giving, praying, and fasting. These acts of worship serve as litmus tests of the reality of our religion. When we perform any of these for show, our religion is a sham.

Giving is something godly people do, but we can give for the wrong reasons. We can give so people will admire us for being generous. If that's our reason for giving, the only reward we get will be a pat on the back.

Fasting is another discipline of godly people. Fasting helps us focus our attention on things that are important. But we can fast for the wrong reasons, too. Some people try to look weak and anemic when they fast so their friends will notice and be impressed with how devout and pious they are. If that's our reason for fasting, the only benefit we'll get from it will be a comment or two from admiring friends.

Righteous people also pray, but they don't have a righteousness that matters with God if they pray loud and lengthy public prayers so others will applaud their spirituality. If we enjoy praying in public so others will admire how marvelously we pray, we have missed the point of the Sermon on the Mount.

Then, within this section on prayer, Jesus provides a model prayer. We call it "The Lord's Prayer." Actually, the prayer is misnamed because the Lord himself could not have prayed this prayer. As the sinless Son of God, He could not join in the petition, "Forgive us our sins." Perhaps the prayer should be labeled "The Disciples' Prayer," since it serves as a primer on prayer for people like us. It helps us to pray, as an outline serves a minister when he preaches a sermon, or as a blueprint serves a builder. It guides us as we go.

The skeleton of the prayer opens with an address to God: "Our Father in heaven." The prayer then has two major sections. First, we are to talk to the Father about the Father: His Person, His program, and His purpose—"Hallowed be your name, your kingdom come, your will be done."

Second, having spoken to the Father about the Father, we are to speak to the Father about His family: the children's need for provision, pardon, and protection—"Give us today our daily bread. Forgive us our debts as we also have forgiven our debtors. And lead us not into temptation, but deliver us from the evil one."

One thing we must do as we work our way through the Scriptures is to understand passages in their context. So the question is, after the Lord's Prayer how does the extended passage of Matthew 6:19–7:12 fit into the context of the Sermon on the Mount? I agree with Robert Guelich that this section stands as a commentary on the Lord's Prayer. Jesus was showing us what a life of prayer looks like.

This extended passage has six sections. The first four begin with prohibitions. For example, in Matthew 6:19 Jesus said, "Do not store up for yourselves treasures on earth." The second section starts at 6:25 with another prohibition: "Do not worry about your life." The third section starts at 7:1: "Do not judge or you too will be judged." The fourth prohibition starts at 7:6: "Do not give dogs what is sacred."

The fifth section beginning in 7:7 is an exhortation to pray based on what has just been said. "Ask and it will be given to you; seek and you will find; knock and the door will be opened to you." And 7:12 summarizes it all with what we call the Golden Rule: "Do to others what you would have them do to you, for this sums up the Law and the Prophets."

Notice how Matthew 6:19–7:12 elaborates on the petitions in the model prayer Jesus gave us. The first section, Matthew 6:19–24, corresponds to the first section of the Lord's Prayer, where we are to pray for God's will to be done, His kingdom to be established, and His name to be honored. In other words, we pray that God will be God to us, that He will be the priority of our lives. The second section, "Do not worry" (v. 25), corresponds to the fourth petition, "Give us today our daily bread." And the third section, "Do not judge" (7:1), corresponds to the fifth petition, "Forgive us our debts as we have forgiven our debtors." And the strange little phrase in Matthew 7:6, "Do not give to dogs what is sacred," corresponds to the last petition, "Lead us not into temptation, but deliver us from the evil one." It is a petition asking God to keep us from Satan's trap, from falling into the hands of the Evil One. The section beginning with Matthew 7:7 exhorts us to pray this way. We are to pray because God, our Father, is a good giver. Then because He gives good gifts, we should also; and this is the basis for the Golden Rule of 7:12.

After Jesus finished His commentary on the Lord's Prayer, He returned to His central theme of how to find true righteousness. He built His case with vivid images—small and wide gates, narrow and broad roads, sheep and wolves, grape vines and thornbushes, fig trees and thistles, good trees and bad trees, rocks and sand. From these images emerge the lonely pilgrim who has taken the road to life, the true prophet who has done the Father's will, and the wise builder who has erected a house upon a rock foundation. These three people reveal in their choices that no true righteousness comes apart from Jesus Christ. He is the Way; through Him we find God. He is the Truth; through Him we know God's will. He is the Life; through Him we have security for eternity.

The illustration of the wise builder is a fitting conclusion to the Sermon on the Mount because lives and houses have much in common. Flesh and blood, as well as brick and mortar, can stand in splendor on an unsure footing. Without the Preacher of the Sermon on the Mount as our solid foundation, we can never live the Christian life, much less understand His Sermon. Life's storms will blow us away. But when we enter into a relationship with Him, when He makes our house His home, we will understand the Master Builder's plan.

SERMON NOTES

How is the Sermon on the Mount a blueprint for living today?

What three qualities of good sermons are evident in Jesus' message?

Good sermons have a single idea—a central thought. Summarize the central subject of Jesus' teaching.

In Matthew 6, Jesus deals with three acts of righteousness that demonstrate our relationship to God. What are they? Explain how these are acts of worship.

In your own life, do you feel these three acts of righteousness always reflect your relationship to God?

Is it possible to perform these acts of righteousness for the wrong reasons? Can you give some examples?

Jesus gives us a model prayer in the Lord's Prayer. Identify the two major sections of this prayer.

THREE-WAY SERVICE

■

Henry James and Edith Wharton, novelists published by Scribner's, were good friends, but they were not equally successful in the income from their writings. Because James was quite sensitive about his meager earnings, Wharton often had to plot in secret to help him. She once arranged with Scribner's to offer James an eight-thousand-dollar advance on a new, forthcoming novel with the understanding that the money would be taken from her own book royalties. Because James never learned that Wharton was his benefactor, he received the money with joy.

The Jewish people had a saying for just about everything in life, including giving. One that the rabbis used was "It is better to give nothing than to give to someone and cause them to be ashamed." In other words, if our giving becomes a public display, we risk not only destroying the gift but also hurting the person to whom we are giving it.

The Pharisees, however, did not live up to this cultural ideal of keeping their giving secret. Figuratively speaking, a Pharisee sounded a trumpet before he gave so that everyone would notice his generosity. Today we would say, "He blew his own horn."

To the Jews, giving ranked as the supreme act of piety. Giving to the needy, said the teachers of the law, was better than sacrifice. When Jesus arrived on the scene He didn't dispute this, but He added a qualifier. More important than giving, said Jesus, was the motive that prompted the giving. He knew the base motives in people's hearts and recognized that even good deeds could be done for bad reasons.

Some people give out of guilt; some give out of a sense of superiority. A friend asks us to contribute to his favorite cause and we feel guilty if we don't. When we help someone, we may picture ourselves as reaching down to help them up. Charity can infuse us with a sense of superiority.

Whether we give out of feelings of guilt, superiority, or for some other reason, most of us want some recognition for our generosity. But if we call attention to our giving, Jesus warned, that attention is all the reward we are going to get.

Jesus said of the trumpet-blowing Pharisees, "They have received their reward in full." This phrase comes from an expression used in ancient Greek commerce. Archaeologists have found it scribbled on papyri identified as receipts and have concluded that it meant "paid in full."

If we give to be seen by others and we receive their applause, we have been paid in full. If we want the praise of men, we can have it; but then God owes us nothing.

If we want recognition from God, however, we should give quietly, not letting the left hand know what the right hand is doing. Then our Father, who sees what we do in secret and knows our motives, will reward us. Good deeds cannot merit more than one payout—if we get our reward from men we will not receive from God.

Jesus was not opposed to having people know about the actions of His followers. Such things cannot always be kept secret or confidential. His concern was that recognition was not His people's motive for giving. He did not want them doing righteous acts for unrighteous reasons.

Fund-raising consultants often approach educational institutions and offer to set up campaigns for these schools. They guarantee that these fund-raising ventures will substantially increase the revenues of the school. Usually their subtle and not-so-subtle strategy includes publishing the names of the people who contribute, listing them in categories according to the amount they donate. Those who give will be trumpeted and by implication, perhaps, so will those who don't give. These firms raise the needed money and get what they want—a percentage of the take. And the contributors get what they want—their names printed on a plaque or program and the subsequent applause of others. In Jesus' words, they have been paid in full.

If we want public acknowledgment for our righteous acts, we have missed the point of Jesus' message in Matthew 6. This applies to our praying as well as our giving.

When we pray, Jesus warned, don't be like the hypocrites who love to stand in the synagogues or out on the street corners and pray where everyone can see them. Like those who receive accolades for their generosity, these showmen receive their reward in full in being recognized for their piety.

Prayer was as important in the Jewish religion as it is in the Christian faith. When Jews awoke in the morning the first thing they did was pray what was called the Shema: "The Lord our God, He alone is God. Help me to love the Lord my God with all my heart and soul and mind" (see Deuteronomy 6:4–5). At the end of the day, as the sun was setting, they repeated this petition. The Jews also had set times to pray during the day, at 9:00, at 12:00, and at 3:00; and they had specific prayers for different occasions. They prayed a certain prayer when they entered a home, when they saw the sea, and when they viewed a river. They prayed a certain prayer when they entered a city, when they left a city, and when they bought new furniture.

Certainly we can applaud this desire to remember God throughout the day and on each occasion, this zeal to commit every area of life to Him. But there is a danger in much praying, for these frequent prayers can become a kind of automatic reaction or rote response done without thought or meaning. For example, have you ever thanked God for your food before a meal and then been unable to remember what you have prayed, or whether you have prayed at all? This is what happened to many Jews; prayer had become something they went through as a thoughtless routine in their daily lives.

Another thing happened. Perhaps figuring that if they prayed long prayers they could pester God enough to gain His attention, they did just that. Their prayers became longer and longer.

These were the kind of folks who could say, "I spend an hour in prayer every morning." Now there is nothing wrong with spending an hour in prayer if it is time spent in true devotion to God. But God doesn't time our prayers, although some people seem to believe that He does. They operate as if somehow God is sitting in heaven with a stopwatch and He is more impressed with an hour-long prayer than He is with a five-minute prayer.

Whether we are trying to impress God or people, Jesus said, praying for effect is hypocritical. He pointed His listeners to those who repeated a prayer over and over as though it were some magic chant or formula. They were just like the pagans, Jesus said, who babbled their empty litanies, thinking they would be heard because of their many words. When Elijah challenged the prophets of Baal on Mount Carmel (1 Kings 18), the pagan prophets repeated "O Baal, answer us!" for half a day. Centuries later the people of Ephesus did the same thing. Attempting to reach the ears of their goddess, they shouted the phrase "Great is Artemis (Diana) of the Ephesians!" for two hours (Acts 19). For the pagans, prayer served as a magic formula. If they found the correct formula and repeated it often enough, perhaps the gods would respond.

"The fewer the words, the better the prayer," said Martin Luther. And the prayer Jesus gave to us as a model prayer has fifty-seven words in Greek and only fifty-two words in English. Yet this short prayer, too, is often mumbled thoughtlessly like some rote formula of faith.

Because prayer had a special place in Jewish religion, religious types schemed to get other people to notice their piety. It's easy to see how they worked that out. You're expected to pray at 9:00 and 12:00 and 3:00 and you want to pick up a reputation for being pious. So you make it a point to be in the marketplace at those hours, or on the top step of the synagogue. Then when it's time to pray you assume the prescribed position—arms stretched out and eyes shut—and it is clear to everyone around that you are very devout. Prayer turns into a performance. Several years ago a Boston newspaper reported on a prayer given by a noted clergyman as "one of the most eloquent prayers ever delivered to a Boston audience."

Again, Jesus wasn't opposed to public prayer. He was against the motive that turned it into a performance. That's why He admonished His followers to go to a room and close the door. In the Jewish homes of the first century the only private place where the door could be locked was the storeroom, and that's the word Jesus used. In a private place no one can see us, showmanship disappears, and we are more likely to talk with God.

The motive behind their worship was what mattered. Jesus also applied the principle to the matter of fasting. "When you fast, do not look somber as the hypocrites do," Jesus warned, "for they disfigure their faces to show men they are fasting" (Matthew 6:16). Traditionally, the pious Jew covered his head with ashes when he was fasting. Again, Jesus refuted this traditional practice, warning that those who let their fasting be known in such a manner had played to an earthly audience, and they would only receive the admiration of men and women. If they wanted God's pleasure and reward, they must change their motives and mode of operation.

Interestingly, fasting does not have a big place in the Bible. In the New Testament, it is never commanded; it is only reported. In the Old Testament, the people fasted once each year, on the Day of Atonement

(Yom Kippur). We are also told that Moses fasted before ministry, as did Jesus.

So why fast if it is not commanded? In the Old Testament fasting always had to do with acknowledging sin. The people of Israel fasted at times of national repentance. If prayer draws us to God, fasting draws us away from self.

The Homily on Fasting from the Articles of the Anglican Church describes this inward attitude in fasting: "When men feel in themselves the heavy burden of sin . . . they . . . are inwardly touched with sorrowfulness of heart . . . all desire of meat and drink is laid apart."

Many people today seem to look at fasting as a way of winning God's approval. Somehow they think that if God knows how miserable they are without lunch He will be more open to their requests. We can't manipulate God. If we fast to wean ourselves away from the ordinary distractions of life so we are more able to concentrate on Him, that's fine—but private.

In the Jewish religion, fasting became theater. The Pharisees fasted twice a week, on Monday and on Thursday. This might have had something to do with the fact that Monday and Thursday were market days when many people came to town. When the Pharisees fasted, everybody in the community knew it. The Pharisees put on a benefit performance, for their own benefit. They donned garments of sackcloth and covered their heads with gray ashes. They wanted the applause of people for their piety, and they got it. They had their reward.

But Jesus told His followers to do otherwise. Wash your face and put oil on your head, He said. Those who really know God should be feasting, not fasting. We ought to wear Easter on our faces, even if we have Good Friday in our hearts.

Giving, praying, and fasting are not things we do for public display. They are private actions done for the good of others or for the strengthening of our own spiritual lives. They are private transactions between ourselves and God.

As human beings we want our piety known. It is difficult to give generously and never be commended. It is hard to pray for an hour without letting someone know of our devotion. It is tough to fast—in fact, most of us don't—and not have someone commiserate with our devout hunger. We forget that in all of this there is an important Onlooker who knows all our motives and cares about our true devotedness to Him. He will see that we are rewarded in His own way in His own time.

We get what we go after. If I want good reviews from the critics in my church for the performance of my religion, I can get them. But that's all I get. I get my reward here and now and I am "paid in full." If I want God's approval, I can get that. This Onlooker is not simply a member of the audience or a judge keeping score. He is "my Father in heaven," deeply concerned about my heart's earnest desires. My giving, my praying, my fasting—my worship—is for Him. My Father who knows my deepest wishes will reward me with treasure that I really value.

In *A Christmas Carol*, Charles Dickens described the tightfisted Ebenezer Scrooge as a man who was "secret . . . and solitary as an oyster." What Dickens expressed negatively about Scrooge, Christ proclaimed to be at the heart of our service for Him. He wanted His followers to carry out their "acts of righteousness" unobtrusively, even secretly at times.

Religion is not a performance; it is faithfulness to a Person. Devotion is not acted out for display and applause; it is our private obedience meant for viewing by our Father in heaven. In our giving, praying, and fasting we are to be in His Majesty's secret service.

SERMON NOTES

Jesus taught that the motives prompting our giving are more important than the acts of giving. Yet it's sometimes difficult to give our tithes in secret or with the purest motives. When is it difficult for you *not* to give, without feeling guilty? Are there times when you should *not* give?

What kind of recognition do people desire for their giving? Is it wrong for others to call attention to our giving, as long as we don't call attention to it ourselves?

How does God show recognition for our gifts?

We don't often see people praying on street corners or other public places. Jesus warns us not to be like these hypocrites. How do we display our piety in public places today?

How often was fasting practiced in the Old Testament? How often does God command it in the New Testament? What are some reasons people fast today?

Why is it important for fasting to be a private affair—between ourselves and God?

Can you think of some other Christian practices that are similar to the showmanship sometimes displayed in giving, praying, or fasting? Why do you think it's so difficult for people to keep their devotional acts private?

DIRECT CIRCUIT

■

When my two children, Vicki and Torrey, were young, I played a game with them. I would take a few coins and put them in my hand; I'd show them the coins and then close my hand over them. My youngsters would crawl up in my lap and try to pry open my fingers one at a time. Once they captured the coins, they would scream with delight and jump down to treasure their prize.

What I enjoyed about that game was having my son and daughter sit in my lap, and feel them close to me. The pennies really didn't mean much to me, but in another way they meant everything to me because, during penny play, my children laughed and talked with me while I expressed, with hugs, my deep love for them.

When we pray we often concentrate on the gifts in God's hand and ignore the hand of God himself. We pray fervently for new jobs or for the return of health. When we gain the prizes, we are delighted. And then we have little more to do with God. If only after the coins, God's hand serves only as a way to make the house payment, buy clothes for the children, or pay for the groceries. After the need has been met, the hand itself means little to us.

Although God in His grace does give good gifts to His children, He offers us more than that. He offers us himself. Those who are satisfied with the trinkets in the Father's hand miss the best reward of prayer—the reward of communicating and communing with the God of the universe.

According to Jesus, when we come to the God of the universe in prayer, we can address Him as Father. Bound up in the word *Father* is a compact summary of the entire Christian faith. It is the answer to the philosopher Lessing's question, "Is the universe friendly?" When Christians bow before God and call Him Father, they are acknowledging that at the heart of the universe is not only ultimate power but ultimate love.

But not everyone can call God Father. It was Jesus who taught us to pray that way. He alone guaranteed that we can enter into relationship with God and become members of His family.

Some believe in the "Fatherhood of God and the brotherhood of man," but this is not the teaching of the Bible. God is Creator of all, and in that sense we are "God's offspring" (Acts 17:29). But the relationship that a creature has with his Creator is not the relationship of a Father to His children, which is our link with God through Jesus Christ.

In the Old Testament the Israelites did not individually address God as "Father." As far as we know, Abraham, Joseph, Moses, David, or Daniel never fell to their knees in the solitude of their chambers and dared to address God that way. Yet in the New Testament God is called Father at least 275 times, and that is how we are instructed to speak to Him. All that a good father wants to be to his children, Jesus told us, God will be to Christians who approach Him in prayer. We can pray as children. Because of Jesus' death and resurrection, when we come to the sovereign Majesty of the universe, the word that should fall readily from our lips is *Father*.

The address "Our Father in heaven," in Matthew's record of the Lord's Prayer, not only recognizes the intimacy that we have with God as our Father, it also speaks of the awe we should have as we come to Him in prayer. The phrase "in heaven" does not refer to God's zip code; it refers to His elevation above all. Jesus was saying that this One to whom we come as Father is the sovereign Majesty of the universe, the God of all power, the God of all authority.

For early Jewish Christians, having a proper awe of God was probably easier than understanding their intimacy with God. Unfortunately, in our day the pendulum has swung to the other extreme. God is often referred to in terms that are anything but awe-inspiring. I cannot conceive of the psalmist saying, "I may not know the answers, but I know the Answer Man." I cannot imagine men and women of the Bible talking about "the big Man upstairs." To say that God is our Father does not imply that God is a great big, huggable teddy bear.

The Bible keeps the tension between intimacy and awe in our thinking about God. The writer of Hebrews said, "Let us then approach the throne of grace with confidence, so that we may receive mercy and find grace to help us in our time of need" (4:16). The fact that we come to a throne should fill us with awe. But because it is a throne of grace, it is approachable. We do not have to parade like the Pharisees or babble like the pagans; we can intimately and confidently talk with our Father.

Yet our Father knows what we need before we ask (Matthew 6:8), so why should we come at all? To put it bluntly, is prayer necessary? Wouldn't it be more pious, more devout, more trusting, to say, "Who am I to tell God how things ought to work?" How will my requests change the course of heaven? Why don't I just leave it up to God and show my trust in Him by not praying at all? Any thoughtful person has asked that kind of question. The answer is in the address itself—"Father in heaven." The sincere cry of "heavenly Father" may in itself be all that prayer needs because we are expressing a relationship of trust and dependence, awe and intimacy. Prayer is not primarily getting things from God but talking with Him.

Being persons is something we hold in common with God, and persons can relate to each other. If a husband and wife are not talking with each other, it is a dead relationship. If a home has become nothing more than a filling station, family life is sterile. Spouses and families need communication and so does every person with God.

We don't come to know God simply because we have feelings. All the beautiful organ music, all the sweet-smelling incense, all the walks down sun-drenched paths cannot substitute for talking with Him and listening to Him as He speaks to us through His Word. When we pray to our Father in heaven, we are communing with a personal God who loves us. The purpose of prayer is primarily to voice to God the priorities of our lives and the needs of our souls. When we talk with Him heart to heart and mind to mind, we affirm our love for each other.

On Father's Day, 1976, my daughter Vicki wrote me a letter. I have saved it and read it several times since then. She wrote in part:

> Dear Daddy, Some of the highlights of my life include the days that I receive letters from you. Your letters are always so bright and thoughtful, so loving and so comforting. Since I can't be with you on Father's Day this year, I wanted to write you a note to tell you how much you are valued and loved by me. I enjoy being with you so much . . . You were so fair to me as a child. Unselfishly you seemed to always put my interest above your own. You've always encouraged and expected the best of me . . . I just wanted to tell you that I love you very, very much.

No longer did she value me for the pennies in my hand. She had grown up now and treasured better and richer things.

No requests, but communication. Out of communication, communion. That letter expresses a wonderful relationship. Are we blind? Our heavenly Father will do for us more than any earthly father can do for his child. Most of all He wants to bring us into a communion with himself.

SERMON NOTES

What is our ultimate reward in praying to God?

In the Old Testament the Israelites did not address God as "Father." Why then did Jesus teach us to pray this way? What does this teach us about a Christian's relationship to God?

How does the Bible balance intimacy and awe in our thinking about God?

Is prayer really necessary? Why? What is its purpose?

Do you find prayer easy? What hinders your prayer life? When you pray, how do you picture God? Does that help or hinder you?

SKYLIGHT

∎

In the Teutonic language, a forerunner of English, the word *king* simply meant "father, the father of a family, the father of a clan, the father of a people." Eventually, the meaning expanded and implied sovereignty. The original Teutonic meaning of *king* is seen in one of the titles given to kings of England. Charles II, a king who did not have full support of his people, was sometimes announced with the epithet "The king, father of his people." But he wanted more than titles. Charles wanted his subjects to truly honor him as a father and gratefully respect his domain and will as a king. He wanted to be set apart in their hearts.

In teaching His disciples to pray, Jesus explained that their view of the heavenly Father's name, kingdom, and will affected their relationship to Him. Jesus told them first to say, "Our Father in heaven, hallowed be your name" (Matthew 6:9). In Hebrew thought, a name was extremely significant. The Jewish people did not give their children names so that their initials would look good on luggage. Parents didn't choose a name because it reminded them of Aunt Hilda or Uncle Harry. They chose names for their children hoping that the name would embody the personality, characteristics, or character that they wanted to see developed in the child.

Early American Puritans did that. They gave their daughters names like Silence, Charity, Hope, Love, and Patience. They hoped that their children, as they grew, would live up to their names. We also see the importance of a name in the New Testament. In times of crisis, if a man's life or outlook changed, often his name was changed to match. When Jesus got hold of Peter, his name was Simon. He was a shifty, sandy, undependable fellow, but Jesus changed his name to Peter, or in effect "Rocky." Jesus renamed Peter before Peter lived up to his new name. It took a while for Jesus to change Peter's shifting personality into rock.

The practice of renaming was seen in more recent days when the cardinal of Poland became the pope. He changed his name to John Paul II because he wanted his life to embody the virtues of his predecessors Pope Paul and Pope John. He chose the name to personify what he wanted to be.

The psalmist proclaimed that those who know God's name will put their trust in Him (Psalm 9:10). He was not claiming that those who can pronounce or read God's name will trust in Him. When we know God's character and His power, we will rest in Him. In hallowing God's name, we are setting it apart, making it something special. We are praying that God may be God to us, that He will be set apart in our prayers in such a way that it will be clear that we reverence God.

Sometimes our prayers are dangerously close to a blasphemy. We often pray as if God were deaf and we have to shout to make Him hear, as if He were ignorant and we have to explain to make Him understand, or as if God were calloused and we have to cajole to get Him to respond. Our prayers betray a very inadequate idea of God.

At other times our prayers reveal that many names on earth are more significant to us than the name of God in heaven. One can be more in awe of an employer, a professor, a loved one, a friend, or a government official than of the God in heaven. We can fear worms of the earth like ourselves more than we reverence and respect the God of heaven to whom we pray.

The petitions in the Lord's prayer cover all that we are to pray about. Whether we pray short prayers or a long ones, we will never pray more than this. Although we often pray for God to increase our devotion and depth of spiritual life, none of the petitions in this prayer is for personal holiness. The first step in spiritual growth is not to pray for inner feeling or inner change but that God will indeed be God in our lives. The focus of the spiritual life is not our inner experience but our honor of God.

We have the command to be holy as He is holy because the spiritual life begins when we determine to allow God to be God in all aspects of life—personal, family, business, recreation—and to allow God to set us apart.

The focus on Him should be true not only in our own inner lives but also in our prayers for others. We should not pray merely that others will be delivered from sin but that they will come to know God. The focus of evangelism is not that people will be won to Jesus Christ, as important as that is, but that people in the world who profane the name of God will come to understand who He really is—the God of holiness, grace, and righteousness. And out of that understanding, they will hallow His name.

Wordsworth well expressed the importance of a special relationship with God when he wrote, "Father!—to God himself we cannot give a holier name."

The second request that we direct to the Father about the Father is not devoted to the person of God but to His program. The second petition is "Your kingdom come." Jesus was speaking here about His future messianic reign upon the earth. All through Scripture, the story of the Bible looks forward to the return of the Messiah, Jesus Christ, who will rule in righteousness when the kingdom of this world will become His kingdom.

This concern for God's rule over the earth and its people is basic to our view of history. Joseph Wittig once noted that a person's biography should begin not with his birth but with his death. He argued that we measure the contribution of life not by its beginning, but by its end. That's how we should think about history. Any thoughtful person wonders, Is history going anywhere? Is it a wheel that moves round and round and never touches the ground? Is it simply a cycle of repeated events headed for no destination except perhaps oblivion? Some people shrug off history as a tale told by an idiot, scrawled on the walls of an insane asylum. Edward Gibbon wrote off history as "little more than the register of crimes, follies, and misfortunes of mankind." Ralph Waldo Emerson dismissed history as the "biographies of a few great men." Henry Ford shrugged it off as "bunk."

In the witness of the Bible, however, history is "His story," and history is headed somewhere—the return of Jesus Christ. The Bible anticipates that day when the angels and the redeemed will sing together. Before us shines that light, and the darker the age, the brighter seems the glow.

So when we pray "Your kingdom come," we look toward that glad time when God's messianic kingdom prophesied throughout the Old Testament will be established by Jesus' return to earth. As we pray, we direct our gaze to the day when worldly realms will become His domain.

When we ask for His kingdom to rule, by implication we also pray that the small bit of earth we occupy now will be subject to Him. If we long for the time in the future when Christ's kingdom will be established on earth—enough to pray sincerely for it—then we must be willing for all of the little kingdoms that matter so much to us now to be pulled down. If we want God's rule over all men and women at some future time, it follows that we will want His control in our lives today. Unless we are sufficiently concerned about making our lives His throne and bringing others into glad submission to Him, we cannot pray with integrity for His kingdom to come.

When I was in my twenties, I heard sermons about the second

coming of Jesus Christ in which I was exhorted to desire the coming of Christ. Well, I wanted Him to come, but not immediately. I had some things I wanted to do before He came back. I wanted to get married, to enjoy sex, to have children, and to establish a ministry. After I got all that done, it would be all right for Him to return. As I was thinking about this recently, it occurred to me that I no longer have any plans that the coming of Jesus Christ would interrupt. Nothing now takes precedence over His coming. May earth receive her King!

We are to pray for the person of God, that His name will be hallowed; for the program of God, that His kingdom will come; and for the purpose of God, that His will may be done on earth as it is in heaven.

Praying for His will to be done provides a foundation for our prayers. We are basically asking for God's will to be done in our lives and in the world. We often get it upside down, though, and pray as if we expect God to change the way He is running the universe because we have given Him our petitions. We treat Him like a genie in a lamp. When we rub the lamp and make a wish, we expect to be granted what we want.

We must recognize the importance of conforming our will to His will. We shouldn't pray for something and then at the end say, "if it be Your will," if we don't really mean it. These words aren't something to tack onto the end of a prayer as a loophole, as an out, so that if God doesn't give us what we want, we won't be embarrassed. Prayer is not getting God to do my will. Prayer is asking for God's will to be done in my life, my family, my business, my relationships, and in the world, as it is done in heaven.

When the Bible gives us glimpses of heaven, we see that the angels stand ready to do God's bidding in heaven; all the hosts of glory respond to His will. In the universe, all the galaxies and all their stars and planets move according to His design. It seems that only here on this third-rate planet, this dirty little tennis ball that we call earth, is there a pocket of rebellion.

For us to live according to God's will on earth as it is done in heaven is to do so in enemy territory. To live in a realm that is controlled by Satan is to recognize that this world is no friend of God's. For us to do God's will on earth as it is in heaven, we must go against the current. When we pray "Your will be done on earth as it is in heaven," we are praying for our friends, our families, our society, but above all for ourselves. We willingly abandon our wills to His unconquerable will.

Charles II never completely received the adulation he wanted. His name was associated with too many mistresses and illegitimate children, his kingdom was too frequently divided over various policies, and his will was too often thwarted by a rebellious parliament. He ruled England for over thirty years, but in just three years after his death almost all his achievements were undone.

As Aristotle put it, "They should rule who are able to rule best." That is why we should hallow God's name, long for His coming kingdom, and submit to His will. His rule is best.

SERMON NOTES

Give some examples from New Testament times to today when people have changed their given names and explain why.

How can we "hallow" God's name?

What does "knowing" God's name involve?

If God wants us to be holy, why do you think Jesus gives us a model for prayer that contains no petitions for personal holiness?

How is our perspective about God reflected in our prayers for others?

What is Jesus telling us to pray for when we say, "Your kingdom come"? Does this pertain solely to the future reign of Christ on earth?

Why do you think it might be difficult for us to always—with integrity—pray, "Your kingdom come"? What does that mean in our day-to-day lives?

Are you wholeheartedly able to pray "Your will be done" at this particular point in your life? Why or why not? How do you feel about God's will?

To carry out God's will on earth, we must do so in enemy territory. Can you illustrate this fact by personal examples or examples from current events?

SUNSPACE

■

Antonio Sanchez was only five years old when he was sent to a Mexican prison for juveniles after supposedly murdering his baby brother. Tony's parents, who had beaten him with chains and tortured him with fire, deserted him and disappeared after telling police he was the killer. In prison other inmates taunted him with the word *murderer* and sometimes abused him. He had to fight for food. No one seemed to care what happened to Tony, until Carolyn Koons, an American professor, heard his story. She battled bureaucracy and a corrupt prison warden for almost three years before she secured Tony's release and adoption at age twelve, but her real struggles had only begun. Somehow she had to meet the needs of a boy who still stuffed rolls into his pockets because of past hunger, who lashed out at others because of his emotional scars, and who seemed enticed by every wrong because of his unbridled life. As a single parent, she was unsure whether she could meet his physical, emotional, and spiritual needs. But she did because she had a heavenly Father, unlike Tony's earthly one, who understood her needs.

When Jesus taught us to pray to our heavenly Father, He gave us a model for praying. The first three requests concern God's name and kingdom and will and focus on our Father; then the last three requests about bread, forgiveness, and temptation center on His family.

Helmut Thielicke, a German theologian, pointed out that the whole of life is captured in the rainbow of these requests. "Great things, small things, spiritual things and material things, inward things and outward things—there is nothing that is not included in this prayer."

Adlai Stevenson once remarked, "Understanding human needs is half the job of meeting them." Perhaps the other half is having the will and ability to meet them. God scores on both counts. Because God understands our needs and can truly meet them, Jesus said that we are to talk to the Father about them. After praying about the cosmic and eternal, we can pray about the earthly and temporal.

When Jesus said, "Give us today our daily bread," He was not suggesting a trip to the supermarket for Wonder Bread. He was making the point that it is proper and right to pray for our daily needs. For after all, we cannot really serve His kingdom and do His will unless we have the strength we need for today. So it is proper to ask God for a job to earn money for food. It is appropriate to turn to God for the clothes we need to work on the job to earn money for food. It is also valid to ask for transportation to get us to the job so that we may earn the bread. God knows our needs, and He is concerned about them.

We are often tempted not to bother asking God for food. "Don't pray for groceries," we insist. "Get out and hustle." In fact, some of the church fathers spiritualized the *bread* to refer to the loaf served at communion. They did this, understandably, because after praying for God's glory, it seemed too commonplace to switch to something as mundane as groceries.

Yet, "daily bread" means exactly what it says. The word *bread* refers to the food that sustains our bodies. In the larger sense, of course, bread refers to all that we must have to live. Our Father in heaven concerns himself with the items on a grocery list. Food for our next meal matters to Him.

The focus of the request is for *daily* bread. The word translated *daily* bewildered scholars for centuries. The Lord's Prayer is the only place that word occurred inside or outside the Bible. Then a few years ago an archaeologist dug up a papyrus fragment that contained a housewife's shopping list. Next to several items the woman had scribbled this word for *daily*. It probably meant "enough for the coming day." The phrase should be translated "Give us today bread enough for tomorrow." When prayed in the morning, it is a prayer for the needs in the hours ahead. Prayed in the evening, it is a request for the needs of the coming day. The implication is, of course, that God will supply whatever we need to honor Him and do His will.

In our culture, with its freezers and refrigerators, we seldom purchase food for a single day. We store up food in such abundance that we mutter only thoughtless words of thanks as we eat.

Jesus did not invite us to ask for everything in the Neiman Marcus catalog, or for a Lincoln convertible, or for Gucci shoes. Pray for bread—the necessities of life, not the luxuries. Ask for bread, not cake. Nor are we invited to request supplies for years to come. We are to ask for the essentials to take us through tomorrow.

Notice, too, that when we pray "Give us today our daily bread," we ask for others as well as ourselves. If I pray this prayer in sincerity, it delivers me from selfishness and hoarding. If the Father supplies me with two loaves and my brother or sister with none, I understand that God has indeed answered our prayers. My extra loaf is not for storing, but for sharing.

God wants to free us. We can bring our small requests to God. We can place before Him our need for bread, a coat, a pair of shoes—all those items that matter to us. If we need them, then they matter to our heavenly Father as well.

After we ask the Father for provision, we should ask Him for pardon. Even though we are instructed to pray "Forgive us our debts as we also have forgiven our debtors," we don't seem to worry much about our sins. Walter Horton speaks to our condition in his book *The Challenge of Our Culture*: "Modern man is certainly worried about something—worried nearly to death. And an analysis of his behavior shows him so feverishly trying to avoid looking God in the eye that it must have something to do with the fear of how he must look standing before God in that position." A cartoon in the morning newspaper pictures a psychologist listening to a patient: "Mr. Figby," the psychologist finally says, "I think I can explain your feelings of guilt. You're guilty!"

"Forgive" follows "give," and Jesus linked the two petitions. In that way when we think of our need for food, we will recognize our need for pardon as well. Also, as we confess our guilt, we consider how we have handled our relationships with others.

In Luke 11, the prayer is "to forgive us our sins" (v. 4). The petition in Matthew 6 "to forgive us our debts" (v. 12) recognizes that sin is not only deliberate disobedience but also a debt. It is a debt we owe to God, which Jesus Christ has paid.

Augustine labeled this request for forgiveness "the terrible petition" because if we harbor an unforgiving spirit while we pray to be forgiven in the same way as we forgive others, we are actually asking God not to forgive us.

Think of how the confession of sin works. If I honestly pray for forgiveness, then I revise my estimate of myself downward and I admit my own guilt. If I see the pollution of my own life, then I see the sins of others in a different light. Without that, I can regard myself as so important, so dignified, so honorable that it would be unthinkable to forgive anyone who dared offend someone as righteous as I. That is self-righteousness. To squeeze pardon from a self-righteous prig is harder than squeezing apple juice from a stone slab. It's simply not in such a person to forgive.

If we honestly know God as our Father, then we are part of the forgiven fellowship. Although at times we may find it difficult to forgive someone who has wronged us, we cannot help but see an individual offense as trivial in comparison to our sin against God. When we forgive others, it is evidence that we have entered into God's forgiveness.

Men and women who live in the relief of God's pardon find it easier to forgive those who offend them.

We are never more aware of God's grace than when we admit our sin and cry out for pardon. We are never more like God than when, for Christ's sake, we extend forgiveness fully and freely to those who have sinned against us.

Having prayed to God for provision and pardon, we go on to seek His protection and so we pray, "Lead us not into temptation, but deliver us from the evil one."

A young woman in a shopping mall sported a T-shirt that proclaimed: "Lead me not into temptation—I can find it myself." She wanted people to chuckle as she passed, but her one-liner raised a question. What are we praying for when we ask, "Lead us not into temptation"?

Why should we have to ask God not to lead us into temptation? To ask Him to keep us out of temptation would be more understandable. Professor D. A. Carson suggests that Jesus is using a figure of speech to express something positive by stating the opposite concept. For example, if I say, "This is no small matter," I mean it is a big matter. When we pray, "Lead us not into temptation," we are really praying, "Keep me away from temptation." We are crying out, "Don't let Satan ambush us. Don't let the foe of our souls catch us in his trap." We are recognizing that God has the power to lead us past all the lures to sin that threaten us. Therefore, we ask, "If the opportunity to sin presents itself, grant that I will not have the desire. If the desire springs up within me, grant that I will not have the opportunity."

Let's face it. We seldom want to be delivered from temptation. It promises too much fun. Some wag has said, "Don't resist temptation. It may go away and not come back." Temptation stirs the blood and inflames the imagination. If we were revolted by it, it would not be temptation at all. Usually, though, temptation doesn't seem very bad, so we play with it, flirt with it, and invite it into our lives. When we pray about sins, it's not temptation that bothers us. It's the consequences of our disobedience that we want removed.

In the context of this prayer, however, we are not merely asking God to keep us from being naughty boys and girls. The work of Satan threatens more severe danger than that. We are surrounded by ten thousand seductions to live life apart from God. In our ambitions and in our successes we are tempted to honor our own names, to build our own kingdoms, to take credit for baking our own bread, and to deny our need for forgiving grace. The enemy of our souls wants us to cast away from God. Only God can make us see sin for what it is. If temptation brought chains to bind us, we would resist it on our own. Instead, it brings flowers and perfume and offers life and good cheer, good times and enlargement. It bribes us with wealth and popularity and entices us with promises of prosperity and unbounded freedom. Only God can keep us from its charms.

The Lord's Prayer reminds us to fear the strategies of Satan. Years ago Helmut Thielicke said of postwar-occupied Germany, "There is a dark, mysterious, spellbinding figure at work. Behind the temptation stands the tempter, behind the lie stands the liar, behind all the dead and bloodshed stands the 'murderer from the beginning.' "

When we pray "Deliver us from the evil one," we recognize Satan's power, admit our weakness, and plead for the greater power of God.

When we truly sense His provision, pardon, and protection, we will recognize His preeminence over all. The Lord's Prayer, as we commonly recite it, concludes with a trumpet blast of praise: "For yours is the kingdom and the power and the glory forever, amen." Since those words seem like an appropriate and fitting way for the prayer to end, it is somewhat unsettling to discover that the sentence does not appear in the earliest and best manuscripts of either Matthew or Luke. Evidently the doxology was not part of the prayer as

Jesus originally gave it. In fact, it appeared for the first time in the second or third century.

Yet the prayer demands a conclusion. Otherwise it stops with the threat of temptation and the warning that the Evil One has set his snares for us. When Christians in the young church offered up this prayer to the Father, rather than finish on a cold and frightening note, they added this affirmation of praise.

Although this doxology may not have been given directly by Jesus, it can claim broad biblical support from the words of David (1 Chronicles 29:11) to those of the four living creatures (Revelation 5:13). This paean of praise, however, is not an assumption that we must accept in order to pray, but rather the confidence to which prayer draws us.

Tony Sanchez was not initially drawn to his new mother, Carolyn Koons. In fact, he seemed more drawn to trouble than anything else. He accused her regularly of not loving him and taunted her with "I won't obey you or anyone." Carolyn never stopped barbecuing those juicy hamburgers he craved, never quit hugging him after his acid words, never ceased rescuing him from fights. Carolyn had almost despaired of Tony ever bonding to her; somehow all those daily little things she had done for him seemed to have no impact. But then Carolyn got a big surprise; Tony made an unexpected speech at his junior high graduation. In almost a stutter he said, "I want to thank my mom for adopting me and bringing me to the United States." Then with tears streaming down his face, he yelled, "I love you, Mom. I love you. I love you." All the glory was Carolyn's that day.

When we recognize our Father's daily care for us, experience the depth of His forgiveness, and sense His ever-present shield, we shout, "Yours is the kingdom and the power and the glory and I love you, Father."

SERMON NOTES

In the Lord's Prayer, what do the first three requests deal with? The last three? What do you think is the reason for the order of these requests?

Explain praying for "daily bread." What are we praying for when we pray for "bread"? Does the word *daily* have any significance to us today?

How does praying for "daily bread" include a concern for other people?

Asking for pardon follows asking for provision. Why do you think Jesus linked these two petitions? Why did Augustine call this "the terrible petition"?

How does our confession and plea for forgiveness change our perception of other people's sins against us?

PERMANENT FIXTURES

∎

Jack Perry spent twenty-five years in the U.S. Foreign Service. "We did not enter government service in order to make money primarily," he wrote in *Light from Light*, "but we were usually sad whenever we took stock after another move and found that we were once again in the hole. We never owned the house we lived in because we knew we would be moving again in a short while. After a Foreign Service career, we emerged without riches, but with a strong understanding that physical treasures of this world are not the important things."

In contrast to Jack Perry, the Pharisees were men of wealth and lovers of money (Luke 16:14). They were not religious professionals, such as priests, but they were religious laymen. Although they made their living in the marketplace, they were known for their strict adherence to the laws of their religious tradition. As a result, they were highly respected and often became wealthy and powerful because of their influence over the people.

Like the Pharisaical viewpoint, the Puritan ethic—the understanding that all work is done before God—has been behind the accumulation of wealth by many in America. In the Puritan ethic, if a person plowed a field, he did it as a sacred service to God. If someone molded a sculpture, it was for the eye of God rather than man. People who took their work that seriously, as something they did as service to God, often ended up being very successful. We pursue the Puritan ethic in work today—not to please the Almighty but to get the almighty dollar.

Hard work often pays off, as it did with the Pharisees; but they made a wrong conclusion. They reasoned that their wealth was a reward for their righteousness. In reality, of course, they made a good living because of their good lives, and that is not the same. Early in the Sermon on the Mount, Jesus demonstrated that their righteousness was not true righteousness. It was simply conformity to an outward standard.

So in His sermon Jesus showed them that their riches, which they thought were a reward from God for their piety, were not true riches, and therefore not a true reward. So in many ways the section on storing up treasures connects to the rest of the Sermon on the Mount, but it is primarily an elaboration, or commentary, on the first two verses in the Lord's Prayer. It shows the implications of what it means to pray the first part of this prayer. If we hallow His name and pray for His kingdom to come and His will to be done, that should affect our view of money.

Some devout people have felt that Jesus' warning about not storing up earthly treasures means that we are not to have a bank account or own property. But that is not the witness of the Scriptures. Paul endorses the principle that parents save for their children (2 Corinthians 12:14), and Proverbs lauds the lesson of the ant who stores for the future (Proverbs 6:6). The Bible has a good word for saving.

The Bible also acknowledges the right to own private property. The eighth commandment about not stealing has no meaning unless someone owns something to steal. Peter rebuked Ananias and Sapphira for lying, not for possessing property. He said that their land and the money they received from selling it were always at their disposal (Acts 5:4).

Jesus neither condemned saving nor asked everyone He met to give everything away. He warned about storing up our goods when our motive was to find our security in our possessions. He abhorred the miserly spirit that desired money and stashed it away, forgetting that money is a trust from God. Money is not for keeping score in the game of life. It is to be used to meet needs.

The rich fool of Luke 12 filled his barns with grain, but God judged him for his greed (v. 20). The rich man of Luke 16 could have helped the beggar Lazarus, but he didn't (vv. 19–20). The picture of this same rich man in torment distinctly portrays the foolishness of shortsightedness— investing in ourselves rather than others. Moths, rust, and thieves will destroy our precious possessions anyway.

In the first century banks did not exist, so people saved their wealth in three ways. One was by hoarding garments. A cache of fine garments was as good as money in the bank. They could be sold in the future. Achan stole a Babylonian robe, and God condemned him for it (Joshua 7:20–21). He didn't take an old suit to wear; his apparel snatch was an investment in the future.

A second way of accumulating wealth was to store grain in barns. Famine was an ever-present reality in the ancient world of the Near East because of the undependable rains. If a man could store his grain until a famine came and prices soared, he could become fabulously wealthy.

The third method of saving lay in exchanging their assets for gold. Instead of locking it in a bank vault, however, they hid it in a pot or buried it in a field.

Jesus pointed to the ways rich people held their possessions and warned that there were no safe investments. For a gourmet moth beautiful garments make a splendid menu, and garments with holes become a lost investment. Grain could be eaten. The word *rust* is just the word *eating*. It is sometimes used for rust because rust eats away at metal, but in this passage it might more naturally refer to the eating done by such rodents as rats and mice. Thieves can steal gold by breaking in, or more literally "digging in." In fact, the thieves in the first century were called diggers. The Palestinian houses were made of baked clay, so a burglar broke in by digging a hole in a wall. People may think their garments, grain, and gold appear secure, but moths, mice, and marauders can demonstrate that earth has no secure investments.

Two thousand years have passed. The situation may have changed but the reality hasn't. Stocks and bonds are at the mercy of a changing market. Inflation, like a rat, can nibble away at a bank account. Currency can be devalued. Houses, boats, and cars are subject to fire, tornadoes, and rust. Even land can lose its value with just one chemical spill. Wherever we put our wealth, there are no guarantees. Only shortsighted investors build up portfolios on this earth. Jesus gave better advice on investments. Equities built up in heaven are more secure and bring better dividends. In the context of the Sermon on the Mount, those who give to the needy are supporting God's work in the world. What we invest in people remains because people are eternal.

Origen, the church father, described Christians as money changers, taking the capital of earth and changing it for the currency of heaven. In other words, we need to invest our wealth in that which will outlast us. The Koran puts it another way: "When a man dies, people on earth ask what did he leave? The angels in heaven ask, what did he send ahead?"

We are to put our treasure in heaven not only because that which is eternal will last and that which is temporal will fade, but also because it will give us the right focus. Notice Jesus is not saying that our treasures follow our hearts. It's the other way around. Where we put our treasures our hearts will be. How can we cultivate a heart for God? By putting our investments in the right place. It's a fact of life that our interests follow our investments.

Investors who play the stock market check the quotes daily to see how their stocks are doing. Although they seldom analyze every stock on the exchange, they rarely miss their own. That is where their concern lies. It goes without saying that with every investment there is a corresponding interest.

If we want a zeal for His eternal kingdom, we must put our treasures there. If our lives are consumed with building a business, buying a nicer home, or trading for a new car every year, God and His kingdom get little more than a tip of the hat or tip money. What is more, if we center our lives on the junkbonds of earth, we find dying difficult.

Samuel Johnson, the eighteenth-century English lexicographer, was once invited to tour a mansion, a place of magnificent beauty surrounded by manicured lawns. As Johnson was leaving he remarked to a friend, "A place like this makes it difficult for a man to die." The more we store up here, the more calamitous death appears, because we leave behind what we have valued most highly. Put it down as a principle of life—wherever you have your treasure you will have your heart.

People who live for the here and now, who can total up their treasures by their bank statements or their real estate investments, live for this age because it is the only age they know. This is all there is. But those who know the reality of God's kingdom understand that Jesus was not making a fund appeal or cozying up to a big giver; He was talking sense.

When we gain an eternal viewpoint, our earthly perspective is never the same. After all, our viewpoint is all important.

A man in New York City had a wife who had a cat. Actually, the cat had her. She loved the cat. She stroked it, combed its fur, fed it, and pampered it. The man detested the cat. He was allergic to cat hair; he hated the smell of the litter box; he couldn't stand the scratching on the furniture; and he couldn't get a good night's sleep because the cat kept jumping on the bed. When his wife was out of town for the weekend, he put the cat in a bag with some rocks, dumped it in the

Hudson river, and uttered a joyful good-bye to the cat. When his wife returned and could not find her cat, she was overwhelmed with grief.

Her husband said, "Look, honey, I know how much that cat meant to you. I'm going to put an ad in the paper and give a reward of five hundred dollars to anyone who finds the cat."

No cat showed up, so a few days later he said, "Honey, you mean more to me than anything on earth. If that cat is precious to you, it is precious to me. I'll tell you what I'll do. I'll buy another ad and raise the ante. We'll increase the reward to one thousand dollars."

A friend saw the ad and exclaimed, "You must be nuts; there isn't a cat on earth that is worth a thousand dollars."

The man replied, "Well, when you know what I know, you can afford to be generous."

If we have any inkling of what it means to be part of God's kingdom, we can afford to be generous. We can establish priorities by the way we give and live.

The importance of having an eternal perspective is what Jesus illustrated with his eye examination. "The eye," He said, "is the lamp of the body. If your eyes are good, your whole body will be full of light. But if your eyes are bad, your whole body will be full of darkness. If then the light within you is darkness, how great is that darkness!"

At first glance that illustration can confuse us. Behind it stands a kind of childlike simplicity. Our eyes resemble lamps that illuminate the inside of us. When we close our eyes, everything inside goes dark. When we open our eyes, light floods in and everything inside seems lighted. If we have good eyesight, the light shines in and it is bright inside of us. But if we have bad eyes, it is as though everything inside us becomes gray and dim. And if we lose our sight, everything inside us is midnight.

Jesus used the eye to symbolize our perspective on life. Putting it another way, if our perspective is eternal, we walk in light. We are not likely to stumble because we see things as they really are. We recognize the difference between the eternal and the temporal. But if we don't see well, if our perspective is temporal, we're likely to trip over every little obstacle, every minor temptation.

Jesus concluded that people whose minds are fastened on the temporal usually think they are in the light. And that, He said, is tragic.

In a sense, they are like people who have been blind from birth. They learn to get around and to "see" in their own way. They become independent and sometimes resent sighted people who tell them which way to go, try to help them, or warn them about obstacles. They have their own reality, their own way of perceiving the world.

We live in a world where people not only spend their lives on what is temporal and give themselves to that which does not last, but they defend it as reality, as light. Men and women believe that this life is all there is and promote their philosophy. Jesus lamented that if we confuse darkness with light, our darkness is very deep.

Our perspective is either one of light or of darkness. And if we can't tell the difference, it's disastrous.

Our perspective, either light or darkness, determines our priorities, which in turn motivate our service and our giving. Jesus warned that we cannot serve two masters, both light and darkness, God and money.

Some people, when they hear this, think Jesus was warning us about moonlighting. Since thousands of people work two jobs, one during the day and another in the evening, they conclude that Jesus was exaggerating when He said it is impossible to serve two masters. It may be difficult, but certainly not impossible.

But Jesus wasn't commenting on working for two employers. He was describing the problem of being a full-time chattel slave to two masters. A first-century slave was the property of the master. He belonged to the master all day and every day. He didn't work for eight hours and have the rest of his time to himself. He did whatever his master wanted him to do, whenever he wanted it done.

If a man got into the impossible situation of becoming a slave to two masters, he would soon learn that he cannot respond to both of their demands. Either he will hate the one and love the other, or he will be devoted to one and despise the other. In Near Eastern thought the concepts of hate and love have little to do with emotions and feelings. They focus on devotion and priorities. In other words, if a man ends up being a full-time slave to two masters, he will have to turn his back on one of them. The demands of the job make it impossible for him to honor both.

The slave must decide which master he will serve. That choice resembles marriage in the sense that when we love one person, we say no to all others. When a man marries a wife, it doesn't necessarily mean that he harbors emotional animosity toward the girls he didn't marry. It's just that the job of marriage requires a twenty-four hour a day commitment.

You can't dance to the music of two orchestras at the same time. You can't be married to two people simultaneously. You can't worship in the temple of two separate gods. And you cannot serve God and money.

In many translations the word *money* is *mammon*. The NIV uses "money" because nobody knows what "mammon" was. It is an Aramaic word that had to do with possessions, with property. It is not necessarily a negative word. Money becomes negative when it gets out of place, when we end up serving it instead of using it.

We all serve something. Something governs our lives, determines our priorities, dictates how we spend our time, affects our daydreams, writes our definition of success. The only question is, What will you serve?

You can serve money in reality and God in pretense. You can serve

God and use money, but you can't serve them both. That's a statement of fact. So the question is, Do you serve God and use money, or do you serve money and use God?

If we pray, "Our Father in heaven, hallowed be your name, your kingdom come, your will be done on earth as it is in heaven," a major application of that prayer has to do with our pocketbooks. When we invest our money in what is eternal, that has a way of affecting our hearts. If we work and walk in the light we see things for what they really are and we realize that the things that are seen are temporal and the things that are not seen are eternal. And when we hold that priority, we will serve God.

How can we know if we are mastered by our money? A couple of questions come to my mind. First, how did we get the money? Did we sacrifice something eternal to get it? If so, we have become slaves to money. Would we put competitors down and destroy them to be sure we got what was due us? If so, money is determining our priorities. Second, what do we do with our money? Let's put it bluntly. Is the cause of God in the world better off because we have been entrusted with money? Or does God only get our spare change?

A boy on his way to church had two quarters—one for the offering and the other for a candy bar. While crossing the street he tripped and fell, and one of his quarters went rolling out of his hand and into the sewer, ker-plunk. Later he told his father what had happened. "Did you put the other quarter in the offering?" his father asked. "No," the boy said, "God's quarter went down the sewer."

If we suffer financial reversals and we change our budgets accordingly, does God and God's work get eliminated? What stands at the top of the budget? Where does God fit in our priorities?

This passage about treasures, eyes, and masters was Christ's commentary on the first three petitions of the Lord's Prayer. When we pray, "Hallowed be Your name," we are saying, "Let God be God to me," and we promise to invest everything we possibly can to see "His kingdom come, His will be done on earth as it is in heaven."

Praying the Lord's Prayer has implications that go deeper than mere words; they reach right into our pocketbooks.

In the game of Monopoly, players buy land and collect money. When one player has enough money and at least one monopoly of properties, he or she can buy houses and hotels and collect rent on them. Eventually one player receives enough rental money through land and building holdings to bankrupt the other players, thus ending the game. Parker Brothers, the makers of Monopoly, take for granted one final instruction—when the game is over, put all the pieces back in the box. People who live for the present, who spend their strength on what cannot last, are like children who play Monopoly as though it were reality. In the end, we all get put in the box and we are gone. What matters is what remains when the game on earth is over.

SERMON NOTES

Describe the work ethic you learned as a youngster. Has it changed as you have grown older?

How has the Puritan work ethic in Western society changed over the years? How does this compare with the way Pharisees regarded their wealth?

Explain the warnings about "treasures," "eyes," and "masters" in light of the first three petitions of the Lord's Prayer.

Do you think the Bible commands us to work hard to earn and save money? How does the use of money reflect our trust in God?

In the first century, people saved garments, grains, and gold. What are some ways we save for the future today? Is our wealth more secure today?

Is there any difference between hoarding wealth and accumulating wealth? Can a Christian be wealthy and still honor God?

Jesus warned that there are no safe investments on earth—the only secure equities are in heaven. How do we go about making these kind of investments?

Do you believe that where your treasure is, there your heart is? Why or why not?

What percent of your time is spent earning and managing your money? Can you give too much time to earning a living?

How does having an eternal perspective affect the way we live? What part does our "eyesight" play in an eternal perspective?

Explain the Near Eastern concepts of "hate" and love." What does Jesus mean when He says we cannot serve two masters—God and money?

How can you determine if you are mastered by your money? Are you?

PRESSURE TREATED

■

Death was walking into a city one morning when a man stopped him and asked what he was doing. "I'm going into the city to claim ten thousand people," Death answered.

"That's horrible," said the man. "It's terrible that you would take ten thousand people."

"Look," Death said, "get off my back. Taking people when their time has come is my job. Today I have to get my ten thousand." Later, as Death was coming out of the city, the man met him. Again he was furious.

"You told me this morning that you were going to take ten thousand people, but seventy thousand died today."

"Don't get on my case," Death said. "I only took ten thousand. Worry and anxiety killed all the rest."

It's true that worry can make us sick. It may even be possible to worry ourselves to death. When we worry, we don't worry with our minds, we worry with our organs. And if we worry long enough and hard enough, we will get ulcers and make ourselves vulnerable to all kinds of other sicknesses. Worry can sometimes even cause people to commit suicide. Gallup ran an interesting study a couple of years ago with young people in the United States. When teens were asked what their major feeling about life is, sixty percent replied, "Fear." That may explain why suicide among teenagers has become a national epidemic. In the last decade, suicide among teenagers has gone up almost four hundred percent. People worry about AIDS; we ought to worry about suicide. It ranks as the second leading cause of death, after accidents, for young people under twenty.

People do all kinds of things to handle their worries. *Time* magazine a couple of years ago said that Americans gulp down seven tons of sleeping pills every day. We gulp down sedatives and tranquilizers until the drugs turn us into addicts.

Other people turn to alcohol. A good stiff drink or a couple of cocktails make their worries seem smaller and make them feel bigger. Edward FitzGerald, in *Rubáiyát of Omar Khayyám*, described that prescription for worry when he wrote, "Ah, my Beloved, fill the Cup that clears Today of past Regrets and future Fears." But when I see the commercials for alcohol rehabilitation centers, it becomes clear that taking a good stiff drink to handle our worries may really give us something to worry about.

People in Jesus' day had just as much anxiety as we do. Some may think life was easier in the first century because the times were simpler and people didn't have as much to worry about. But anyone who thinks that doesn't understand conditions in the first century. Most of the people in the ancient world lived like members of the third world today. Laborers were paid every day because they needed the money to live the next day. The government gave them no security. They had no safety net. Some estimate that the average citizen in Palestine paid at least forty percent of his wages in taxes. Times may be hard today, but they were concrete tough then. Yet to people then and now, Jesus said, "Don't worry."

Jesus began His discussion of worry with the word *therefore*, so we know it is related to what Jesus spoke about previously. If we take seriously the Lord's Prayer, He said we will be concerned about where we put our treasures. If we are concerned about God's kingdom and that which is eternal, we will not be had by what we have.

What we value determines how we live. If we have double vision— if we look intently on earth and try also to look at heaven—we will stumble and fall flat on our faces. We have to choose. If we value that which is eternal, we will choose to serve God. If we value that which is temporal, we will serve money. The fact that we will serve something is taken for granted; we give our lives to something. What that will be is up to us.

If we commit ourselves to Him, He commits himself to us. If we become a slave to God, He will free us from anxiety and worry. This also ties into the fourth petition of the Lord's Prayer. Having prayed that God's will and His kingdom will be first in our lives, we can then pray, "Give us today our daily bread." That privilege alone should remove worry from our lives.

God committed Himself to two things. He committed himself to what goes into our bodies: food and drink. And He committed himself to what goes onto our bodies: clothes.

When Jesus declared "Don't worry," He didn't mean we shouldn't think about tomorrow. The King James Version translates this as "give no thought for tomorrow." The verb really means "don't give anxious thought." That is, don't worry about it. Jesus was not against thinking about tomorrow. That is part of being human. We are not warned against forethought but against foreboding.

"Don't worry" doesn't mean "Don't work." Jesus used birds as an example. Every self-respecting bird works hard for food and shelter. But it doesn't worry. In fact, when Paul wrote his second letter to the Thessalonians, he said, "If a man will not work, he shall not eat" (3:10). God is not against working; He is against worrying. He was saying to His disciples, "Don't worry about the necessities of life." If we commit ourselves to Him, He commits himself to us.

That sounds good on paper, but Jesus' words may give us the uneasy feeling of someone patting us on the back and saying "Don't worry" just after we have totaled our only car. Words by themselves don't calm anxiety. But Jesus didn't stop with the command. He followed it with seven reasons in support of a worry-free life.

Jesus took His first reason for not worrying from the logic of Creation. Life is more important than food and clothing. If God did the greater thing—gave us life and created our bodies—surely He will do the lesser thing—give us food to sustain us and clothes to keep us warm. If God has done the big thing, we can expect Him to do the little thing. For instance, if a jeweler gave you an expensive diamond ring as a gift, would you not expect him to give you a box to put it in?

"Is not life more important than food, and the body more important than clothes?" Jesus asked. We may not appreciate the full force of this argument because we are not sure it is true. We tend to get our self-identity from what we eat and what we wear. Advertisers reinforce this belief. The underlying message in many advertisements is that we are what we wear or eat.

But Jesus said we are more than that. God gave us life, and He will surely give us what we need to stay alive.

Worrying about the basic necessities of life is not only needless, Jesus concluded, but secondly it is also senseless. At our house we have a bird feeder. Sometimes I watch the birds while I eat my breakfast. Few people work harder than birds. I never see robins sitting on a branch hoping that heaven will drop a worm into their mouths. I see them scratching and pecking to find their meals. But they don't worry. They sing. Jesus wasn't suggesting that we not work. He was saying, "Be like the birds who don't worry." Their Creator takes care of them and your heavenly Father will take care of you.

Nor was He proposing that we stop sowing, reaping, and storing away in barns. God is not against farmers or farming. He was simply reminding us how much better off we are than the birds. They can't sow, reap, or store, yet they don't worry. Why then, He asked rhetorically, should we who have these abilities spoil our lives with worry?

Behind this argument about God's provision for the birds stands the Bible's model of the universe. In this model God stands outside the universe and also within the universe. This view says that God created all things and sustains all things. He designed the universe to act according to certain laws of nature. We who are in this universe can observe what is happening and learn those laws. In fact, that is our commission. We are the keepers of the universe. We are the ones to whom God has given the mission of guarding what He has made.

This view is not mechanistic—it is not tied strictly to scientific laws or cause and effect relationships—for God, if He chooses to do so, can break into that universe and set aside the natural laws. He did so when He raised Jesus from the dead. God created the universe, sustains it, and can overrule it when necessary. It is held together by His sovereignty, by His power.

There are two distortions of the biblical model of the universe. One is deism, which views God as the creator of the world but not necessarily as the sustainer. Deists believe that God made the universe in the same sense that a watchmaker makes a watch. When He finished, He went off to make other watches and left the universe to tick away on its own. When we discover the laws that keep the watch ticking, we learn about an infinite God; but this view leaves no room for a personal God.

The second distortion is seeing God as sustainer of the universe but not recognizing Him as creator. These people are much like the pagan animists, the people who believe that what they do affects the gods or spirits and that the gods or spirits in turn affect the people's lives. Animists believe the gods are capricious; they can be happy one day and sad the next. But by pacifying the gods, they can get the gods to bless them.

Like these animists, many well-meaning Christians believe God's work in their lives is always immediate. For them, everything is a miracle, even finding a parking place on a crowded city street. They have three miracles before breakfast, five before lunch, and another six in the afternoon.

Instead of having spirits to placate, these Christians placate God. The laws of nature do not mean a great deal to them. They see God as sustainer, but they don't acknowledge His work as creator because they don't recognize that God works according to the laws of nature He established at creation.

The implications of a proper view of the universe are amazing, almost overwhelming. In the biblical view God is infinite—He is above His creation—but He is also personal—He is involved in His creation. This understanding of the universe recognizes science as well as miracle. It says that the universe runs according to laws. In addition to the natural laws that govern the universe, there are moral laws that govern human behavior. In a moral universe we can discover things about the way people live and the results of their behavior. When we acknowledge that behind the universe stands a righteous God who has set His physical and moral laws in motion, we acknowledge that we don't break God's laws. We simply break ourselves on His law.

When Christians look at nature, they see evidences of God's providence and design. In this example Jesus implied that God provides for the birds of the air as part of His process of Creation. That is His way of sustaining birds, and He sustains us in much the same way. He gives us the brains, the bodies, and the forces of nature necessary to provide for ourselves. That is why we thank Him for our food. When pagans hear us thank God for our meals, they may think we believe that He brings food directly to our tables. But when we thank God for food, we do not thank mother nature but our heavenly Father who provides for us through the processes set in motion at Creation.

If God as Creator and Sustainer has set in order the process to feed the birds, surely He has made provision to feed us as well.

The third reason Jesus gave for not worrying is that it is useless. Worrying won't add a moment to our lives nor an inch to our height.

In other words, it doesn't change anything. Worry does nothing to meet our basic needs. And since it is useless, we ought not worry.

People who have read *MAD* magazine recognize Alfred E. Newman as the fellow with the good-natured smile whose motto is "What, me worry?" He is not so confident or secure that he has no reason to worry; he is simply a dolt who does not have enough sense to worry.

A friend of mine has a plaque in his office that says, "If you can keep your head when all around are losing theirs, it is obvious that you don't understand the situation."

It is true that some people don't worry simply because they are mindless. Certainly Jesus was not commending people who are thoughtless, reckless, shiftless, and who neither work nor think. Too much of the Sermon on the Mount applauds people who take life seriously.

But some folks take life far too seriously. In fact, they are so careful about life that they let it fill them with care and anxiety. These folks can blow a small incident into major proportions. They turn worry into a life-style.

People like that sometimes come to me for counsel. If I show them how to solve a problem they argue with me. "Yes, but . . ." they say, and then they bring up something else. I get the unsettling feeling that they don't want to stop worrying. These folks always live with worse-case scenarios. If they read about a problem with Social Security, they are certain they will not only lose their benefits but will have to pay additional taxes as well. They worry about the bank failing, and if it doesn't fail they worry whether or not they have enough money in it. They worry about their investments, their family, their friends, and the nation's summit conferences.

The way we look at life, Jesus said, has a lot to do with how much we worry. If we focus our attention on temporal things, such as bank accounts, careers, and physical appearance, we have reasons to worry.

For example, if we build an extensive wardrobe we'd better worry about moths. They can make a great dinner out of woolen suits. If we have a big bank account, we'd better worry. The bank could fail tomorrow. If we find security in our house, we'd better worry. The house might catch on fire. If we stockpile treasures to put inside our houses, we'd better worry. Professional thieves can break into any house. Everyone who focuses on earthly things has reason to worry.

On the other hand, if we focus on that which is eternal—God's kingdom and His work in the world—our hearts will be at ease. As we commit ourselves to God, He commits himself to us. And He promises that if our hearts are where His heart is, He will take care of our needs.

The fourth reason we should not worry is because it is faithless. "Why do you worry about clothes? See how the lilies of the field grow. They do not labor or spin. Yet I tell you that not even Solomon in all His splendor was dressed like one of these. If that is how God clothes the grass of the field, which is here today and tomorrow is thrown into the fire, will he not much more clothe you, O you of little faith?" (Matthew 6:28-30).

The flowers Jesus spoke about were ordinary field flowers, red poppies or anemones that still grow in Palestine. They are like wild grass. As a fuel for baking bread a housewife would gather this grass, cut it, let it dry, put it in the oven, and then light it. It would make a hot fire for an instant or two, just long enough to heat the oven. She would then remove the burned grass and put her loaves into the heated oven until they were baked. Although the grass was good for nothing but making a fire, God dressed it in great beauty—more splendid than one of Solomon's robes. Solomon dressed himself, but God dressed the flowers.

Jesus not only compared grass to Solomon's finest attire but also to people. Grass is passing, but people are permanent. We will live some place forever. And if we belong to God, we are not only permanent, we are of special value to Him. So the contrast is great. If God clothes the passing flowers in great glory, surely He will give us who are permanent an ordinary wardrobe.

When Jesus said we have little faith, I think He meant that worry shows our faith to be insufficient and thoughtless. Some people have sufficient faith to believe God will get them to heaven but not enough to believe He will get them through the next twenty-four hours. They are absolutely confident of the sweet by-and-by but are terrified by the nasty now-and-now. Others thoughtlessly focus on everyday events but forget the ultimate issues of life.

The fifth reason we should not worry is because it is godless. Worry shows that we are little more than pagans. The Jews considered the Gentiles pagans because they believed in lesser gods or in no god at all. The mythical gods of the Greeks and Romans were insufficient gods that lied, cheated, got angry, murdered, and were actually less than human. To the Jews, those gods were the opposite of the God of righteousness.

Worrying was natural for the Gentiles because they couldn't trust their gods. Our worry testifies that God cannot be trusted, that the God we worship is no different from the gods of pagans. This is a form of atheism and an affront to God.

The absence of worry ought to distinguish people who live for what is eternal. We are people who trust in God, and that should make a difference in the way we handle life.

The sixth reason we should not worry is because worrying denies family ties. Jesus made plain that our heavenly Father knows our needs. The emphasis throughout the Sermon on the Mount is that the God we trust relates to us as our heavenly Father. We belong to God and to His family. Therefore we ought not worry because God will do no less for us than a good earthly father would do for his children.

The Jews of the Old Testament did not think about God this way. No one in the Old Testament called God *Father*. They did not pray to Him as a heavenly Father. But again and again Jesus told us that our Father is God, that God is our Father. When He introduced the Lord's Prayer in Matthew 6:8, He said, "your *Father* knows what you need before you ask him." He followed that by saying we are to pray to our *Father* in heaven. When He spoke about the way we should give, pray, and fast, He said that our *Father* who sees in secret will reward us openly. Then He told us that our heavenly *Father* feeds even the birds of the air.

The fatherhood of God is a constant emphasis in the Sermon on the Mount. This is incredibly significant. It means that at the heart of the universe is not only ultimate power but also ultimate love. We are part of God's family. We bear the family name. And God has committed himself to us as a father commits himself to his children. As children we don't always know what we need. Sometimes we confuse necessities and luxuries, but God gives us what we need. Sometimes we ask for things that could destroy us, but our Father doesn't give us those. God does for us what a good earthly father does for his children. If we believe this is true, we have no reason to worry.

Because we are our Father's children, if we worry about anything it should be about His kingdom. Jesus pointed this out with a touch of humor when He said, "Do not worry about tomorrow, for tomorrow will worry about itself" (Matthew 6:34). He had been talking about misdirected concerns that grow into worry. In this statement He took a slightly different approach. He acknowledged the human propensity to worry and said we should at least worry about something important. If we're going to have concern, we should have it about big things, about things that concern God, like God's kingdom.

Again, this ties in to the Lord's Prayer. The first section of the Lord's Prayer deals with praying to the Father about the Father—that

His name will be hallowed, that His kingdom will come, and that His will will be done. Then we can ask for daily bread. In other words, we are to seek His kingdom first, to make that the aim of our lives, and then these things will be given to us, leaving us no reason to worry.

The word *seek* was used to describe the activity of a hunter who hides in a blind to hunt birds. He is hunting for food, not just for sport. He focuses his mind on those birds. His eye always looks for them. He keeps his bow and arrows ready. The birds will be within shooting range for only a moment, so he is constantly alert.

Just as a bird hunter makes birds the center of his attention, we are to make God's kingdom the center of ours. Then all we need, in addition to His kingdom and His righteousness, will be given to us. And that too takes us back to the context.

Righteousness is what Jesus has been talking about. He said, "Unless your righteousness surpasses that of the Pharisees and the teachers of the law, you will certainly not enter the kingdom of heaven" (5:20). Then He explained that the righteousness we are to seek has nothing to do with keeping rules and rituals; it has to do with relationships. It has to do with our relationship to God, which is kept intact with pure motives, not outward motions, and with right attitudes, not religious acts. This righteousness is shown in the way we perform religious deeds—giving, praying, and fasting. We don't do them for applause; we do them for God and for His kingdom. To seek His kingdom is to seek His work in the world. To seek His righteousness is to live the kind of life that pleases Him, which leads to another truth about righteousness. It has to do with our relationship to others. A righteous life seeks the highest good for others. Whether we deal with foes or friends, we seek their highest good because that is what God does. In business affairs or family affairs we are to seek the best for others. As we seek what is best for others, God gives us what is best for ourselves.

And so we must choose. Will we continue to worry about our own needs or will we decide instead to fasten on God and His kingdom and trust Him to give us what we need? To choose earth is to lose everything; to choose heaven is to gain everything. If we live only for earthly things, we lose heavenly things; if we live for heavenly things, we get earth thrown in.

Worry is needless, senseless, useless, faithless, godless, pointless, and last, it is impractical. "Each day has enough trouble of its own" (v. 34). One of the most difficult things to do is to live one day at a time. People keep ruining all their todays by mixing spoiled yesterdays or unripe tomorrows into their stew. Some people live with yesterday's slights, grudges, and guilt. Something bad happened to them, and they can't forget it. Other people live with tomorrow's threats, evil, and sorrow. Something fearful might happen to them, and they can't ignore it. Helmut Thielicke called this "wandering in times not our own."

If we don't live a day at a time, Jesus argued, we spoil all of life. God divided life into bite-size chunks called days, and trying to chew more than one at a time can choke us.

People seldom, if ever, are destroyed by what happens on one particular day. What really does us in is our worry about what might happen tomorrow.

A farmer drawing water from his well started to wonder what might happen if his well went dry. Before long his wondering turned to worrying. Soon he couldn't enjoy the water he had because of his concern that he might not have any the next day.

God can't control that kind of worry; He can't help us with the future until we get there. And when we get there it is no longer tomorrow; it is today. And God has promised to take care of our todays. He told us to pray for bread daily, not weekly or monthly. If He can supply our needs for one day, He can do it for every day and every week.

And the reality is, most of the crises we anticipate never happen at all.

Wally Morgan, a friend of mine in Dallas, is fond of repeating, "Don't tell me worry doesn't do any good. When I really worry about something it doesn't happen! "

Ian McLaren asked, "What does your anxiety do? It doesn't empty tomorrow of its sorrows, but it empties today of its strength. It does not allow you to escape the evil, but it renders you unfit to cope with it when it comes."

Jesus was telling us not to let tomorrow's worry affect today. Doing so only robs power from today. Can we trust God to supply our needs for the next twelve hours? The next twenty-four hours? That is all He has committed himself to. Every time we bite off a hunk of today, God commits himself to meet our needs. And when we think of it, that is all we need; no crisis has ever happened in the future.

On the way to his inauguration, Abraham Lincoln stopped in New York City, where he spoke with Horace Greeley. Greeley asked Lincoln the question that was on everyone's mind. "Will the nation be plunged into a civil war?" Lincoln responded to Greeley's question with an anecdote about some lawyers from Illinois. They followed the judge from town to town to argue cases. As they traveled they had to cross a number of rivers, including many that were swollen. They were particularly worried about the Fox River. In a small town where they had stopped for the night, they met a circuit riding preacher. He had crossed the Fox River many times, so they asked him about it. "I have one rule that helps me cross the Fox River," he said. "I don't cross the Fox River until I get there."

SERMON NOTES

What do you worry about most? Why?

List the seven reasons Jesus gives for not worrying. Do some of these reasons seem more significant for your life than others?

What does constant worry reveal about our faith? How do our values determine how we handle life?

Explain how worry can be a form of atheism.

What *should* Christians be concerned about?

How can the pursuit of a righteous life free one from worry?

What could you do to keep from worrying about tomorrow? Will you do it?

TOLERANCE

∎

"You can't be a Christian," the female caller said to Dr. Gordon Lewis, a professor at Denver Seminary. "Jesus said, 'Judge not that ye be not judged,' " she continued. "And here you are judging whether or not a cult or some individuals are really Christians." Dr. Lewis, who specializes in the study of cults, was on a Denver talk show to discuss the New Age movement. During the program listeners were invited to call and ask questions. Many of the callers asked about particular cults and wanted to know whether or not they were Christian. In a warm and gracious way, Dr. Lewis had been answering their questions.

The woman's accusation put Dr. Lewis in a difficult situation. He could not defend himself without getting into a lengthy discussion of Matthew 7, and a talk show wasn't the place to do it. Apparently the woman was unaware that later in Matthew 7, Jesus warned His listeners to beware of false prophets. "Watch out for false prophets," He said. "They come to you in sheep's clothing, but inwardly they are ferocious wolves" (v. 15). I don't know any way to beware of false prophets without making some judgment about prophets and their messages.

A few years ago, a friend who is a pastor in Southern California heard that a treasurer in his congregation was having an affair. He asked the man if it were true. The man admitted it and added that he felt it was a very positive addition to his life and he had no intention of repenting. Later the pastor and an elder of the church, a respected and godly man, confronted the treasurer again. They pointed out his sin and the damage it was doing. The man still refused to change his ways. They took the matter to the leadership of the congregation, and they asked the man to appear before them, which he did. But in an arrogant and defiant way, he said that for the first time in his life he had found out what true love was and he was not about to give it up. And so, reluctantly, the church excommunicated him. The man did not take it easily. He went through the community saying that the pastor and congregation were unchristian because they were judging him. They had no right to do it, he claimed, because Jesus himself said, "Judge not that ye be not judged."

I suppose no sentence in the Bible is more familiar, more misunderstood, and more misapplied than "Judge not that ye be not judged."

Leo Tolstoy, who was intent on applying the Sermon on the Mount to society, decided that Matthew 7:1 was a basis for getting rid of law courts. According to his interpretation, judges and juries act in direct disobedience to Jesus when they judge who is wrong in a legal matter.

Part of the problem here is deciding what we mean by judging. In both Greek and English the word has a multitude of meanings. Sometimes it means a simple evaluation. And sometimes it means censorship and condemnation.

Is Jesus saying it's wrong to judge a cake-baking contest? A talent competition? Is it unchristian to give a recommendation for a student who wants to go to college? Is it sinful to evaluate someone who applies for a job? Are employers wrong to give their employees job reviews?

The only way to answer these questions is to determine what Jesus means by *judge*. And the only place to find His meaning lies in the context of what He said. To understand the context we need to review what Jesus has been preaching in His mountainside sermon.

It begins in Matthew 5 with the Beatitudes—the attitudes that ought to characterize men and women who are part of Christ's

kingdom. Jesus says that Beatitude people, in contrast to the Pharisees, who were very good at keeping rules and regulations, are concerned about inner righteousness.

The righteousness that characterizes people who belong to Jesus
has nothing to do with externals; it is an inner relationship with God
that shows up in relationships with people. It changes the heart first,
not behavior.

For example, in 5:21 Jesus said that if we are really concerned about
being righteous we don't draw the line at murder, we draw it at anger.
We recognize anger as the internal counterpart to murder, and as followers of Christ we deal with it.

The same is true of adultery. In verse 27, He said we should not be
content simply because we have never committed the act of adultery.
Lust is the internal counterpart to adultery. If we take Jesus seriously,
we will be as concerned about lust as we are about adultery.

Oaths were another example of the conflict between motives and
actions. People in the first century had oaths that mattered and oaths
that didn't matter. They were like children who promise something
and then say it doesn't count because they had their fingers crossed.
Jesus said we're not to do anything like that. When we write contracts
we're not to focus on every word and punctuation mark to allow ourselves loopholes to get out of keeping our word either in letter or in
spirit. Our biggest concern should be honesty and integrity. When we
say yes, we mean yes. When we say no, we mean no.

In Matthew 5:38, Jesus talked about revenge. We are not to try to
get back at people. We're to deal in generosity. We don't say, "We invited them over last time. It's their turn to invite us." Or, "I picked up
the check last time. This time it's her turn." Instead we are generous.
If someone asks a favor, we do more than she asks.

Finally Jesus said we are to be people of love. No matter with whom
we deal, we are to seek their highest good. We love other people.

The point of all this is that we are to have inner righteousness. Christ has called us to a righteousness of motive, not a righteousness of rules and regulations.

In chapter 6 Jesus turned His attention from principles of righteousness in relationship to the Law, to deal with the practice of righteousness in relationship to religion. He singled out three acts of religious people. They give, they pray, and they fast.

We're not to do these so that others will notice and think well of us. If we do, that's all the reward we will get. If we want a reward from God, we will do these things in quietness so that only He will know.

Beginning in 6:19, Jesus elaborated on the Lord's Prayer. He began a series of negatives: "Do not store up for yourselves treasure on earth" (v. 19); "Do not worry about your life" (v. 28); and now "Do not judge or you will be judged" (7:1).

Matthew 7:1 is an elaboration of the fifth petition in the Lord's Prayer: "Forgive us our debts, as we also have forgiven our debtors." And the commentary in 6:14 says that if we forgive others when they sin against us, our heavenly Father will also forgive us. But if we do not forgive others their sins, our Father will not forgive ours.

What Jesus meant by judging, therefore, is the opposite of forgiving. To judge means to condemn people rather than forgive them. When Jesus said, do not judge, or you too will be judged, He was saying that as His followers we must not have a spirit of condemnation toward other people, or a spirit of harsh criticism, a spirit that puts other people down. That kind of judgment often characterizes people in our society and it comes out of self-righteousness.

The reason we criticize people, the reason it is great sport to point out other people's faults, is that by pulling others down we think we can build ourselves up. If we point out someone else's sickness, we think we highlight our health. If we point out another's failures, we think we showcase our successes. Harsh and vitriolic criticism that condemns and judges is the mark of a self-righteous person trying to gain a righteous reputation by delighting in the faults and flaws of other people. But once we recognize our own poverty of life and our own sinfulness, once we recognize our own desperate need and have come to hunger and thirst for the righteousness of God and have cast ourselves with reckless abandon upon His grace, we will no longer condemn or judge.

So when Jesus said, "Do not judge, or you too will be judged," He meant that a person who manifests a critical, judgmental, condemning spirit is a person who doesn't know God at all. He still stands under God's judgment. A forgiven person is a forgiving person.

Two things are important here. First, we are to look at the manner of our judgment, at the measure we use. In the same way we judge others, we will be judged. When we make judgments about other people, what is our attitude? Is it one of forgiveness or condemnation? Is it an attitude that shows concern for the person and a desire to restore him? Or is it an attitude that wants to use her fall as a step to raise ourselves?

If we judge with an attitude of putting people down, God will put us down. If we judge with an attitude of helping other people, God will help us. What measure we use will be measured to us.

The rabbis would say that God deals with two measures: the measure of mercy and the measure of justice. That was a common saying in the first century, and I think that is what Jesus meant. We can judge in mercy or in justice. If we want justice for others, we'll get justice for ourselves. If we want mercy for other people, we gain mercy for ourselves.

When we judge we usually say that what we want is justice. But when we judge someone, when we deny them our forgiveness, we put ourselves in the place of God. We intimate that we don't have that weakness, that failure; we imply that we occupy a position of perfection. And none of us dare make that kind of judgment on another person. All of our judgments are partial at best. We don't know the entire story of anyone else's life.

When a man fails to resist temptation and falls into sin, we don't know, can't know, how much temptation he resisted before he fell. In fact, if we understood the whole story instead of criticizing him, perhaps we would commend him for his courage. All of our judgments are not only partial, they are fallible. Even when we know the facts, we are not always right in our verdicts. That's why we have hung juries. Twelve honest and true people look at the same facts presented by the same attorneys, and some see guilt while others hold out for innocence. Hung juries loom as constant reminders that human verdicts are fallible.

We have no basis for judging or demanding justice. Yet we do it. And if this attitude dominates our lives, we are on dangerous ground.

If a man commits adultery we know he has sinned. The Bible prohibits sexual looseness. But what is our manner? What is our measure of judgment? Is it one of condemnation? Do we insist that the sinner be punished? If so, do we apply that standard to ourselves? Perhaps we haven't committed the act, but again we may not have had the opportunity. Maybe we have kept our uniform clean simply because we haven't had a chance to get into the game. What about our fantasies, our reading, our thoughts? What about the things we'd do if we had the chance? If we demand justice for others, we expect strict justice for ourselves. Or do we?

If we have coworkers who lie, how are we to respond? We can't simply say lying doesn't matter; it does matter. But do we respond in mercy or justice? If we are concerned about their lies, are we equally concerned about our own? Do we shade our stories to make ourselves look good? Do we change the facts a bit to bolster our cases? Do we cheat on our income taxes or change our expense accounts? If we insist on justice for our coworkers, then we must expect justice for ourselves.

Our attitudes toward other people and their sins speaks volumes about our attitudes toward ourselves and our standing before God. A forgiven person is a forgiving person.

Frankly, when I stand before God I don't want justice, I want mercy. But only those who give it will receive it. Mercy is a family trait.

After showing us the absurdity of being judgmental, Jesus showed us what hypocrites we are. "Why do you look at the speck of sawdust in your brother's eye and pay no attention to the plank in your own eye? How can you say to your brother, 'Let me take the speck out of your eye,' when all the time there is a plank in your own eye?" Jesus pictured a person with a tiny speck of sawdust in his eye, which of course can hurt and irritate. Then along came an ophthalmologist to remove the speck, but a huge log sticks out of his eye. It was an absurd scenario. It sounds like a comedy routine. But in life itself it comes close to reality.

When the prophet Nathan told king David a veiled but pointed story about a sheep thief, David flew into a rage. The king had a keen conscience about stealing sheep, but somehow he didn't have any conscience about stealing wives. He was trying to remove a speck of sawdust from a man's eye when he had a log in his own. It happens all the time.

A businessman, convicted of embezzling hundreds of thousands of dollars from his corporation, resembled a mother bear guarding her cubs when it came to the petty cash box. Every day everyone had to account for every cent taken. While he monitored the trickle of petty cash, he was pulling the plug on the corporate bank account. He was big on other people's accountability but oblivious to his own.

Not long ago a preacher in Maine had an affair with a woman in his church. The story made national news because he had campaigned against pornography. He preached against it and led campaigns to abolish it in his community. He was death on sexual looseness in magazines but apparently blind to it in his own life. The man railed against the sawdust of the 7-Eleven down the street but could not see the telephone post sticking out of his face.

Jesus did not contend that sin in other people's lives was unimportant. He simply pointed out the absurdity of concerning ourselves with specks in others without paying attention to our own planks.

So what are we to do? Jesus said, "You hypocrite, first take the plank out of your own eye, and then you will see clearly to remove the speck from your brother's eye" (7:5).

The word *hypocrite* is close to our word for *actor*. Jesus called this kind of judgment hypocrisy because it pretends to show a concern for righteousness. Hypocrites feel righteous when they spotlight the sins of others. To them, the essence of religion is concern about sin, but someone else's sin, not their own. If we are really concerned about sin, and we ought to be, we will first of all be concerned about our own. If we are really concerned about righteousness, we will be concerned about righteousness in ourselves. To be concerned about another person's sin and not our own is to playact religion. We play a part designed to impress an audience, but we don't care much about authenticity in our own experience.

After we remove the plank from our own eyes, we have two things going for us. First, we can see clearly the sin in someone else's life. Second, we are in a position to help that person deal with that sin.

If we take seriously the sin dogging our own lives and come to the poverty of spirit such insight gives us before God, that affects the way we look at sin and how we deal with it.

When we let God operate on the sin in our lives, that changes the way we deal with people. When we see their sin in the light of what we have wrestled with, we approach them with grace and concern.

We can encourage others to repent because we know the agony of sin and the relief of God's forgiveness. Oswald Sanders captured what Jesus meant: "What God has done for me, he can easily do for you. You have only some sawdust in your eye, but I had a huge log in mine."

That spirit of grace is what Paul spoke of when he said, "If someone is caught in a sin, you who are spiritual should restore him gently" (Galatians 6:1). The King James Version says we are to "restore such an one in the spirit of meekness." Where does meekness come from? It comes from sensing our own desperate need for mercy and from knowing the work of God in our own lives. Knowing how God has handled us, we can minister gently to others. We approach them not as a judge to condemn, but as a brother or sister to restore.

A good place to look for a post in your own eye is to take a look at whether you judge others. Do you frequently pass judgment? Why do you do it? How do you do it? If you do it out of a sense of condemnation, you have put yourself in the place of God. And that's about as far from God as you can get. You cannot know the mercy of God and refuse to extend it to others.

Colonel Protheroe, the magistrate in Agatha Christie's *Murder at the Vicarage*, didn't have much patience with lawbreakers. In fact, he thought they should all be punished alike, without exceptions.

"Firmness," he said to the vicar. "That's what is needed nowadays—firmness! Make an example. If you catch someone on the wrong side of the law, let the law punish him. You agree with me, I'm sure."

"You forget," said the vicar, "my calling obliges me to respect one quality above all others—the quality of mercy. When my time comes, I should be sorry if the only plea I had to offer was that of justice. Because it might mean that only justice would be meted out to me."

SERMON NOTES

How does the command "Do not judge or you too will be judged" relate to the Lord's Prayer that precedes it?

What basic issue do you think Jesus is addressing with this command?

Explain the difference between judging in mercy and judging in justice.

Sometimes we have double standards when it comes to demanding firm justice for others and not expecting it for ourselves. Give some examples of ways we do this.

Jesus shows the absurdity of being judgmental by calling a hypocrite the one who tries to remove the speck from another's eye, while having a log in his own. How can judging a person in *justice* be hypocrisy?

After we "remove the plank" from our own eyes, what two things are we able to do? How might this affect the way we react to other people's sin?

The King James Version of Galatians 6:1 states that we are to "restore" in the "spirit of meekness." Where does meekness come from?

It comes from God as we remember what we were.

How can we view people who sin with a spirit of grace and concern rather than with a spirit of condemnation?

It's a remembrance of who we were (are). Hate the sin love the sinner.

WRECKING CREW

■

I n the 1700s missionaries from the London Missionary Society
faced a multitude of obstacles and temptations in the South Pacific. Many of their problems on the island of Tonga came from other
Europeans, who considered the missionaries a threat to their freewheeling lifestyle. One of the tactics used to undermine the work of
the missionaries was to taunt them and mock them for their sexual
purity. George Veeson, one of the ten missionaries on Tonga, could
not withstand the pressure. He gave in and joined the Europeans in
their promiscuous life among the natives. He took land, servants, and
a harem of wives. But he did more than that. He disgraced himself,
the London Missionary Society, and God.

Through the centuries, many committed Christians have turned
their backs on God when their passion for short-term personal pleasure has blinded them to the long-term cost.

Jesus warned us about giving in to these inevitable temptations
when He said, "Do not give dogs what is sacred; do not throw your
pearls to pigs" (Matthew 7:6). In other words, we are not to throw our
lives to the world and invite humiliation and scorn.

Many commentators have wrestled with this verse and been
thrown to the mat by it. They are not quite sure what it means. Jesus had been talking about not judging. And a little later He talked
about asking, seeking, and knocking. But sandwiched in between sits
a warning about dogs and pigs. What did He mean?

The metaphor itself isn't hard to understand. Dogs and pigs were
despised animals. The dogs we read about in the Bible were not like the

cuddly creatures that jump in our laps to have their heads scratched. They were scavengers, more like wild animals than pets.

When Jesus cryptically pronounced, "Don't give what is sacred to dogs," He was referring to the meat offered to God in the temple of Jerusalem. The temples we know of today are much different from those in the first century. To get the right idea about temples we must clear our minds of images of St. John the Divine in New York, or St. Peter's in Rome. The temple in Jerusalem may have been a beautiful structure, but at its center was a slaughterhouse. The Jewish people who came to worship brought animals and sacrificed them to God to show Him they were serious about their sin.

At the end of the day not all the sacrificial meat had been consumed, so something had to be done with it. But no one was quite sure what. If they put it in the garbage heap, scavenger dogs would spend the night ripping it apart and eating it.

We have somewhat the same problem today with old flags that are worn and tattered. How are we to dispose of them? Out of curiosity I called the Air Force base and asked one of the officers what to do with an old flag.

"Well," he said, "in an appropriate ceremony, you could burn it. Or you may wrap it and bury it. One thing you don't do—you don't throw it in the dumpster because other people will throw garbage on it and you will desecrate the flag."

I have the same problem with worn-out Bibles. I have a collection that I don't know what to do with. They are too torn and tattered to give away, but I don't feel right throwing them in the garbage. I don't want to desecrate them because the book means so much to me.

The priests had that problem. So they took great care to burn the meat and bury it so scavengers would not get it.

Those who have lived on farms know that when you feed pigs they squeal, push, and shove to be first at the food trough; they pay no attention to Miss Manners or Emily Post. If for some insane reason you would feed them pearls instead of grain, the pigs would go after it thinking it was something to eat. But as soon as the swine realized the pearls were not grain, they might go after you.

Like dogs and temples, first century pigs were different from the plump, well-scrubbed Miss Piggys we think of today. They were half-wild creatures derived from the European wild boar, and they didn't sing love songs to Kermit the Frog.

Knowing this, it's not hard to figure out that Jesus was warning us not to give something sacred and valuable to those who won't recognize or value it. But what is not so easy to figure out is what all that had to do with everything else Jesus was saying. Why did Jesus say that at that particular place in his sermon? And when He was talking about dogs and swine, whom did He have in mind?

We get some help from the Bible in the references to dogs and pigs. For example, speaking about the death of Christ a thousand years before the Crucifixion, the psalmist wrote, "Dogs have surrounded me; a band of evil men has encircled me" (Psalm 22:16). David, a righteous man who was being persecuted, foresees our Lord on the cross surrounded by those who, with great delight, pinned him there. And they are like a pack of savage dogs, circling, ready to jump, ready to tear the victim apart.

And in Philippians 3:2, Paul wrote, "Watch out for those dogs, those men who do evil, those mutilators of the flesh." Even more interesting is the discussion of false teachers in 2 Peter 2. Peter compared them to dogs who return to their vomit and to washed sows who go back to wallowing in mud. Unless we somehow change the inner nature of a dog or pig, the dog will revert to form and delight in vomit and the pig will thrive on mud baths.

Apparently the dogs and pigs Jesus called attention to in this part of His sermon were people in opposition to Him and His message.

So we're back to our question: How does this sentence about dogs and pigs fit the context of what precedes and follows it?

Some commentators say the verse refers to evangelism, that we ought to be discriminating as to whom we tell the good news about Jesus Christ. We ought to be sure we're not giving it to people who will scoff, mock, jeer, and despise it.

There are times when it is wise not to speak, when it is better to let your life say something before your words, to let people hear the music before you sing the lyrics. This is especially true when people are mocking. I was on a plane awhile ago and a fellow next to me and a fellow across the aisle had had too much to drink. One of them saw me studying my Bible and asked if I believed it.

"Yea, I guess I do," I answered.

"Don't touch him," said the guy across the aisle. "If you start attacking him you'll tear him apart, and that poor guy is going to lose everything that he holds dear."

"Do you want to get into a discussion," I asked. "Do you want to argue? Tell me the kind of life you are living. You're drunk. You can't even hold your own beer, and you're telling me you are better off than I am. By all means, let's talk about it."

I wasn't evangelizing. In that conversation it would have been ridiculous for me to give them the gospel. I wanted to say, "Look, if you think you have something better than I have, I'll listen to you." It wasn't the right time to throw the gospel before those two men. There had to be something done before that.

There are times, even in evangelism, when it is wiser to be quiet than to speak. And sometimes in the silence there is a great deal of eloquence.

This is a fairly common view, and there is some support for it. Luke 23 tells how Jesus stood before Herod prior to the crucifixion. Herod was eager to interview Jesus. He wanted to ask Him many questions, and he hoped Jesus would perform a miracle. But Jesus answered him not a word. Herod was not an ignorant person. He already had more than he was living up to. He simply had a heart of stone, so Jesus refused to answer him.

So there is some support for this view from the ministry of Jesus. Jesus didn't tell everything He knew to everyone He met. Bishop Gore used to say, "Don't shriek the highest truth of our religion on the street corners." There is wisdom in that. A lot of common sense. To present God's truth to mockers who blaspheme and degrade it can be like offering pearls to pigs.

But is this what Jesus is saying here? Jesus has been warning about judging, and He goes on to talk about prayer. Why would He stick in two sentences to urge us to be careful about whom we evangelize? What does witnessing to the Gentiles have to do with the Sermon on the Mount?

Early Christians referred this passage to the Lord's Table. When they gathered for Communion an elder would begin it by saying, "Holy things are for holy people." This food, this bread, this wine, were not offered to anyone who happened to drop into the service.

The *Didascalia Apostolorum*, the oldest book of church order we have, gave this instruction: "Let no one eat or drink of the eucharist, that is the communion service, except those baptized into the name of the Lord. For as regards to this the Lord has said, give not that which is holy to dogs!"

It wasn't that early Christians did not desire to win men and women to God. They simply wanted to keep the fellowship pure. Engulfed by paganism, they labored to keep what was distinct about their faith separate from the influences that would have swept in, immersed it, and destroyed it.

The principle of not giving what is sacred to dogs could apply to the Communion, but the question remains: Was that what Jesus meant here? Was He talking about the Lord's Table? If He was, the lesson appears at a strange place. No where else in the Sermon on the Mount did He mention the Eucharist. Although it is not an impossible application, it doesn't appear to fit the context of this passage.

There is another direction we can take to interpret this verse. It grows out of the broader context of the Sermon on the Mount. These two verses go back to the beginning of chapter 6, where Jesus gave us a model prayer.

The final petition in the Lord's Prayer is "lead us not into temptation, but deliver us from the evil one." It was a prayer for protection from Satan, who isn't particularly concerned about whether we commit adultery, murder, lie, or steal. His mission focuses on anything that separates us from the Father.

Satan appears as an angel of light Paul tells us. He fell because he wanted to be like God. Satan's finished product is often a church deacon or elder who lives a very righteous life but doesn't have much trust in God. Self-righteousness serves his purposes as well as unrighteousness. And as long as the Evil One can lure us from God, he doesn't care how well behaved we are.

Jesus once said to Peter, "Satan has asked to sift you as wheat. But I have prayed for you" (Luke 22:31). That's what Satan wanted to do. In the last petition of the Lord's Prayer, we are to pray for protection from the Evil One. As commentary on this request Jesus warned, "Do not give dogs what is sacred; do not throw your pearls to pigs" (Matthew 7:6). He was concerned that we not turn our backs on the Lord and give what is sacred—our lives—to dogs, that we not take what is precious—our relationship with God—and throw it to pigs who will tear us apart.

Jesus made essentially the same point in Matthew 5, where, after speaking about persecution, He declared, "You are the salt of the earth. But if the salt loses its saltiness, how can it be made salty again?

It is no longer good for anything, except to be thrown out and trampled by men" (v. 13).

When I was a chaplain with the Dallas Cowboys, one of the team members came to faith in Jesus Christ. Even though professional football is a tough arena to serve Christ in, this man demonstrated a changed life. Several months later the team was in Philadelphia playing the Eagles and a couple of the guys on the team struck a deal with a call girl. They gave her one hundred dollars and said, "If you can get that guy to go to bed with you this weekend, we will double it, and you can have anything he gives you."

I am happy to report that my friend withstood the tremendous temptation. When he told me about it he said, "I didn't know what was coming off, but they were watching me. They would have ripped me apart if I had gone to bed with that girl."

He was right. They would have ripped him apart, because they wanted to believe that what happened in his life wasn't worth having, that it wasn't real. But it was. Life is not cheap; it is sacred.

If we turn our backs on our commitment to Christ and dishonor Him, the world outside will be like a pack of ravenous dogs, like a pack of boars that will tear us apart. They will trample us and what we believe into the dirt.

If a man who has followed Christ decides to turn his back on Him, we might think that those people who don't know God would say, "Welcome home, friend. We're delighted to have you back." But they don't. They tear him apart.

When I was teaching at another school, I had a student who was very gifted. He went through seminary and became a pastor of two churches that both grew during his ministry. But then he committed a very serious crime. He was caught and convicted. I have kept in contact with him in a penitentiary in Texas. When he went before the judge, the judge said, "You are supposed to be a Christian. You are despicable. I have only contempt for somebody like you." In a recent letter he wrote, "I am despised by the other prisoners who are here. They go out of their way to cut me down because of who I was and what I have done. I am here for ten years; I don't know if I can take it."

His experience simply confirmed what Jesus said. The convicts in that penitentiary have committed crimes worse than his. Some of them are in for life. Some serve sentences for murder. But they take great delight in attacking him, like dogs devouring meat, or pigs turning on someone who feeds them pearls.

The most difficult thing to handle when talking to scoffers who have no time for God is that they throw up all the Christians they know or have read about whose lives betray the Savior. Like dogs and pigs, they take great delight in savaging Christians.

People living a trivial existence justify themselves by despising righteousness. As a result they revel in followers of Christ who have fallen into one of Satan's traps. A Christian's sin makes them feel superior. They can behave like a pack of wild dogs or ravenous swine. When a Christian falls for a seduction of the Evil One, they rejoice.

Some non-Christians know this phenomena so well they draw back from following Christ because they are afraid they can't hold out. They hesitate to take on a commitment they couldn't carry out. The truth is, no one can hold out. That's the purpose of the Lord's Prayer. We fight in a spiritual battle and evil men will attack those being attacked by the Evil One. We can't go it alone.

How do we protect ourselves? By a constant dependence on the Father in heaven. He will protect us from the Enemy who schemes to separate us from Him. That explains why we must fervently pray this final petition in the Lord's Prayer and why Jesus goes on to urge us to keep on asking, keep on seeking, and keep on knocking. The price of victory is constant vigilance.

Martin Luther understood what Jesus was saying and captured it in the battle hymn of the Reformation.

> A mighty fortress is our God,
> A Bulwark never failing;
> Our helper He, amid the flood
> Of mortal ills prevailing.
> For still our ancient foe
> Doth seek to work us woe;
> His craft and power are great,
> And armed with cruel hate,
> On earth is not his equal.
> Did we in our own strength confide,
> Our striving would be losing;
> Were not the right Man on our side,
> The Man of God's own choosing.
> Dost ask who that may be?
> Christ Jesus, it is He;
> Lord Sabaoth is His name,
> From age to age the same,
> And He must win the battle.

SERMON NOTES

What is Jesus referring to when he talks about "dogs" and "pigs"? What do these animals represent?

How does this sentence about "dogs" and "pigs" fit the context of what precedes and follows it?

Why do you think Jesus refused to answer Pilate (27:12–14)?

Explain the relationship of Matthew 7:6 to the petition in the Lord's Prayer, "Lead us not into temptation, but deliver us from the evil one."

Can you think of ways that dogs and pigs operate today in our society?

DOOR KNOCKER

∎

I rving Berlin has no place in American music. He *is* American music," said Jerome Kern. America's favorite songwriter did not earn that distinction by composing a tune every now and then. Berlin has written as many as fifteen hundred songs. "Berlin's songs are his life," said *Time* magazine on the occasion of Berlin's one hundredth birthday. One of Berlin's nine rules for composing a song is "work and *work* and then WORK." Irving Berlin knows all about persistence in songwriting. Jesus urges us to have this same persistence when we pray. In Matthew 7:7–12, Jesus motivates us to pray. He urges us to persevere. Ask, seek, and knock are three different ways of talking about prayer. In the Old Testament, asking and seeking have to do with finding the mind of God. Jeremiah 29:12–13 uses those two words together. Although *earnest* may include repetition, Jesus' emphasis is on persistence, not vain recitations.

What is not captured well in English is that each of the words—ask, seek, and knock—are in the present tense, which denotes a continued action. It is more like a motion picture than a snapshot. The verbs here mean we are to keep on asking and it will be given to us. Keep on seeking and we will find. Keep on knocking and the door will be opened. The emphasis is not merely prayer but persistence in prayer. Pray about different things, but be persistent.

In any discipline, spiritual or physical, repetition enables us to perfect it. Florence Joyner did not become an Olympic runner by jogging around the block once a week. Ansel Adams did not become America's leading black-and-white landscape photographer by taking a few snapshots of his family. Magic Johnson did not become the NBA's most valuable player by shooting baskets only when the weather was nice. It is the nature of any discipline, physical or spiritual, that we persist at it to do it well. We practice again and again. And so Jesus was coaching us to persist in prayer.

We are not to keep at prayer because God needs to be nagged into a response. It is the opposite. We are to persist, to keep at it, because God has committed himself to answering our requests.

The bride-to-be was late to the wedding rehearsal. The groomsmen were getting a bit impatient so they began to kid the groom. They told him she wasn't coming. "Let's all go home," they said. "You might as well call the whole thing off."

But the groom waited. The couple had made a commitment to one another, and he knew she would arrive. He persisted because of his confidence she was coming.

The emphasis here is that we are to persist because God has promised to answer. "Everyone who asks receives," He said. The word *everyone* is limited by the context. This is not a blanket promise. When He introduced this section on prayer in chapter 6, Jesus pointed to the hypocrites who prayed three times a day in the marketplace. They pray to be seen, but Jesus made it clear that God made no promise to them. Then He described the pagans who babble the same phrase over and over again. They look for the magic word to move their god's heart. They persist, they stay at it, of course, but that kind of useless repetition has no effect on the true God. *Everyone* here refers to the disciples to whom He was speaking, those who wanted to make God's rule paramount in their lives.

A century or so ago people sometimes closed their letters with the phrase "Your obedient servant." That closing strikes us as odd, old fashioned, and even insincere. After all, the letters were not written by servants, and we suspect the writer had no intention of obeying the person to whom he wrote. But then our "Yours truly" isn't much better. I get a letter from the IRS signed "Yours truly." I don't believe that. I may belong to them, but they don't belong to me. And it's not enough to be *yours*, we must be truly yours. That's about as meaningful as getting a valentine from boys at the garage.

But in a sense prayer resembles a letter to God, a letter of petition. And those who close that letter with "Your obedient servant" are His disciples. The people who say to God, "I am truly yours, I want to be your person." That is the kind of person to whom this prayer is addressed. To those who persist in prayer because they believe God answers and who want what God wants for them.

So the first thing Jesus indicated was that we persist because we believe God has committed himself to answer us. That means prayer is dangerous business. In fact, if we took that promise alone, we would be afraid to pray. Sometimes on my knees I ask for ridiculous things. Sometimes I catch myself asking God for what could destroy me. So Jesus said, "Which of you, if his son asks for bread, will give him a stone? Or if he asks for fish, will give him a snake. If you, then, though you are evil, know how to give good gifts to your children, how much more will your Father in heaven give good gifts to those who ask him!"

The imagery is clear. And the pictures are interesting. The stones He mentioned are found in Palestine, on the shores of the Dead Sea or the Sea of Galilee, and in the wilderness. They are all over Israel. They are small, white stones that have the shape and color of small loaves of bread. But would a father give his hungry child a stone instead of bread? Or a snake instead of fish? No.

Jesus meant that we don't have to be afraid that God will give us something harmful, something that will destroy us. God won't mock us like that. This was a new thought to the Greeks. They believed their gods often mocked them. In fact, in one Greek legend, Aurora, the goddess of the morning, fell in love with a handsome mortal named Tithonus. Zeus asked Aurora what she wanted for a wedding present. She asked that Tithonus might live forever. Zeus granted the request. But Aurora had not thought to ask for her husband to stay young forever. So Tithonus got older and more feeble, but he couldn't die. Because Aurora asked foolishly, Zeus mocked her.

Jesus assured us that God doesn't do that. We have a heavenly Father who is willing to answer and wise enough to give us what we need. The emphasis is on God's wisdom. We often don't know what to ask for. But God knows what we need.

When our daughter Vicki was a baby, she had a habit of waking up in the middle of the night. When she woke up she didn't want to be alone, so she made enough noise to wake up the household. I'd go staggering into her bedroom.

"What do you want, Vicki?" I would ask.

"I want my bear."

I would go find something that looked like a bear and give it to her. She would take one look at it and throw it on the floor.

So I would try again. "Vicki, just tell daddy what you want."

"I want my dolly."

So daddy would go looking for a dolly, return to her bedside, and place it gently beside her. She would hold it for a minute and then throw it on the floor with the bear.

By this time my wife Bonnie had gotten up and gone into the kitchen and warmed a bottle. As soon as she put it in Vicki's mouth, Vicki was silent. That was what she wanted all along. She had been hungry but was too young to know what would satisfy her. I am convinced that Vicki thought she wanted a bear and thought she needed her dolly. But what she really needed was a mother who knew that she needed warm milk.

When we lay our requests before God, we can ask Him for things we think we really want and be assured that God will not give us something that will hurt us. He will answer according to our needs, as any good father would. Even though we are imperfect, we want to give our children good gifts. But our heavenly Father does even more. We don't always know what to give our youngsters, but our heavenly Father knows exactly what we need.

A while ago I sat with a good friend whose son had kicked the traces. He had been convicted of trafficking in narcotics and was about to go to the penitentiary for a ten-year sentence. I sat with that father, a man of wealth and influence, in his living room.

"You know, I've given him everything he ever asked for," he said. "I think that is what destroyed him."

That father loved his son. I have no doubt about it. And what the boy asked for he received.

"I can't hold this back from my son," I had heard him say. "He knows I have the money to give him whatever he wants."

And so the boy was given his heart's desires, but he was destroyed by the gifts. Fathers don't mean to do that. But they sometimes do.

God does not indulge our whims, but He will give us what we need. As the sage put it:

> I asked for strength that I might achieve; he made me weak that I might obey. I asked for health that I might do great things; he gave me grace that I might do better things. I asked for riches that I might be happy; he did not give them so that I might be wise. I asked for power that I might have the praise of men; I was given weakness that I might feel a need of God. I asked for all things that I might enjoy life; I was given life, that I might enjoy all things. I received very few of the things that I asked for; but I received the things that I had hoped for.

In the act of prayer we acknowledge that we can't go it alone. When we ask, a Father answers. When we seek, we find a Father's face. When we knock, a Father, not a servant, opens the door. It's the Father, and we need to know that. Prayer is our way of knowing that.

What do all children need? They need a father's love and care. We look at a boy from a wealthy suburb and say he has everything, everything except his dad. The father has given his son a catalog of expensive gifts, but hasn't taken the time to give him himself.

What do we really need? Gifts? Yes. God knows we need bread and fish to eat. But what we really need is God. If we persist in music, sports, or business, we may gain recognition and wealth; but the greatest gift from persistent prayer is God himself.

SERMON NOTES

Talking about prayer, Jesus tells us to "ask," "seek," and "knock." What is His point? How long should we persist in our prayers?

What do we gain by persisting in prayer? What must we believe about God if we pray this way?

Explain the verse, "Everyone who asks receives." Does God answer all the prayers of everyone? Have you ever asked God for something you didn't receive?

How does God deal with us when we make ridiculous or unwise requests? Does it really matter *what* we ask for—or just that we ask?

So how *do* we know what to pray for?

Aside from getting answers to our prayers, what does praying to God accomplish?

LEVELING ROD

∎

I love to have enemies. I fight my enemies. I like beating my enemies to the ground," said Donald Trump, whose name has become
synonymous with glitz and greed. His get-even game plan stands in
glaring contrast to what we know as the Golden Rule, a commonly
accepted moral standard that some have called the Mount Everest
of ethics. "Do to others what you would have them do to you" (7:12)
is, I am sure, the most famous statement that Jesus made. Folks who
know very little about the Bible know the Golden Rule. But it isn't
original with Jesus. The rule, in one form or another, goes back centuries before Christ. Isocrates, a Greek philosopher who lived about five
hundred years before Jesus, used it. Socrates gave it. Confucius, who
lived in the Far East about five hundred years before Christ, taught it.
Philo, the philosopher theologian, imparted it. What is interesting,
however, is that outside the Bible it is usually stated negatively.

Shami, a stern and rigid Jewish rabbi, was approached one day by
a pagan. "I am willing to convert to your religion if you can sum up
your law while I am standing on one leg," the pagan said.

Shami drove the man from his presence with a big stick. I don't
blame him. The man presented ridiculous conditions for becoming
a convert.

The man then went to another rabbi, Hillel, with the same proposition. Hillel's response nailed the pagan. "What is hateful to yourself,
do not do to others."

Tsze Kung, a disciple of Confucius, asked for one word that could
be a rule for life. "Reciprocity," Confucius responded. "What you do

not want done to yourself, do not do to others." That is often called the silver rule because it is negative. What we don't want others to do to us, we shouldn't do to them.

It is not a bad rule, but it isn't particularly religious. We don't have to embrace religion to recognize that it makes good sense. We don't have to endorse any ethical system, any theology, to understand that we can't live in society unless we follow that precept. It is little more than calculated shrewdness to avoid retaliation.

But Jesus was being positive. He said, "Therefore in everything, do to others what you would have them do to you, for this sums up the Law and the Prophets." In the Greek text and in many translations, the word *therefore* precedes the statement. The principle does not stand alone. It is not a nugget that we can take out of the Sermon on the Mount. The word *therefore* takes us back to what lies before.

At the end of Matthew 5, Jesus spoke about our relationship with others, which grows out of our relationship with God. And He summed it up by saying that we are to love our enemies, just as God does. God doesn't make the sun shine on only the good people. It shines on everybody. And we are to emulate that kind of goodness. When we love our enemies we are very much like God who does not discriminate.

In Matthew 7:11 Jesus concluded that the reason we go to God in prayer is because God gives us good gifts. So the word *therefore* refers to our relationship to God. Because God is our Father, because God is a good giver, because we are His children, we should be known for doing to others what we would have them do to us.

Although Jesus earlier commanded that we are to love our enemies, here He is even more specific. We are to do to others what we want them to do to us. In other words, we are to start with ourselves. We are to ask ourselves what we want the other person to do for us. I want the other person to be kind to me; therefore, I will be kind.

I want the other person to be honest with me; therefore, I will be honest. I want people to help me when I am hurting; therefore, I will help them when they need it.

Conversely, I don't want people to make life difficult for me, so I will make it a point never to make life difficult for them. I don't want other people to bring out the worst in me, so I will endeavor not to bring out the worst in them. The important thing to note is that we are to take the initiative.

We are to govern our lives by doing for others what we want them to do for us. "This," Jesus said, "sums up the law and the prophets."

If you read the laws in the Old Testament with what Jesus said, you can see this connection to the Golden Rule. I recently went back to the Old Testament and read many of the laws. In doing this, I began to see the connection to the Golden Rule. For example, the Law says, "Do not oppress an alien; you yourselves know how it feels to be aliens, because you were aliens in Egypt" (Exodus 23:9). There it is, the Golden Rule in the Old Testament. The Israelites should have known how to treat outsiders because they themselves had been outsiders. They were to treat strangers in the same manner they themselves would have wanted to be treated.

Look at another example from the case law in Exodus. "If you come across your enemy's ox or donkey wandering off, be sure to take it back" (23:4). I don't own an ox, but if I did I wouldn't want it lost or killed. I would want the person who found it to be kind enough to bring it back to me. I, therefore, should do the same even if I find my enemy's ox.

What applied to oxen applied to donkeys. "If you see the donkey of someone who hates you fallen down under the load, do not leave it there; be sure you help him with it" (23:5). A donkey that has fallen under its load, unable to get to its feet, is in grave danger. If that were my donkey, I'd appreciate it if somebody would help him get up so the poor beast wouldn't lie there paralyzed. If that's what I want someone to do for my animal, that's what I should do—without asking whose donkey it is, without weighing how the owner has treated me in the past.

The principle starts with us as a very practical application of the rule of love. It is active, not passive; positive, not negative.

The story of the Good Samaritan could have taken place in downtown Denver, Chicago, or New York. A traveler was stripped, mugged, and left in a pool of blood beside the road to die. Two men saw him but went on about their business. One was a priest and the other was a Levite. They practiced the silver rule. They didn't do evil to this man, but they didn't help him either.

If I were the victim I would want someone to aid me. I wouldn't care whether assistance came from a Jew or a Samaritan, nor would I care at all about the color of his skin.

We do not help others because they have helped us. That is not how God deals with us. God's help has nothing to do with our merit. God doesn't love us because of what we are; He loves us in spite of what we are. We never have dibs on God. God doesn't owe us; He owns us.

Is the Golden Rule an absolute?

Probably not. We must be sure that what we want to receive from others is what we ought to receive. For example, I may want to be flattered, to have others say nice things about me whether or not they are true. So I flatter people to get them to flatter me. Eventually the whole process becomes destructive manipulation, and obviously that wasn't what Jesus was trying to generate.

Or suppose a man commits a very serious crime and is captured and brought to court. If I asked him what he would like the jury to do for him, no doubt he would say he wanted to be let off. That also would be true, I'm sure, of the jury members if they were guilty of a crime. Does the Golden Rule mean, then, that the jury should let the man go free? Should we always give people what they desire?

It is important to realize again that this is connected to the rest of the Sermon on the Mount, and the topic of the sermon is righteousness. Jesus was pointing out that we are to act righteously toward others so they will act righteously toward us. If we understand God's righteousness, we will not twist the Golden Rule into an excuse for unrighteous behavior.

If we walk with God, we are concerned about sin. The whole essence of the Sermon on the Mount is that when we recognize our desperate need, we come before God in mourning and we hunger and thirst for His righteousness.

If we fail to put the Golden Rule in the context of the Law and the Prophets and the Sermon on the Mount, we do great damage, instead of great good, to the society in which we live.

One other thing to remember is that the Golden Rule, as Jesus gave it, is a guide and not a goal. He was not saying we are to be nice to others so they will be nice to us. Receiving kindness from others should not be our motive for being kind. Although the Golden Rule expresses the way we are to conduct ourselves, it does not guarantee any results. In fact, early in the Sermon on the Mount Jesus alerted us against that expectation. "Blessed are you when people insult you, persecute you and falsely say all kinds of evil against you because of me" (5:11).

Several times in the Sermon on the Mount Jesus warned that people may take advantage of us, slander us, and persecute us if we live truly righteous lives. Let's be realistic: treating people kindly is no guarantee that others will treat us kindly. Chances are some people will take advantage of us. Living a godly life can put you at a disadvantage in the game of life. This doesn't mean, however, that we will necessarily come in last. We'll escape a great deal of disappointment if we realize that the motive for being nice isn't to get others to be nice to us. The Golden Rule is not a goal, it's a guide.

Then why do it? Because we live for the approval of our heavenly Father. It doesn't matter whether my enemy throws appreciation banquets for me after I bring his ox back to him. It doesn't matter whether others deal honestly with me after I deal honestly with them. We do not take our lead from the crowd but from our relationship with the Father. We represent Him to a society whose leaden rule is to do others before they do you. But if we are serious about our relationship with God, we live in love toward friend and foe, neighbor and enemy.

So I ask myself what I would want in any given situation. And when I answer that I don't ask further questions about the other person, I simply respond as God responds to me.

This is enough to make us uneasy. The Golden Rule should guide us in all our activities: at home in our relationships with our spouses and children; on the highway; at the football stadium; and in the office. It is not a precept we practice when it is convenient or when we want warm feelings.

When we sense our bankruptcy, our utter selfishness, we realize how seldom we put others' interests first. When that hits us, we find ourselves driven back to the Beatitudes, the foundation of this sermon.

"Blessed are the poor in spirit, for theirs is the kingdom of heaven." I suddenly recognize how much I need the grace of God. "Blessed are those who mourn." When I strip away all my excuses, I realize that I am far from what God wants me to be; and I come with a sense of submission before God, a sense of deep need. And then I read, "Blessed are those who hunger and thirst for righteousness, for they will be filled." And out of that, "Blessed are the merciful. Blessed are the pure in heart. Blessed are the peacemakers." And I realize how being sure of my relationship with God affects my relationships with others.

Jesus was not telling me to turn over a new leaf. He was saying that this kind of righteousness demands a new life. He was not saying that I need to make up my mind to keep this rule. I can't do it on my own.

I recognize my desperate need for God's righteousness. I go to the Bible, but I can't keep all of God's rules and regulations. In fact, I can't even remember them all. How in the world can I reflect God's love? How am I to think? How am I to behave?

I am to determine that what I want others to do for me, I will do for them. I'll start by asking myself what I would want in that situation. Then I'll do it. The person who does that fulfills the kind of righteousness that God requires. And to do it consistently the person needs the righteousness that only God can give, righteousness that is a relationship of grace first with Him, and then with others.

Charlie Brown is a kind-hearted, do-good kind of character. Despite the abuse he receives from the other inhabitants in Charles Schulz's cartoon strip, *Peanuts*, Charlie Brown continues to practice the Golden Rule. Even though it rarely works to his advantage, Charlie Brown keeps doing for others what he would have them do for him.

In one strip Charlie and Lucy are lined up behind a bunch of other kids to see a movie.

"Have you been here long, Charlie Brown?" Lucy asks.

"No, I just got here. Actually, I shouldn't be going to the movies at all. I have homework to do. If it weren't for the fact that they're giving away free candy bars to the first fifteen hundred kids, I wouldn't even be here."

Lucy, who has been listening to the ticket agent counting kids while Charlie Brown talked, asks him, "Do you mind if I get ahead of you, Charlie Brown?"

"No, please do. 'Ladies first' is always my motto. I don't think this is a very good movie. I just came because of the free candy bars for the first fifteen hundred kids. I really should be home doing my reading, but you know how it is when they're giving something away free," Charlie Brown continues as Lucy pays for her ticket.

"Fifteen hundred!" announces the ticket agent. "Sorry, kid, that's the way it goes."

The world is full of Lucys. When you practice the Golden Rule, don't do it for them; do it for your Father in heaven. He pays off with more than candy bars.

SERMON NOTES

Rabbi Hillel and Confucius both stated the Golden Rule negatively, while Jesus stated it positively. What difference does it make how it is stated?

In many translations the word *therefore* precedes this verse. What does it refer to? Why is it important?

This verse tells us to "do." It is a command to act. What actions might you take to follow this command?

How does the Old Testament Law relate to this verse? Did Jesus "rewrite" the Law?

The Golden Rule is a guide—not a goal. Why should we live by it? What enables us to treat others with love?

Do you think that following this command is practical in our "dog-eat-dog" world?

SERVICE ENTRANCE

∎

J ohn Calvin profoundly influenced Christian theology as well as the culture at large. As a young man he was thoughtful, reverent, and studious. By age 27 he had written the first edition of his *Institutes of the Christian Religion*. By the time he died in 1564 he had laid down the planks for Reformed theology. In addition, he had laid some of the planks for democratic government. He died almost penniless, but measured by the standards of history he was a success. The treasure he gave the human race still enriches us today. John Calvin had a brother named Charles. Charles Calvin was a profligate. He led a dissolute life. All that John Calvin was, Charles Calvin was not. He died a miserable wretch.

What made the two men different? Not genetics. They came from the same parents. Not the environment. They grew up in the same home. Not education. They went to the same schools. In fact, in their early years they had nearly the same influences. But one man reached for the heights and the other didn't make it out of Death Valley.

What distinguishes us from one another are the choices we make. We make decisions and then those decisions turn around and make us. A lot of folks spend a great deal of money going to psychiatrists or therapists to find out who they are. But if we unpeel ourselves one layer at a time to find out who we are, we may end up with nothing more than what we get when we peel away all the layers of an onion: tears.

A playwright in New York City wrote an article about some of the men who had worked with him over several decades. He lamented the fact that many of them began with great promise but ended a lie.

Summing up his observations he said, "In the final analysis very few lives are hits that end up on Broadway. Most lives are flops that finish out of town in New Haven."

His verdict holds a great deal of truth. Most people desperately want to be successful, but when life is over, measured by their own standards, they have failed. Why does that happen so frequently? We often blame heredity, environment, or genetics. Although all of those factors possess a shaping and molding force, they don't explain everything.

We are what we are committed to. If you tell me what you are committed to, I can tell you what you are. Certainly that is a theme of the Bible. Again and again biblical leaders call people to choose. Moses preached five sermons just before he died. Then he said, "This day I call heaven and earth as witnesses against you that I have set before you life and death, blessing and curses. Now choose life, so that you and your children may live and that you may love the LORD your God, listen to his voice, and hold fast to him" (Deuteronomy 30:19–20).

In Moses' audience that day stood a soldier named Joshua. When Moses died, Joshua took up the reins of leadership and led the people into the land God had promised them. When Joshua gave his farewell address he said, "Choose for yourselves this day whom you will serve, whether the gods your forefathers served beyond the River, or the gods of the Amorites, in whose land you are living. But as for me and my household, we will serve the LORD" (Joshua 24:15).

Moses and Joshua called the people of Israel to choose, and that has been true of preachers through the centuries. The really outstanding ones preached for a verdict. Someone said that a great sermon is a speech that ends with a motion to act. Effective sermons are not given for an audience to consider; they are preached to get people to decide. Jesus' preaching makes us nervous because He was asking for a radical decision.

Some people are attracted to Christianity because they have a leaky faucet and they want God to fix it. Perhaps they struggle with a destructive habit and they would like to tap God's power to help them break it. Or maybe they have broken relationships that they want God to mend. But they learn from the Sermon on the Mount that God is not a plumber. They learn that leaky faucets are minor league to Him. God wants to tear out the plumbing and deal with the well itself. He wants to change what comes out of the faucet. But really we want to settle for a minor repair, not a major renovation.

A friend of mine bothered by blurred eyesight went to her ophthalmologist to get a change of prescription in her glasses. He discovered a cancer behind her eye, a melanoma, and wouldn't even let her go home. He placed her in the hospital, removed the cancer, and treated her eye with radium. My friend wanted new glasses and ended up having radical surgery.

That is what Jesus does. His kind of righteousness isn't a prescription for glasses; He performs major surgery. We don't get His kind of righteousness with new glasses. We need major surgery. Jesus doesn't deal with leaky faucets; He deals with wells.

As Jesus delivered His sermon He wasn't preaching for applause. He demanded a decision. He pictured two gates, two ways, two trees, and two foundations. Travelers must choose their way; hearers, their message; and builders, their foundation. Listeners to Christ's message need to choose.

In Matthew 7:13–14 Jesus painted a scene depicting a narrow and a wide gate and a narrow and a wide way. The imagery behind those verses was common to someone living in the first century or to someone living today in the Near East. Most cities in the ancient world had walls, some wide enough for chariot traffic. And the walls of the city had gates. Jerusalem had twelve gates wide enough for two-way traffic. Throngs of people moved in and out to do their business and shop.

In the ancient world those gates were closed at night. If the city came under attack, the doors would be shut against the invader. In the door itself or next to the gate there usually stood a small door to allow citizens known to the guards to enter at night. This helped the soldiers let citizens in while keeping enemies out.

Jesus had that image in mind. There are two roads and two gates, not three. We have a choice to make. If we have been listening to Him, we know that we are to enter the narrow gate and travel the narrow road. In fact, He told us that up front, just after the capstone was laid in the Golden Rule. "Enter," He said, suddenly, starkly, directly. It is a command. We are to enter the narrow gate and travel the narrow road.

That unsettles me a bit. I don't like to think of myself as narrow. Narrow people come through as dwarfed spirits with tunnel vision, folks with no breadth to their lives, country bumpkins who measure the whole world by their small towns. They have trouble seeing beyond their back fences. I think of narrow religious people in the same way. They measure everyone by their limited experience. They tell everyone what is wrong with the world, but they are not better, just smaller. Yet they think everyone is evil except them. They have a warped view of life and of God.

No. I don't want the reputation of being narrow. But in a sense truth is narrow.

When I was growing up I was not particularly adept at arithmetic. We usually studied it first thing in the morning, and I hated school because I dreaded that first hour. By the time I was six or seven, you see, I had developed an appreciation for broad-mindedness, but my arithmetic teacher didn't. She and her narrow math tables said that three times three equalled nine, but I took a more expanded view of arithmetic than that. I was willing to settle for seven, eight, or ten. Why be a stickler about one number more or less? That's why I never got into accounting. At the end of the day, week, or quarter if I were fifty dollars short, I would simply throw in the fifty bucks and forget about it. Good accountants don't do that. They tend to be narrow about numbers.

Narrowness not only governs math and accounting, but also it is an essential of marriage. When a couple stands at a marriage altar, they make a commitment. As their minister, I want them to enter into all the poetry of that relationship. I want to see it grow and develop. So I say, "Henry, will you take Agnes to be your lawful wedded wife, will you comfort her, cherish her, cling to her; forsaking all others, will you take her alone?" And Henry responds, "I will." That's limiting. Of all the women on earth he chooses Agnes. He makes a narrow commitment to her.

Some folks in our society don't like that restriction. They are broad-minded. That is one of the reasons homes get shattered and people wounded by the shrapnel—they have never grasped the narrowness of a deep relationship.

The way is narrow; the gate is narrow; the truth is narrow; our relationship with God is narrow. And narrowness, even in Jesus' day, was unpopular. In fact, so many people are surging down the highway to destruction that Jesus said only a few would find the narrow path to life. In other words, we can't find the right road by sampling majority opinion. The crowd does not applaud the individual who enters the narrow gate.

This can be disconcerting. All of us gain confidence when we surround ourselves with people who think the way we do. Likewise, we lose confidence when we stand alone with our beliefs. Although some like smaller crowds than others, we all like the comfort of being with like-minded individuals. It's the "birds of a feather flock together" syndrome.

I don't like being the only Christian at an academic meeting and hearing speakers take cheap shots at the Christian faith. In fact, I don't appreciate it when I witness to the businessman next to me on an airplane who says, "You've got to be kidding me. You don't believe that, do you?" I don't like that at all. I like to play with the winners. I like to cheer for the champion. I'm not comfortable sitting alone. I don't enjoy being mocked for my narrow-mindedness when I tell people there is only one way to God—through Jesus Christ.

Our society is ripping apart at the seams because we poll the majority to define morality. If we expect to find truth by surveying the crowd, we will end up in disillusionment because the crowd consistently travels in the wrong direction. Going with the crowd is not the way to determine what really matters.

In the days of Athanasius, one of our church fathers, the great religious debate concerned the deity of Christ—whether or not Jesus Christ is God. It almost split the church. Orthodox Christians now believe that Athanasius was true to the Scriptures, but during his day he stood almost alone. People said to him, "Athanasius, give it up. The world is against you." To which Athanasius replied, "Then it must be Athanasius against the world."

When we make important decisions we must make them without considering whether or not they will make us popular. If popularity is our major concern, we are carbon copies of the Pharisees who lived for the applause of men instead of the approval of God.

Jesus warned us that the kind of life He is calling us to invites persecution. People will say evil things against us, dismiss us as odd, or accuse us of parading our righteousness. Folks don't seek out friends whose lifestyles show theirs to be wrong. If they live in darkness, they don't like what the light reveals. And rather than clean up their mess, they'll try to put out the light.

If we don't like to be narrow or unpopular, why choose the narrow road? We decide on the narrow road for the same reason we choose any road—for its destination. As Alexander McCartney said, "the main thing about a road is where it goes." Jesus said that the broad road leads to destruction. It may be an eight-lane, well-traveled highway; it may have beautiful scenery and marvelous accommodations along the way; it may be free of potholes. But Jesus said it ends in destruction. If we let the crowd decide our direction, we'll be destroyed with them.

The destination, not the road conditions, determines whether or not we're headed the right way.

Several years ago my son Torrey and I decided to go to the top of Mount Princeton, a 14,000-foot peak. Coming from New York City, I had never driven a jeep nor ridden on a mountain trail. I was not accustomed to hairpin turns that made me feel as if we were going headlong over the edge. Every time we turned another one I wished we had taken Highway 70 instead of the twisting trail. But Highway 70 didn't go to the top of Mount Princeton. To reach the mountain-top I had no choice but to take the jeep trail with its ruts and hairpin turns.

Likewise, Jesus said that only one road leads to life, and it's not a wide, well-traveled freeway. But we choose it—not for its comfort and convenience but for its destination. And when we do, we learn that folks who walk that narrow road are not narrow people. In fact, they are anything but narrow. They are broad in their sympathies. They take the initiative to do things for others that they would want others to do for them. They do good to those who despitefully use them, and they pray for those who persecute them. They're concerned not only about family and friend, but also about foe.

They are broad in their purposes. They have sworn allegiance to another king and to another kingdom. They pray regularly, "hallowed be your name, your kingdom come, your will be done on earth as it is in heaven." Their purposes are not limited to their own concerns.

They don't put their lives into their own houses, lands, or bank accounts. They live with a sense of the eternal. They take what is perishable and turn it into treasures that outlast them. They are not narrow in their goals.

They are also broad in their hopes. One of my major frustrations is that I want to do so many things and I know I don't have time to do them all. At times I look in the mirror and say to myself, "What's a young man like you doing in an old body like that?" Life for all of us ends more often with a whimper than a bang.

But if we are traveling the narrow road, our destination is life. Death is not the end of the road; it is a bend. Death is not a period; it is a comma. For us, the best is yet to come. We will do and be more than we ever dreamed possible.

No, the folks who choose the narrow gate and travel the narrow road are not narrow people. To walk with Jesus Christ gives us sympathies as broad as all mankind, purposes as great as heaven itself, and hope that is eternal.

To get on this road, however, we must make a choice. We don't stumble on to it by accident. We don't wake up one morning and discover that we are Christ's disciples. We become Christian men and women only when we recognize that we are bankrupt before God, that we possess a desperate hunger and thirst for righteousness. We recognize that we can't work up righteousness ourselves, and we cast ourselves with reckless abandon on the grace of God. We understand that God will make us merciful, will make us peacemakers, and will make us pure-hearted, which will mark us out in society as His children.

Our Puritan forefathers would not be overly impressed with some of our evangelistic methods: signing a card, raising a hand, or walking to the front of a church. They emphasized a covenant with God. In fact, they urged people to write out the covenant they had made with God as they would write out a business contract. They swore allegiance to a new king, to a new citizenship. They renounced their rights to themselves and gave themselves to God, to His work, and to His kingdom. Like enlisted soldiers, they gave up their rights to themselves and to their time. After writing the covenant they would sign it, seal it, and that would settle it. Not a bad thing to do.

When Charles Colson opened *Mere Christianity*, he found himself "face-to-face with an intellect so disciplined, so lucid, so relentlessly logical that I could only be grateful I had never faced him in a court of law," he wrote in *Born Again*. "Soon I had covered two pages of yellow paper with *pros* to my query, 'Is there a God?' "

The more Colson read of Lewis's mighty little book the closer he came to God. "I knew the time had come for me," he wrote. "I could not sidestep the central question Lewis (or God) had placed squarely before me. Was I to accept without reservations Jesus Christ as Lord of my life? It was like a gate before me. There was no way to walk around it. I would step through, or I would remain outside."

SERMON NOTES

We are what we are committed to. Can you think of some choices people have made that have changed their lives. If someone were going to describe you by describing what you are committed to, what do you think they would say?

What were Moses and Joshua urging their followers to commit to? What kind of choices were they facing?

What radical decision does Jesus urge us to make? Have you ever made it?

In your own words, explain what Jesus meant by the narrow gate and the narrow road.

By choosing the narrow road, we invite unpopularity, even persecution. Why take the narrow road? Why not another?

How do we get on the narrow road?

OUT OF TRUE

∎

Years ago the Metropolitan Museum of Art in Amsterdam put some of their priceless originals next to copies and held a contest to see how many visitors could tell the false from the true. Of the 1827 people who took part in the experiment only seven were able to tell the genuine from the fake.

What is true of paintings is true of prophets. People in our society believe their senses. So if something looks like a duck, waddles like a duck, and quacks like a duck, we believe it is indeed a duck. Generally that is true, but not always. If an animal looks like a sheep, sounds like a sheep, and is covered with wool, it is probably a sheep; but not necessarily. It may be a clever wolf.

Like a wolf in sheep's clothing, true and false prophets share many features in common. A lot of things we normally associate with true prophets can lead us astray.

For example, we cannot identify true prophets by the way they dress. They may or may not wear a clerical collar, a cassock, a cross around their necks, a business suit, or carry a Bible. They may have been ordained by some Christian denomination. They may flash all the credentials that go with ministry. Although they may exhibit the marks of a genuine calling, they may be false prophets.

Nor can we identify true prophets by their works, no matter how miraculous. Jesus said, "Many will say to me on that day, 'Lord, Lord, did we not prophesy in your name, and in your name drive out demons and perform many miracles?' Then I will tell them plainly, 'I never knew you. Away from me you evildoers!' " (7:21–23).

Evidently false prophets as well as true ones cast out demons, display spiritual powers, and perform miracles. Judas, along with the other disciples, had power over the forces of hell. And speaking of the last times, Jesus said, "At that time if anyone says to you, 'Look, here is the Christ!' or, 'There he is!' do not believe it. For false Christs and false prophets will appear and perform great signs and miracles to deceive even the elect—if that were possible" (Matthew 24:23–24). Just because someone heals the sick does not mean he or she is a true prophet. We cannot identify true prophets by the miracles they perform.

Religious vocabulary is not a reliable test of true prophets either. The false prophets Jesus mentioned did all their works in His name. In fact, "in your name" is repeated twice in verse 22. Saying "Lord, Lord" was an important part of their religious vocabulary. But they were impostors. Jesus will say to them, "I never knew you."

True prophets perform their ministry in the name of Jesus, but false prophets also know how to use those words. We cannot tell them apart by their theological vocabulary. Just because a preacher on television speaks the name of Jesus does not necessarily mean he is a prophet of God. He may be a prophet of another power, using the right words to get across the wrong message. Historically, one way heretics brought false doctrine into the church was by using orthodox words but filling them with different meaning. Sometimes it is done deliberately, but not always. Some false prophets honestly believe they are right. We cannot distinguish authentic prophets from counterfeits by their vocabulary.

Perhaps even more disturbing is that we cannot identify true prophets by their sincerity. False prophets are not necessarily charlatans who intentionally use a religious message to line their own pockets. Quite often they are dedicated. They build churches, raise money, preach decent sermons, and do it all in a sincere way. In fact, they are so sincere and effective that when they stand before God they will be shocked to discover that the God whom they thought they represented does not know them at all.

It is difficult to distinguish the false prophets from the true. It is hard to spot the counterfeits from the original. We cannot tell them by the clothes they wear, the ministry they perform, the words they speak, or even their sincerity.

So how do we identify the prophets of God? How do we separate them from false prophets? Jesus answered that question twice. "By their fruit you will recognize them," He said in verse 16 and again in verse 20.

We usually apply this passage to morality. We assume Jesus was saying that we can identify good people by their good deeds, by the lives they live. But having studied so much of the Sermon on the Mount, we know that cannot be what Jesus was teaching. In fact, some of those He singled out as being false prophets, the Pharisees and the scribes, kept all the religious rules and regulations. If "fruit" means the same as "good works," the Pharisees would be the first to qualify for a medal of righteousness.

Many cultured people in the world do good deeds and don't even pretend to be Christians. And many men and women who live moral lives make no time in their schedules for religion. No, we can't know the authenticity of prophets merely by examining the quality of their conduct.

The fruit of an orange tree is an orange. The fruit of an apple tree is an apple. The fruit of a grapevine is a grape. And the fruit of a prophet is prophecy. The primary question about a prophet is whether or not his teaching is true to the Word of God. Is the word of the prophet the same as what Jesus preached in His Sermon?

Throughout the Old Testament, the litmus test of a prophet did not lie in his ability to predict the future. And it had nothing to do with scolding the congregation. Today when someone says, "He has a prophetic message," they usually mean that he speaks with a pious snarl and severely criticizes the world and the church.

The test of a prophet was always whether or not he spoke for God accurately. A true prophet teaches what Jesus taught. He tells us that we stand before God bankrupt, that we have nothing to give God to acquire right standing with Him. He does not tell us to straighten up and get our act together or to turn over a new leaf. He does not urge us to simply shape up our moral conduct. The true prophet preaches that we have something radically wrong deep inside us. That's why Jesus started His sermon by saying, "Blessed are the poor in spirit, for theirs is the kingdom of heaven." A true prophet makes us aware of the depth of sin in our lives. And this awareness makes us feel a sense of mourning about our sin. "Blessed are those who mourn, for they will be comforted." This mourning leads to a craving for righteousness. "Blessed are those who hunger and thirst for righteousness, for they will be filled."

The true prophet does not tell us to conform to a list of rules and regulations. He doesn't tell us how to dress or how to wear our hair. True prophets deal with what we are inwardly. They make us aware of who we are before God. So when we give, fast, pray, or worship, we don't do it to impress the minister, the deacons, or our spouses. We don't do it to be an example. We do it because our Father who sees in secret will reward us. True prophets make us concerned about His approval.

His righteousness not only gives us a relationship with Him, it gives us a relationship with others, a relationship of love, a relationship out of a pure heart. We become aware that anger and homicide are not that far apart. The seed of unresolved anger can yield the weed of murder. Lust can flame into immoral conduct, divorce, ruined families, and shattered relationships.

God's righteousness at work in our lives produces genuine concern about integrity. Our promises don't depend on contracts written by shrewd lawyers. We deal honestly because we want to please God. And our honesty makes us merciful, pure in heart, and peacemakers.

The message of the Bible doesn't have to do with self-image, self-help, success, making money, winning, or staying healthy. Its truth has to do with our sinfulness before God and being made right before Him, and that comes about because Jesus Christ who preached this sermon went out and died to make it happen. He paid the penalty for all our sin.

Ultimately there are only two kinds of religion in the world: the kind that we have to carry and the kind that carries us. Religion that we have to carry—that depends on our strength, determination, and zeal—belongs to the false prophets. The religion of the Bible carries us. It depends on what Christ has done to declare us righteous.

Beware of false prophets, Jesus cautioned. They are here today; they were there nineteen hundred years ago. We can hear them on the radio or watch them on television or see them in front of a church. We cannot recognize them by their vocabulary, their effective ministry, or their sincerity; we can only measure them by their prophecy, by their fruit.

The first question Jesus asks of me is, "Are you staying true to my Word?" The second question He asks of me is, "Is your life true to the Word you preach?" In the day of judgment people will expect many of their actions to pass muster with God, but they won't make it at all. People who have been involved in religious work, who have learned all the right phrases, have carried on religious missions, and have preached moving sermons will hear from Jesus Christ, "I never knew you. Away from me, you evildoers!"

A soul is a dangerous thing to lose. We had better be careful whom we listen to, whom we watch, and what we read. Some who seem like gentle sheep may be ravenous wolves.

Elmer Gantry was a fictional example of a great deceiver. When Sinclair Lewis wrote his novel in 1927, many Christians felt he had sensationalized the story of the corrupt evangelist. Unfortunately, it has turned out that Lewis was a prophet of sorts. Elmer Gantry could substitute for one of a number of modern-day preachers.

Gantry, though guilty of immorality, deception, and hypocrisy, eventually discredited his accusers and, in the last scene of the book, faced his congregation.

"Without planning it, Elmer knelt on the platform, holding his hands out to them, sobbing, and with him they all knelt and sobbed and prayed, while outside the locked glass door of the church, seeing the mob kneel within, hundreds knelt on the steps of the church, on the sidewalk, all down the block.

" 'Oh, my friends!' cried Elmer, 'do you believe in my innocence, in the fiendishness of my accusers? Reassure me with a hallelujah!'

"The church thundered with the triumphant hallelujah."

And so do thousands of deceived believers today. But Jesus himself is not in the crowd.

SERMON NOTES

Why is it difficult to tell the difference between true and false prophets? Name some ways we *cannot* identify false prophets.

How does Jesus tell us to identify true prophets of God? Does "fruit" mean "good works"?

What characterizes the teaching of a true prophet? Does a true prophet deal with external moral codes? How does a prophet of God deal with our inward depravity?

Are prophets of God always popular? Are they always unpopular? Would you choose to serve as a prophet of God?

FOUNDATION

∎

Twenty-five years ago I had a conversation with a Dallas home-builder, a Christian who tried to make his faith effective in his business. My friend believed it was important to build good houses with solid foundations, sturdy walls, and good insulation. He paid attention to details the buyer couldn't see. Other builders, however, were more concerned with getting business than with building quality homes, so my friend was losing to the competition. His competitors knew that the couples buying homes were primarily concerned with appearance—bric-a-brac and decorations. This placed an honest builder at a disadvantage. If he gave attention to the foundation and put insulation in the walls and attic, he didn't have money for many decorative touches. If he put in the decorations, he had to raise his prices. What bothered him most was that the folks buying the homes didn't care about what was hidden. They only expected to live in the houses a couple of years, so appearances meant more to them than quality.

My friend solved his problem by getting out of the residential building business and getting into commercial property. Buyers there were more interested in what was put into the foundation, the walls, and the roof.

A few years ago I was back in Dallas and I drove through the neighborhood where my friend had tried to build homes. It looked like a slum. When we don't pay attention to what is hidden, a time comes when what is hidden will be revealed.

At the conclusion of the Sermon on the Mount, Jesus expressed concern about good housing. That should not surprise us; He was a carpenter. As part of the firm of Joseph and Sons in Nazareth, He had built the furniture that people put into their houses and He had probably built some of the homes as well. Jesus knew the difference between a solid building and a shoddy one. Therefore at the end of the Sermon on the Mount, this carpenter-preacher talked about sensible and stupid builders.

In the last illustration in His sermon, Jesus described two men who had built homes. The builders had several things in common. First, both were building permanent houses. They weren't putting up tool-sheds or erecting tents. They wanted to settle down, raise their families, and pass on a home to their children.

They were probably building similar dwellings as well. Jesus put no emphasis at all on any difference in design. For all we know they may have used the same blueprints—same plates for the windows, chimney, porch, doors. They may have been situated in a slightly different position on the ground, but for Jesus' purposes the two buildings could have been identical. The differences would not be seen by the average person. The houses looked the same. The casual observer could not see there were different foundations. Although that difference was not obvious, it was fundamental.

One man built his house on a foundation of rock, the other put his house on a foundation of sand. It seems like a scene from the theater of the absurd. It is difficult to imagine anyone stupid enough to build a house on sand. But the picture is not as absurd as it appears. In early summer many of the areas in Palestine, or even in the United States, look like lovely places to build homes. The land is smooth, the view is magnificent, and the sandy plain baked by the sun looks like an inviting place to live.

Besides, building on sand takes a lot less. Digging into the rock requires more sweat and time. Erecting mansions on the sand has distinct advantages and that's why people build there today. On the West Coast people build their homes on or next to faults. Others build on the cliffs overlooking the Pacific Ocean. They have a marvelous view of the sunset. But when a storm comes it eats away the ground underneath the house, and some of those lavish homes slide down the hill. Some actually tumble into the Pacific. Even after such disasters others insist on constructing houses on the slippery hillsides again.

Storms, Jesus said, reveal the difference between houses that appear identical. The pounding rain reveals the stability of the foundation; the wind tests the strength of what we have built.

When we review the Sermon on the Mount, we recall that Jesus wasn't very concerned about appearances. They can be deceiving. In His preceding story Jesus talked about guarding against wolves in sheep's clothing. False prophets and authentic ones also resemble one another. They speak the same language, wear the same clothes, carry on the same kind of ministry. The foundational difference is their prophecy.

When Stanford University was built, it had a great arch like the great Roman victory arches. It was built in memory of Leland Stanford, who gave an enormous amount of money to start the university. That arch, built so grandly, solidly, and splendidly, looked as if it would stand forever. But when the earthquake came the arch collapsed in ruins. Apparently the builder had tried to save some money. Instead of building that arch of solid rock and going as deep as he could go, he erected it on top of rubble. The earthquake revealed the builder's wretched choice.

Obviously, Jesus wasn't talking about the construction business. Nor was He giving instructions on how to build houses. He was driving home a lesson on building a life. Although we can use many pictures to describe our lives, Jesus chose a building metaphor. Our lives resemble houses. Everyone is building a house of some sort. But our lives are not just made up of brick and wood, nails and mortar. All of us have a foundation for our lives. Something on which we build. It may not be much more than shifting sand or it may be solid as a rock.

Some people build their lives on possessions—how much they own. Some build their lives on passions—the satisfaction of desires. Some build their lives on position—the jobs and offices they hold. And some build their lives on what is eternal.

All of us are building a life according to some scheme, some design. We don't build at random. We all have a world view. We all have a philosophy. We all have something important to us on which the building blocks of our lives rest.

Jesus said all of us will have the foundation of our lives tested. All of us—wise builders and foolish builders, Christians and atheists—will be exposed to the storm. Christians don't get a free pass. God doesn't pamper His people. The benefit of being a Christian is not protection from the hurricanes that blow our way in life.

The storms are what test us. Living in the sunshine of life doesn't tell us much about ourselves. Anybody can build a house that will stand firm when the sun is shining and the wind is still. It is the storms that reveal the strength of our foundations.

Sometimes the storm breaks us with the fury of a great temptation. In the last two weeks I've had conversations with men undergoing enormous temptation. One man, who works for a financial institution, has debts he cannot pay. He has access to the funds at work and is tempted to "borrow" some. He intends, of course, to pay them back before anyone finds out. Another man is strongly tempted to throw aside his marriage, his family, and his reputation. He is romantically overwhelmed by a young woman he knows. What we really are is exposed by the storm of temptation.

Sometimes the storm is a crushing personal loss. You may lose a job that not only provides income but also provides you with self-esteem and personal security. A carefully built stock portfolio suddenly destroyed can be like a tornado roaring through the comfortable life you have built for yourselves. When we realize that we haven't built up the security we counted on and everything in our lives comes tumbling down, we see exposed the faulty foundations of our lives.

Sometimes the storm roars in as we are pounded by sickness or the fear of death. You can lose your health and anguish, pain, and the prospect of death may come between you and the leisurely retirement you've anticipated. You begin to question the strength of the life you've built. And when someone you love goes out into the mystery of death, a not-so-solid foundation can start coming apart. Times like these reveal the foundations of our lives.

For others, the foundation is tested by prosperity. Prosperity comes to us like a gentle spring rain. At first we're convinced it will make our lives green and healthy. But when prosperity keeps coming, it can develop into a large destructive force as damaging as a storm. What we gain, not what we lose, often serves as the supreme test of our foundation. More men and women have been knocked off their spiritual foundation by great wealth than by great reversal.

For all of us there comes the storm of judgment as certain as the fact of life, of death, of God himself. We will all stand at the judgment bar of Christ and give an account for the living of our days. That storm will be the final test of whether our foundation is rock or sand, whether we have built on what is secure or on what is fleeting.

We are all building, Jesus declared, and what we are building will be tested, not in the sunshine but in the storm.

The third thing Jesus conveyed is that some will stand while others will fall. Jesus said that those who hear His words and practice them build wisely.

Many religious people deceive themselves into believing that knowing the Bible is the same as obeying it, that memorizing verses is the same as applying them, that assenting to the doctrines of Christ is the same as practicing them. Jesus said "not so." To hear the Word is essential, of course, but to *do* it is to know it. We must know our desperate need of God, and then we must cast ourselves upon Him to supply that need. We must know we are dependent on God, but then we must be obedient as well. The center, the focus, the foundation of our lives must be Jesus Christ. People who build on that foundation will stand when the storm comes. In the day of judgment that foundation will hold us secure.

But not all houses will stand. In fact, the Sermon on the Mount ends with a severe note of judgment. We like sermons that end positively, on an upbeat note, that send us away feeling good about ourselves. But Jesus issued a storm warning at the end of His sermon.

Jesus had a lot to say about judgment and hell. In His sermon He mentioned two doors, two roads, and two voices. Those who choose the broad way will end up in destruction, and those who follow the false prophets will be like refuse thrown into the fire. In chapter 5 Jesus talked about hell and compared it to Gehenna, the garbage dump outside Jerusalem. He pictured judgment and its destruction like being thrown on the garbage dump of the universe.

Jesus used all kinds of images—darkness, fire, a garbage dump—to tell us that destruction is coming for those whose houses don't stand. God takes us very seriously, even though we may not take ourselves seriously. But the decisions we make and the foundation on which we build has eternal implications. We are not flotsam and jetsam. We are not leaves tossed about by the winds of life. We make choices, and they make us what we are. And those who choose to build on sand will one day find their house has crumbled.

Therefore, we must not only be careful how we build, we must choose carefully what we build on. What is the foundation of our lives? What really matters to us? That's what will be revealed at the judgment.

When we take friends to church with us, one of the first questions we ask after the service is "What did you think?" We want to know if they liked the sermon, the preacher, and the service. Most of us don't hear the rave review that Jesus got. In Matthew 7:28 we learn that His hearers were astonished by His teaching. They were amazed at two things: the matter and the manner of His teaching.

They were astounded by what He taught. He differed from anyone they had heard before. He didn't urge them to new forms of religion, to give more money, or to attend services more often. He didn't summon them to a greater commitment to a religious routine. He kept going back to their motives, to what they were deep inside. He said that what mattered to God was their relationship with Him. He said that true religion wasn't a performance, it was a deep reality. Out of it came complete trust in God, and out of that came a love that would cause them to seek the highest good for others.

That wasn't the religion of the first century and frankly it isn't the religion of today. Our religion emphasizes ceremonies and attendance, things that don't matter much, and it ignores the weightier matters of what we are deep inside.

In addition to their astonishment at the matter of His teaching, the people were impressed by the manner in which He taught: He taught as one having authority, not as the teachers of the law. Rabbis were highly educated. They knew their two thousand years of religious tradition inside and out, and they had studied all the learned opinions. But they did not teach as if they had authority. In most of their teaching they simply quoted the experts. Listening to them was like listening to someone read an extended footnote.

Jesus didn't teach like that. Standing two thousand years away from the Sermon on the Mount, we may not appreciate the significance of this difference. Jesus was about thirty years of age, not very old by the standards of the ancient world. He had grown up in Nazareth, a small town of little importance. When Nathanael heard that Jesus came from Nazareth, he said, "Can anything good come from there?" (John 1:46). Jesus was a carpenter, an artisan. He had not gone to the schools the rabbis had attended. He had never studied the religious traditions. And yet, at thirty years of age, this son of a carpenter, from a fifth-rate little village, spoke with an authority that the older scribes and the teachers of the law did not possess.

When the prophets spoke in the Old Testament, they introduced their message by saying, "Thus saith the Lord." That little phrase appears almost three thousand times in the Old Testament. The prophets did not speak with their own authority; they spoke with the authority of God. It is striking that Jesus never used that phrase. He spoke with His own authority.

In Matthew 5:17 Jesus said that He had come to fulfill the law. In His own life, by the way He lived, He embodied all that the Law pointed to. Not only in actions, but in motives. In addition Jesus said that He fulfilled all of the Old Testament, all of its prophecies pointed forward to Him, all of its promises related to Him, all of its history ultimately touched on Him, and all of its future depended on Him. He was the One of whom all the prophets spoke. And He himself would be the Judge of all people.

The Judge of all the earth preached this sermon. And eternal destinies will be decided by what people do with Him and what He does with them. He spoke with authority all through the Sermon when He interpreted or reapplied the law, when He promised, when He commanded, when He prohibited. Not in the name of God, but as God himself. The people had never heard anyone do that because no one like Him had ever appeared on earth before.

After studying the Sermon on the Mount, we recognize it is not merely another moral code. It has a way of condemning us, of revealing our motives, of unscrewing the top of our hearts and looking in.

And we come away, as Jesus said in the first Beatitude, with poverty in spirit, which drives us back to Him.

When the Sermon ended the people were driven back to Jesus. They were astonished by the content and the manner of His teaching. In the end, any sermon worth preaching drives us back to Jesus Christ. Christianity doesn't exist without Him. The essence of Christianity is a relationship to a person, not to a code of conduct. A relationship to a Lord, not to a law. And that's an eternal foundation; He's the only base on which we can safely build our lives.

After a disagreement with World Vision board members, Bob Pierce, founder of the relief organization, signed away his life's work.

"I gave them everything—my films, my office, my work. I told them if they wanted it so badly they could have it. I started with nothing; I'll leave with nothing," Pierce explained to his family after his decision.

In *Days of Glory, Seasons of Night*, Pierce's daughter, Marilee Pierce Dunker, described the family's reaction.

"Jesus was still the foundation our lives were built upon, the solid Rock which is the same yesterday, today, and forever," Dunker wrote. Yet she also said, "Suddenly there were no clear-cut definitions, because the thing that had controlled and defined the purpose of our existence—the ministry—was gone.

"Everything had emanated from that—our friends, our family relationships, our attitude about ourselves. We lived in that quiet assurance that we belonged to something truly remarkable, something that gave our lives a special meaning and purpose."

Jesus said that when we build our lives on anything other than himself—even a religious cause—we risk losing everything. Dunker described her father during those days as "a king exiled from an empire of his own making. He mourned his loss with angry bellows and stormy silences, and we all watched with growing concern as his inward turmoil began to manifest itself in uncontrollable shaking and choking spells."

Pierce's ten-year-old daughter, Robin, spoke for the whole family the day she asked, "Who are we now, Mama?"

Those who belong to the Solid Rock Construction Company always know whose they are.

SERMON NOTES

What makes a solid foundation for a house? What makes the best foundation on which to build our lives?

Think about the types of unstable foundations on which people build their lives. Why do they do it?

Name some ways in which our foundations might be tested in today's culture. What is it that will ultimately reveal the strength of our foundations? Has yours been tested? How?

When you think about your life, your choices, your priorities—what is your foundation? Should it be different?

EPILOGUE

Years ago Joe Bayly, the late *Eternity* magazine columnist, visited some German Christians who had been devoted soldiers in the German army during World War II. Two of them had been put up for promotion to become second lieutenants in the Nazi army. The commandant told them he would approve the promotion on one condition: that they join the Officers' Club. Being members of the club would require them to attend some wild and rather permissive weekend dances. These young men believed that dancing was wrong because it promoted sexual looseness, and sexual looseness would lead to immorality. Because of their convictions, they turned down the promotion.

Later in their military careers these same men were assigned to the death camps where thousands of Jews were stuffed into ovens and killed. Even though they did not directly participate in the slaughter, they knew what was going on. Yet they never voiced any protest.

When Joe Bayly talked to them many years after the war, they looked back on their experiences with no regret, convinced they had made right decisions. For them, not conforming to social pressure and refusing to dance was an act of righteousness. And conforming to patriotic mass murder, and remaining silent while thousands of Jews were burned in ovens, left them with no feelings of unrighteousness.

When we set our own standards of external righteousness, we are capable of any evil. When we are filled with His righteousness, no good is too great.

SERMON NOTES

What is the most meaningful lesson you have learned from the Sermon on the Mount?

Take a sheet of paper. Then imagine that you had heard the Sermon on the Mount. Write a letter to a friend telling about the Sermon and what Jesus said about living a successful life.

NOTE TO THE READER

∎